ÉTIENNE SOURIAU

THE DIFFERENT
MODES OF EXISTENCE

TRANSLATED BY
ERIK BERANEK AND TIM HOWLES

Les différents modes d'existence
by Étienne Souriau
© Presses Universitaires de France, 2009
Translated by Erik Beranek
The Different Modes of Existence

Le sphinx de l'oeuvre
by Isabelle Stengers and Bruno Latour
Translated by Tim Howles as
The Sphinx of the Work

First Edition
Minneapolis © 2015, Univocal Publishing

Published by Univocal
123 North 3rd Street, #202
Minneapolis, MN 55401

Designed & Printed by Jason Wagner

Distributed by the University of Minnesota Press

ISBN 9781937561505
Library of Congress Control Number 2015956998

Table of Contents

THE SPHINX OF THE WORK

THE SPHINX OF THE WORK

ISABELLE STENGERS[1] AND BRUNO LATOUR[2]

What we have here is the forgotten book of a forgotten philosopher. But not the book of some wretched philosopher sequestered in his attic, working up, unknown to all, a radical theory whose fate was to end up the object of general derision (before perhaps gaining some belated recognition). On the contrary, Étienne Souriau (1892–1979) forged a good career, accrued responsibilities and honors, and was bestowed with all the rewards held in store by the Republic for its deserving progeny. Today, however, his name and his work have disappeared from

1. Despite the oblivion that has swallowed up his work, I owe my discovery of Souriau to that intellectual deep sea diver, Marcos Mateos Diaz, who unexpectedly put into my hands, during a stay in the Cévennes, the book *L'instauration philosophique*. From that moment on, the question posed by Souriau, his work and its fate has continually prompted between us further reflections, fresh points of departure and conversations—"a confidence with no possible interlocutor" as Deleuze put it [Deleuze and Parnet, (1987, 1977), p.3]. May this Foreword do nothing to interrupt the course of that conversation!

2. Dazzled by this book first brought to my attention by Isabelle Stengers, my immediate reaction was to seize upon it as a close relative to the inquiry into modes of existence that I had been pursuing separately for a quarter of a century. I quickly wrote an article that was a little too self-interested to be faithful. And so when it became a matter of writing a preface to the republication of this compelling book, I naturally called upon Isabelle for help, only retaining a few paragraphs from my earlier article.

11

memory, like a liner going down at sea, to be covered over by the enclosing waters. At best we might recall that he was responsible for the development in France of the branch of philosophy that is called aesthetics. It's hard to explain why, having been so well known and so well established, Souriau would have then vanished entirely from view.

We are reduced to speculations as to why such an all-encompassing silence has reigned over him since the 1980s.[3] It's true that his style is pompous, stiff, often technical; that he makes a haughty display of erudition; that he mercilessly excludes readers who might not share his encyclopedic learning. It's true as well that he seemed to embody everything the post-war generation of angry young men learned to despise, those who wanted to say "no" to the world, from the tree-root that caused the nausea of Roquentin to the staid bourgeois ideology that was masquerading as moral and rational virtue. There's no doubt about it, Souriau was one of those mandarin philosophers whom Paul Nizan hated, a member of the Sorbonne hierarchy that Péguy was already denouncing.

By contrast with the various thinkers of that time who remain known today, the approach taken by Souriau is insolently patrimonial. He heedlessly took advantage of a vast legacy of progress in the sciences and in the arts, strolling around in the midst of it indulgently in the manner of his first teacher Léon Brunschvicg, who had described the advances made by the sciences as furnishing a sort of cabinet of curiosities out of which the philosopher might freely extract, in an ever more pure form, the laws of thought. Étienne Souriau was not a *tabula rasa* thinker. And yet this indulgence is not enough to explain the oblivion that has befallen his work, an oblivion even more complete than that which has engulfed Brunschvicg or André Lalande (a fate which Gaston Bachelard managed to avoid only by subjugating his thought under a gesture of negation). It seems as though, even for those of his generation who did not participate in the frenzy of rupture, Souriau, loaded with honors, was nevertheless viewed as "uncategorizable," pursuing a journey that no one dared to engage with so as to comment on his work, to contextualize it, to take it forward or to plunder

---

3. The collected work: *In memoriam, L'art instaurateur*, (1980) is hardly any more enlightening than the thesis of one of Souriau's former students: de Vitry-Maubrey, (1974).

from it. It's as if in one way or another he had "scared them all off" thereby ensuring that a vacuum, albeit a respectful vacuum, grew up little by little around him.

In any case, the book being republished here must have generated wholesale incomprehension at the time, even for those few philosophers who would have claimed some prior "familiarity" with Souriau. It must have been as if in these 170 dense pages, published in 1943, written on the inferior paper necessitated by wartime restrictions, Souriau was giving a new twist to the tradition in which he strolled around with such self-assurance, without however betraying it. As if this tradition was suddenly being transformed in such a way that all its certainties were being made to falter. In republishing *The Different Modes of Existence*, as well as the lecture entitled "Of the Mode of Existence of the Work to-be-made," delivered thirteen years later to the *Société française de philosophie*, and representing a kind of epilogue to it, we are wagering that Souriau's audacity will be encountered today with as much force as it was back then.

Gilles Deleuze was not mistaken about it, as those who have some familiarity with the author of *Difference and Repetition* will discover.[4] We have to wait until nearly the last moment, in a footnote from *What is Philosophy?*, for an acknowledgment of this affinity, even though it is as plain to see as the famous purloined letter of Edgar Allen Poe.[5] It is true that, in acknowledging his indebtedness to Souriau, Deleuze was not only conceding that his inspiration came from one of the earliest of Bergson's opponents, he was also allowing himself to be championed by the old Sorbonne on which he desperately wanted to turn his back. Today that Sorbonne has foundered and the air is full of petty quarrels whose cacophony neither Souriau nor Deleuze could have anticipated. Despite the outmoded style of this 1943 book, the shock it now generates comes above all from the encounter with a philosopher who, magnificently and without reserve, "does" [*fait*] philosophy, one who constructs a problem out of what he calls a "questioning situation," a situation that

---

4. As one example among others, there is "problem of the work of art to-be-made" which, in *Difference and Repetition*, is referred back to Proust, but which is developed in such a way as to bring about an extraordinary union between Mallarmé and Souriau, in Deleuze, (2011, 1968), p.246. Cf. also p.264 of that book, where the virtual is defined as a task to be performed.

5. Deleuze and Guattari, (1994, 1991), p.41, fn.6.

requires an answer, that unleashes a veritable hand-to-hand combat of thought, and that refuses any form of censorship with respect to what "we know very well" we are no longer supposed to talk about—for example God, the soul or even the work of art. Without ever having been fashionable, Souriau is well and truly a philosopher who is now "out of fashion." And yet today his writing takes on the force of a burning question: what have you done with philosophy?

This question must be brought to our attention once again. Certainly *The Different Modes of Existence* is a book that is tightly-woven, concentrated, almost harrying, a book in which it is easy to get lost, so dense are its thoughts and so vertiginous are the perspectives that perpetually threaten to disorient the reader. If we are offering this long introductory essay, it is because we have frequently found ourselves lost in it too.… We reckoned that perhaps (by putting our two heads together!) we might manage to ensure the reader won't take it merely as some meteorite that has fallen in the desert. To appreciate it as something other than a strange little treatise of disconcerting complexity, we must first throw it into relief by demonstrating the trajectory within which it is situated. And as it happens, for Souriau everything comes down to a *trajectory*, or rather to a *journey*.

"WORK IT OUT, OR THOU SHALT BE DEVOURED"

Great philosophies are difficult only on account of the extreme simplicity of the experience of which they seek to take hold, for which they find in common sense only ready-made concepts. Such is the case with Souriau. His favorite example, to which he returns every time, is that of the work of art [*l'œuvre d'art*], the work in the process of being made [*l'œuvre en train de se faire*] or, to use the title of his lecture, as it was then taken up by Deleuze, the work to-be-made [*l'œuvre à faire*]. This was the crucible in which during the course of his work he continually recast his philosophy; the philosophical capstone of his great corpus. We encounter this *experimentia crucis* in the 1943 book, and then in the 1956 lecture in an even more concise form. It first introduces itself in a surprisingly banal guise, almost as a cliché:

> A lump of clay on the sculptor's bench. A *réique* existence—undeniable, total, accomplished. But nothing yet exists of the aesthetic being, which has still to bloom.
> Each application of the hands and thumbs, each action of the chisel accomplishes the work. Do not look at the chisel, look at the statue. With each new action of the demiurge, the statue gradually emerges from its limbo. It moves toward existence—toward an existence, which in the end will burst forth in an intense and accomplished, actual presence. It is only insofar as this heap of earth is consecrated to being this work that it is a statue. Existing only weakly, at first, through its distant relation with the final object that gives it its soul, the statue gradually frees itself, takes shape, exists. The sculptor, who at first only senses it, accomplishes it, little by little, with each of the determinations he gives to the clay. When will it be finished? When the convergence is complete, when the physical reality of the material thing meets the spiritual reality of the work to-be-made [*l'œuvre à faire*], and the two coincide perfectly; to such an extent that in both its physical existence and its spiritual existence, the statue now communes intimately with itself, the one existence being the lucid mirror of the other. (127-128)

We might say that Souriau has provided himself with some ammunition here: the sculptor standing before his lump of clay can serve as the *topos* par excellence of free creation imposing its form upon shapeless matter. What, then, might be the use of such a classical example? Especially if it serves to recall the ancient Platonic idea of a "spiritual reality" as a model to which the work must conform? Why did Souriau flirt in this way with the possibility of what would be in effect a monumental misunderstanding? Because for him it is the construction of the problem that counts, not the guarantees required by the spirit of the age, the assurance that would have come from being in step with the rejection of the Platonic model. By means of this example he wanted thought to map out for itself an apparently straightforward route by which it would endeavor to distance itself from the various models previously utilized in the history of philosophy, one after the other, in order to render an account of them. It is the banality of the cliché that will cause the originality of the treatment to stand out. He intends to subject his reader to a particularly difficult trial (we can testify to the truth of that!): to travel the entire length of the journey from sketch to work, without having recourse to any of the available models of realization, construction, creation, emergence or planning.

If the reader wishes to undertake the trial, it wouldn't be a bad idea first of all to read the 1956 lecture that is reproduced here. In fact, it was by means of this lecture that Souriau tried to interest the eminent members of the *Société française de philosophie* in his ideas (Gaston Berger, Gabriel Marcel, Jacques Maritain, all of whom are more or less forgotten today), those who had a very different idea of their discipline than the one that had taken hold amongst those in the avant-garde of art, thinking and politics. Souriau begins with an exaggerated generalization of the concept of an outline:

> In order to ensure that my problem is well-posed, I will begin with a rather banal observation, which you will surely have no difficulty in granting me. This observation—and it is also a great truth—concerns the existential incompletion of every thing. Nothing, not even our own selves, is given to us other than in a sort of half-light, a penumbra in which only incompleteness can be made out, where nothing possesses either full presence or evident patuity, where there is neither total accomplishment, nor plenary existence. (220)

The journey that goes from sketch to work, as we can see, is not limited to the lump of clay and to the sculptor or potter. *Everything* is a sketch; *everything* requests accomplishment: not only simple perception, but also our interior lives and society itself. The world of sketches awaits us to take hold of it, but without pledging or dictating anything to us. And here is the lump of clay again:

> The lump of clay—already molded, already shaped by the chisel—is there on the sculptor's bench, and yet it is still no more than a sketch. In its physical existence, of course, this lump will always, from the beginning all the way up through completion, be as present, as complete, and as given as such physical existence can require anything to be. The sculptor, however, leads it progressively toward that final touch of the chisel, which will make possible the complete alienation of the work in its current form.

And for the entirety of this development, the sculptor is ceaselessly calculating, in a manner that is clearly both comprehensive and approximate, the distance that still separates the sketch from the completed work. This distance is constantly diminishing: the work's progression is the progressive coming together of its two existential aspects, the to-be-made and the made. The moment the final touch of the chisel is made, the distance is abolished. It is as if the molded clay is now the faithful mirror of the work to-be-made, which in turn has become incarnate in the lump of clay. They are nothing other than one and the same being. (236)

It would be an error of interpretation to think that Souriau is describing here a passage from form to matter, the ideal of form passing progressively into reality, like a potentiality that is straightforwardly realized by the intervention of the more or less inspired artist. The journey of which he speaks is actually the exact opposite of a *project*. If it were conceived as a project, its completion would entail nothing more than the final coincidence of a plan with reality, the two finally conforming. But completion is not the submission of the clay to the image of what in turn might be thought of as an ideal model or imagined possible. For it is completion itself that ends up creating a statue made in the image of—in the image of what? Why, of nothing: the image and its model attain to existence together. We must altogether modify our representation of a mirror, since it is the completion of the copy that causes the original to be reflected there. There is no resemblance, but only co-incidence, the eradication of the distance between the work to-be-made and the work that is made. It's all a question of learning to pass from the sketch to its completion without recourse to the various reflexes of mimetic philosophies. Nothing is given in advance. Everything plays out along the way.

Despite the old-fashioned style of writing, the reader will begin to understand that this is by no means a reversion to the Idea of the Beautiful of which the work is the expression and the artist the medium. There's no need to count on a strategist, a creator or a director, nor even an artist. There is no author at the controls. There's no pilot at any point of this particular journey. Don't reckon on a human being walking the paths of freedom. In the heyday of Existentialism, Souriau inverts the claims of Sartre: a world of contingencies in which the only thing that shines forth is the freedom of man, who has the solemn responsibility to make something of himself. Certainly for Souriau everything is contingent, or rather everything is sketched out, but the full weight of the work to-be-made rests upon man—and yet the work gives him no original to copy. With Souriau, it's as if Roquentin's tree-root were to demand of him that he should get to work and set about the task of bringing its sketch to completion! We see how the trial that began with the banal cliché of the clay and the sculptor has already become more demanding. No fear of collusion with the notion of creation or, worse still, of creativity.

We might object that Souriau has only succeeded in identifying the most unremarkable of problems and that if, as we well know, the realization of a project runs up against the modifications of reality and the resistances of matter, we can usually hobble along from one to another, until the original and the copy end up coinciding. But this is not at all the quaint notion that Souriau is marking out. He draws our attention to something vertiginous, something that the strategists, the directors, the creators and the constructors take great care to keep in the background: everything, at every moment, can fail, the work as well as the artist. Souriau will transform the apparently ever so straightforward journey by which an idea becomes reality into a veritable assault course, for the very good reason that at every step of the way the work of art is in jeopardy, as is the artist—and the world itself. For yes, with Souriau, the world itself might fail.... Without activity, without anxiety, without error, there is no work, no being. The work isn't a plan, an ideal, a project: it's a monster that poses a question to the agent. This is what he dramatizes, in 1956, by invoking a conceptual persona that he calls *the Sphinx of the work* and to which he attributes the deadly maxim: "work it out, or thou shalt be devoured":

> I must insist upon the idea that as long as the work is under construction, it is in jeopardy. At each moment, with each of the artist's actions, or rather *as a result of* each of the artist's actions, it can live or die. The nimble choreography of the improviser, who, in the very same moment, is able to perceive and to resolve the problems posed to him in the work's hasty advance; the anxiety of the frescoist, who knows that a single mistake will be irreparable and that everything will have to be completed in the time that remains before the plaster will have dried; or the work of the composer or the author, seated at his desk, who is able to contemplate at leisure,

to touch up, to redo—there is nothing spurring or goading these people on other than the expenditure of their own time, strength, and capacity; and yet, it remains the case that every one of them will have to respond, ceaselessly, to a more or less rapid progression of the ever-recurring questions of the sphinx: "work it out, or thou shalt be devoured." (229)

As we see, the trial faced by the artist, just as by the reader, has become much more perilous. Where the project proposed the straight and narrow, we now find a path of vertiginous hesitation, pockmarked along its entire length by what Souriau calls the fundamental "errability" [*errabilité*] of the journey.

We might argue that errability of this sort holds true only for the artist, who is a little bit crazy anyway, and that if we were to ask an engineer, an expert, a business-person or an architect, they surely would know how to plan, anticipate, create and construct, prevailing over the unforeseen resistances of matter little by little. But Souriau doesn't agree. If he speaks of the work and the artist, it is because he needs the most topical and expressive example: the one that furnishes everywhere else with metaphors, contrasts and oppositions. But for him it really is a matter of journeying to that "everywhere else," for everywhere the "to-be-made" responds to the great truth of existential incompleteness.

We can appreciate the irony of the label "aesthetician," which is attributed to him by those who have some familiarity with the name Souriau. It is true, of course, that he is the principal author (along with his daughter) of the *Vocabulaire d'esthétique* and that he did teach this branch of philosophy for a long time.[6] And yet, somewhat surprisingly for the founding father of aesthetics, he treats contemporary art with the same studied indifference that he does existentialism! Marcel Duchamp doesn't get him thinking any more than Jean-Paul Sartre does. With mandarin tranquility he speaks about the work to-be-made at the very moment when artists were struggling to secure the supreme freedom of the artist, proclaiming "down with the work of art!" This wholly untimely thinker, ensconced at the Sorbonne, pursuing a work far removed from the passions of the contemporary artist, battling with the avatars of iconoclasm, furnishes an exemplary case of the Deleuzean idiot, the one

---

6. Souriau and Souriau, (1999). This is the only one of his works that is still in print.

for whom "there is something of greater importance" which prevents him from adhering to what mobilizes everybody else. In this most caricatured example of an unfashionable artist in front of his unfashionable lump of clay Souriau seeks the secret of a journey that is never far from the riddle of the Sphinx capable of devouring us.

Moreover, let's not allow ourselves to see this as a celebration of the freedom of the artist. There's no freedom here, for the artist must devote himself to the work, and yet this work neither announces anything to him, nor prepares him at all. It worries him, it bothers him, it keeps him up at night, it is full of demands. But it is mute. Not mute like the tree-root encountered by Roquentin, whose very inertia is an insult to the freedom of man. But mute like the Sphinx of the work. So we have a Roquentin who no longer vomits, but who finds himself trembling at the thought of not being commensurate to this mute tree-root, which is like a sketch that demands to be completed.

The reader now understands that he's going to be confronted with at least two riddles: the one proposed by the Sphinx, and the one proposed by Souriau to grasp the work as a journey and not immediately transformed into a project. To describe this trajectory and avoid conflating it with any other idea—whether it be creation, emergence, fabrication, planning, or construction—Souriau initially gives it the wonderful name of *instauration*, before later, even more mysteriously, describing it as *progression* or *anaphoric experience*:[7]

> In a general way we can say that to know what a being is you have to instaure it, construct it even, either directly (happy are those, in this respect, who *make things*), or indirectly, through representation, up to the moment when, lifted to the highest point of its real presence and entirely determined for what it thus becomes, it is manifested in its entire accomplishment, in its own truth.[8]

---

7. The efficacity of anaphora, a stylistic device which makes use of reprise and repetition, in particular to create a sense of heightened intensity that seizes the reader or the listener, but also the speaker himself, is understood by readers of Charles Péguy. And yet this was the same Péguy who speaks in *Clio* of the "awesome responsibility" of the reader on whom the fate of the work depends: "by our hands, by our attention, by our hands alone can it receive an accomplishment not presently secured," in Péguy, (1992), p.118. Péguy is the thinker *par excellence* of anaphora, that is, of creative repetition, and a proud Bergsonian in the face of the eternal.

8. Souriau, (1938), p.25.

To speak of "instauration" is to prepare the mind to engage with the question of the work in an entirely opposite way to constructivism, if the latter is understood as being indelibly characterized by a dispute over responsibility. Instauration and constructivism are perhaps related terms, but instauration has the distinct advantage of not being weighed down by all the metaphorical baggage of constructivism—baggage that could be called "nihilist" insofar as it is always eschewing anything that might be able to prevent a term from being attributed with one exclusive responsibility, whatever that term might be. If an appeal to the notion of "construction" always renders a critical note, it's because it is usually applied not to those who see themselves as creators, claiming this exclusive responsibility, but against those who seek to attribute responsibility for what they make to something other than themselves. But perhaps all this goes back to the image of the potter—or the image of God the potter—imposing a will unilaterally upon a lump of clay that has to be taken as indifferent—or even non-existent, with God as the creator *ex nihilo*. The world becomes so much mud permeated by the divine breath. A *fiat*! It is this image of a potter that Souriau is revisiting when he takes up his example of the sculptor and his lump of clay. To say of a work of art that it is "instaured" is to prepare oneself to see the potter as one who welcomes, gathers, prepares, explores and invents—just as one "invents" a treasure—the form of the work.[9] If they originate from a sketch, then works endure, resist and exert themselves—and humans, their authors, must *dedicate* themselves to them, which is not to say, however, that they serve as a mere conduit for them.[10] The time of the Muses has passed and the question of responsibility has shifted. If the sculptor is responsible, it is in the sense of "having to respond to," and it is the confrontation with this lump of clay that he has no idea know how to help reach its completion that he must respond to.

For Souriau, every being must be instaured, the soul as well as the body, the work of art as well as the scientific existent, an electron or a virus. No being has substance; but if it subsists, this means it has been instaured. Apply instauration to the

---

9. In French, the legal term for one who locates a hidden or lost treasure is *inventeur*; this would be the equivalent of the English "discoverer" or "uncoverer." [TN]

10. This is the same relationship that one of us has previously attempted to describe by means of the neologism "factish," cf. Latour, (2011).

sciences, then, and you will transform all of epistemology; apply instauration to the question of God, and you will transform all of theology; apply instauration to art, and you will transform all of aesthetics; apply instauration to the question of the soul, and you will transform all of psychology. What falls by the wayside in all these cases is the idea, at bottom fairly absurd, of a mind that would be at the origin of the action, whose consistency would be transferred, by way of ricochet, to a matter that would have no other stability, no other ontological dignity, than whatever we would condescend to give it. The alternative to this, which some incorrectly label as a "realist" position, is in fact only the ricochet of that ricochet, or its return via a boomerang effect: this would be when a work, a fact, a divinity or a psyche established itself in this way and then offers in return its consistency to a human now stripped of the means to discover them. Instauration allows exchanges of gifts that are interesting in other ways, transactions with many other types of beings, in science, in religion, in psychology, as well as in art.

As he never tires of repeating, the concepts Souriau is putting in place here have no meaning independently of the experience that calls for them, nor do they have any value apart from what one might call the possibility of their being dramatized. We might say that Souriau is attempting to renew empiricism, but his empiricism is not at all the one bequeathed to us by Hume and his various successors. That there is before me a white patch, and that I infer from it that here is a stone is the sort of thing that holds no interest for him. What gets him thinking is what is called for by the experience of "making a work" [*faire œuvre*], one which is grasped without reduction to any kind of social, psychological or aesthetic conditioning. In this regard Souriau is a follower of William James: he wants nothing but experience, certainly, but at the same time he wants *all* of experience. Without a doubt, what is usually called reality is still desperately short of realism.

A MONUMENTAL PROJECT

We are beginning to sense where Souriau is going, what preoccupies him: the Sphinx, or what he calls elsewhere "the Angel of the work" (206). But where is he coming from? As we'd expect, Souriau's intellectual biography was bound to follow the same journey as his thought about the work to-be-made: it follows a route, of course, but not one that could ever be conceived as the realization of a project. In fact, although he never stopped considering the relationship between the question of reality and that of the work, he was continually reworking the formula. In his thesis, published in 1925, entitled *Pensée vivante et perfection formelle*, the word "instauration" makes an appearance, without being thematized as such.[11] It is picked up again in 1943, and then again in a more minor key in 1956. Instauration, up to that point understood merely as the conquest of reality, now adduces the question of modes of existence.[12]

To begin with, let's consider the notion of reality as conquest. It's in relation to science that Souriau first outlines this position, which makes him the most explicitly, and the most positively, anti-Bergsonian of philosophers. Here's how he set out his inquiry at that time:

> Whoever speaks of science speaks of a work that is abstract and collective, of the higher, social life of the human mind, of the expansive utilization of the victory that was secured earlier in more humble contests, which has enabled individual ideation—that phenomenon among phenomena, that singular event, driven hither and thither on the tide of places and times—to sink its teeth simultaneously into distinct points or moments, to shatter the frameworks of the *hic* and the *nunc*, without however ceasing to take its being and its lifeblood from the breast of reality.[13]

Thought must not lament its abstraction, the way in which it conquers a knowledge of things; this is the work of reason, a sign of the stability, the consistency and the inflexibility of the reasoning process. It works in this way to achieve its own

---

11. Souriau, (1925).

12. The expression "mode of existence" becomes fashionable later on; cf. Simondon, (1958) and Haumont, (2003).

13. Souriau, (1925).

accomplishment. "The conquest of our thought goes hand in hand with that of the external world; they are both one and the same operation."[14] It is not enough merely to think, or simply to have an idea, which may escape us the very next moment. If to have consciousness is to be able to live one's life in (relative) continuity, to be able to remember in the "here and now" what we were thinking elsewhere or at some previous time, then even consciousness itself is a conquest.

> That which we call bearing a thought in mind is in truth to re-make it each time we may have need of it; and that which we call remaking it is to remake it into some other thing that has the same form.[15]

The first formula that Souriau uses to describe the journey to completion, then, is that of the *form* just mentioned, which presents itself as the key to attaining a continuity that is not given in advance, but which must be conquered.

And yet these forms will not prove to be the exclusive preserve of epistemology. We must recall that Souriau was an aesthetician, this time remembering that if he worked somewhat against the current this was also because he had a grand ambition, a monumental project, in mind for his field, one that began to take shape after 1925. Aesthetics must become a type of scientific discipline directed toward the multitude of beings that constitute works, beings that are now understood in terms of the forms they realize. These works therefore constitute what Souriau calls a pleroma,[16] a world of beings instaured in "patuity": each one in its total radiance, its own singular and fundamental presence. Aesthetics must learn how to decipher architectonic laws just as the natural sciences do for the world of things. Or, to be more precise, in the same way that physiologists or anatomists came to understand the constitution of the human body by comparing a great many living specimens, so aesthetics must learn to examine the pleroma of works, each

---

14. Souriau, (1925), p.232. We will encounter this important theme again in the definition of "*réiques.*"

15. Souriau, (1925), p.234.

16. This is a term inherited from Classical philosophy denoting "plenitude." For Souriau, there are many pleromas, one example being the "philosophemes" brought into existence by the work of philosophers, cf. Souriau, (1939).

one also being endowed with an order, with a hierarchy and with constituent norms. Souriau wanted to be something like the Georges Cuvier or the Claude Bernard of the strange, living things that works are. This ambition, which preoccupies him throughout his *Vocabulaire d'esthétique*, left incomplete upon his death in 1979, committed him to an idea of the work that was being explicitly deconstructed by his contemporaries: Souriau is without a doubt the philosopher of monumentality,[17] a monumentality that is organic and coherent, conquering ground by means of successive, methodical determinations. For it is to the extent that reality is monumental that it can be read, that is, that its laws can be deciphered. Such a statement is what will be put to the test in the reading of this text.

Nevertheless, the book we're about to read is no more about aesthetics than it is about epistemology. To appreciate it rather as a work of philosophy, or of metaphysics, we will have to avoid the trap of connecting Souriau's forms in a privileged way with the knowable, which risks reducing the journey of knowledge into a simple act of co-operation between a knowing subject and a known object—assigning responsibilities sometimes to one and sometimes to the other. If these forms do not belong either to perception or thought, as conditions for their possibility, then neither do they belong to the thing itself, as if residing there calmly, waiting to be discovered. Instead, these forms are concerned with the problematic way in which realization is conceived of as a conquest. They reveal themselves in the very movement by which both thinking and that which is thought about become concrete together. Forms, as Souriau wrote in *L'instauration philosophique*, possess "the keys to reality."[18] But they're not keys that open the door, because reality must be instaured. Instead, these keys refer to the riddle to which realization provides the solution. Before any discipline takes shape, whether it be scientific, psychological, aesthetic or philosophical, the forms are what in Souriau's opinion link the notion of reality with that of *success*. This is precisely what classical

17. We might thus read Deleuze and Guattari's chapter on the "plane of immanence" in *What is Philosophy?* as an audacious attempt to rescue the instauration of the "philosopheme" from Souriau's monumental conception, cf. Deleuze and Guattari, (1991). The plane of immanence itself also needs to be instaurated, but by means of the creation of concepts, provisionally, in a kind of zig-zag way, and, being hewed out of chaos, it will never be identifiable by the concepts that populate it.

18. Souriau, (1939), p.18.

empiricism has always lacked: this handhold is lacking. No assurance is given. If realization must conform to the demand of the forms, the satisfaction of this demand cannot be conceived as a straightforward submission to some general conditions, whatever they may be. It insists upon choices, renunciations and decisions. It is what sets the instaurative agent on the adventure of his work. This is certainly true of the scientist who neither projects forward, nor discovers, but instaures, deploying as he does so "efficacity in the art of asking questions."[19] Instauration, in this case, designates experimental apparatuses, a careful readiness to observe, and the production of facts endowed with the power of demonstrating whether the form realized by a given apparatus is suitable for grasping it or not. But it is also true of the artist. For each kind of instauration there is a corresponding kind of efficacity which determines the realization of a being. The single characteristic in common is what instauration requires of the agent, the one for whom realization is the reward: fervor and lucidity. These are the "spiritual arms" that Souriau claims for himself.

Souriau wants these arms to be anti-Bergsonian. Picking up again the notion of the antitype, traditionally associated with the impenetrability of extended beings, occupying a place within a mode that excludes all the others, he maintains the incompatibility of forms with one another. A realization entails sacrifices and denials. Getting started is a matter of fervor, but lucidity is required in order to differentiate. Souriau therefore addresses himself to the philosopher of compenetrability and osmosis, and to the critic of that which separates and sifts, by writing:

> One must be a philosopher, a cerebral type, a seeker of beautiful, abstract constructions to arrive at a conception of time as an enrichment, which, in conserving the past integrally, continuously completes it through the integration of an ever-novel present. But for all those who are living, for those who butt up against life's rough edges and are injured by its hard knocks, time is composed of annihilation.[20]

19. Souriau, (1925), p.248.

20. Souriau, (1925), p.153.

Souriau, that voracious reader of Bergson, refuses to follow him insofar as he discerns in the notions of creative evolution and time as *durée* the danger of a certain laxity. For Souriau, it's all about conquest, not coincidence. What motivates his thought is not a Bergsonian sympathy but Bergson himself, as he grapples with his words, the rhythm of his phrasing and his arabesque development.[21] For Souriau's world is one in which projects are broken in pieces, a world in which dreams evaporate, in which souls experience injury and diminishment, and even obliteration.

But suddenly, in the closing pages of his thesis, the young philosopher unexpectedly reveals an ambition that overbears in a vertiginous manner the calm domain in which the forms have hitherto circulated, whether they've been of the Aristotelian or of the Kantian type. Here, in a single movement, Souriau extends the concept of instauration to lived existence itself. For a life must also be instaured, that is, it must be supported by a form:

> To come to self-awareness in one of these forms that harmony and perfection preserve from all failure and from all deviation, this is the initial condition of the full life, of the sublime life, of a life that is truly worthy of the name. To maintain this form through thick and thin, through whatever may happen, is henceforth the foundational act of this life: it is also known by the name Fidelity.[22]

This is no longer only about scientific knowledge or artistic creation, but about fidelity to oneself. The example is no longer drawn from science or from art, but, strangely enough, from the drama that plays out as adolescence draws to a close and "the impalpable *élan* of youth in its quest for life gives way to life itself," when:

> [...] the power of dreaming begins to diminish; the vivacity of fancy, the wealth of invention, the soft-focus that conceals shortcomings, the purple haze that hides the objective, when all that withers

---

21. Thus in *L'instauration philosophique* he writes: "Bergson! We hardly need to remind ourselves to what extent his philosophy was accomplished and finished *ad unguem*; but also the enormous damage it did to philosophy, its refusal to account for a great number of aspects of the world and of existence, and how this is linked to the complete closure of the determination of what he is prepared to accept" in Souriau, (1939), p.358.

22. Souriau, (1925), p.273.

away and is impoverished [...] It is at this point that many neuter the dream, abandon themselves to fate, deny themselves and thus renounce life, for, as we have seen, to deny oneself is to commit the one transgression that may be fatal. In one way or another, they substitute a different form for the first one and try with the time that is left to them to forge a new life, and spend the rest of their days without ever managing to live.[23]

Taking up certain Stoic themes, Souriau calls on us to become "sons of our works," right at the point where the Bergsonian conjuring-trick, Circe-like, might suggest we abandon ourselves to the delights of a becoming that will enrich itself. The soul must "make an appearance" and aim for that which it alone can confer:

> [...] on action, on the effectual work of realization, a structure that is so solid and so generative of sincere vows that it consists of nothing less than the power of a sworn oath, of a pledge made to oneself.[24]

He provides a more lapidary formula for this pledge in the final lines of *Avoir une âme*, published in 1938, when it is called into action for the second time[25]:

> It is not in its own power for a soul to make itself immortal. It is only within its power to be worthy of immortality. If we are to perish at the usual age, it is at least in our power to *render this an injustice*. To have a soul is to act in such a way that, if it must perish,

23. Souriau, (1925), p.274.

24. Souriau, (1925), p.273.

25. During the First World War Souriau spent some years in captivity. In his book *Abstraction sentimentale* (1925), in which he intended to pursue an objective study of affective life, he chose as source material a text, which took the form of a document, that met the requirements for objectivity because, as he explained, it had not been written as a response to this question. This text was none other than his own prison notebooks. And what the long excerpts taken from those notebooks recount is in fact a good deal more readable than the theses they are mobilized to support: they report the daily struggle of one trying to accept an interrupted life, in all its harshness, but without succumbing to the false hopes or melancholies that preoccupy the dreams of the one experiencing captive life, that is, the one who is "idle" [*désœuvré*]. It does not stretch the imagination to suppose that the philosopher who *contra* Bergson committed himself to a hard life and to his sworn oath came into being within the walls of Ingolstadt.

its final cry [...] will with good reason be the sigh of Desdemona from beyond the grave: *O, falsely, falsely murder'd!*[26]

AT THE FOOTHILLS OF THE WORK

We are now at the threshold of *The Different Modes of Existence*. The trial is well defined: whether it has to do with science, with art, or with the soul it will be necessary to pass from sketch to reality without relying on an outline that would realize itself secretly and on the quiet: a substance, a plan, a project, an evolution, a providence, a creation. Neither must we hand over the treasure of the discovery of beings to human freedom alone, lost in a clearly contingent world. Such is the trajectory into which this book inserts itself. It is up to us to march in step and to undergo the trial by passing over the same burning coals.

On the one hand, we have the sense that Souriau is continually thinking the same movement of reality, on the other hand, that he suddenly rearranges his entire equipment. It's as if he casts the dice anew, convinced that the trial will be flunked every time if we don't replay the game in its entirety.

Let's get our bearings. Souriau positioned the problem as early as 1938, in his *Avoir une âme*, when he defined what would be the principle of his investigation, an investigation that seems however to belong to the domain of psychology (the author presents himself in that text in the guise of one listening to students and friends who have come seeking counsel or to confide their troubles):

> We do not have the right to speak philosophically of a being as real, unless at the same time as we state the type of direct or intrinsic truth we have found in it (I mean its way of being in its maximum state of present lucidity), we do not also say on what plane of existence we have, in a manner of speaking, sounded the kill; in which domain we targeted it and overwhelmed it.[27]

---

26. Souriau, (1938), p.141. [The words of Desdemona are cited in English in the original. {TN}]

27. Souriau, (1938), p.23.

The contrast is striking between this requirement and the way in which he referred to existence in *L'instauration philosophique*, which did appear in the same year, although it had been prepared at a much earlier date.[28] In that work, "to exist" was plainly a synonym of what in 1925 he was calling "to live":

> You suppose, children, that you exist and that the world exists, and you deduce from it your knowledge of that which is, as a simple combination, as a simple mutual adaptation of these two things. Now I am not saying that you do not exist at all, but that you only exist weakly, in a muddled way, half-way between real existence and this lack of reality, which may even entail an absence of existence. For existence itself needs reality in order to be real existence, in order to be the existence of something or someone. Or at least there are many sorts of existences. But our real, concrete and individual existence is almost always proposed as a to-be-accomplished [*comme à accomplir*]. You would accomplish your reality if you could be, manifestly and for yourselves, in your "aseity,"[29] as Prémontval said, or in the "patuity" of your being, as Strada said, in its total radiance, in a presence that is at once singular and essential—and this poses a problem of truth. And so you yourselves, you who believe yourselves to exist, you only exist to the extent that you participate more or less in that which your real existence would be, and it is only in relation to what that would be that you exist, you, presently.[30]

An additional contrast, which we will see is correlative to the first: in *The Different Modes of Existence*, Souriau no longer refers in the first instance to instauration, but, as we have already pointed out, to "anaphoric variation." While instauration nods toward a realizer and realization, anaphoric variation dramatizes the progression of what was in the beginning a lump of clay and ends up as a work. Here, man is the one who must dedicate himself. And it is what is required by this dedication, this

---

28. It's not inconceivable that Souriau, predicting that he would be enlisted (for the second time), wrote up *Avoir une âme* in haste, a strange composition between philosophy and psychological studies, ending the work with a flurry of propositions that are barely elaborated. Does it testify to a "what could have been?"

29. "Aseity," existence through oneself—a Scholastic term—is the antonym of abaliety (*ab alio*), which is existence with reference to or in dependence to an other (a note from the presenters).

30. Souriau, (1939), p.6.

efficient help provided to the anaphor, and what it testifies to, that is the primary theme of the 1956 lecture.

The Different Modes of Existence engages the investigation in an indisputably metaphysical direction. We shouldn't think in terms of a conversion for, as we've seen, Souriau will continue his monumental project by means of a science of aesthetics. Indeed, Souriau himself made the case for continuity, maintaining in 1952 that his various writings follow "the succession of grand problems he sought to address, throughout his entire philosophical career, *in a certain order.*"[31] Was his memory smoothing over events here? Or was Souriau in the process of producing a "monumental" version of himself? In fact, it's pointless to ask ourselves whether this venture in metaphysics does indeed belong to this journey into the "grand problems" that Souriau had anticipated addressing right from the start, or whether he was reacting to external circumstances (the recurrence of war, and then the advent of a new generation of philosophers who were contemptuously turning away from the ambitions of their predecessors—down with Brunschvicg and Bergson!—in order to think according to the Hegel of Alexandre Kojève, with Husserl and with Heidegger). For even if Souriau did define the list of problems he would have to address, it wasn't the conception of a program that simply had to be executed, which would have been wholly contradictory to the notion of instauration itself. There's no dotted line waiting to be traced over in pencil. Souriau is a man of the journey and not of the project, and his reference to a "certain order" could equally imply "at the moment that's too much for me to carry out." All that we can say is that this small, dense, apparently labyrinthine book, strangely brief, written during a period of massive uncertainty, must have arisen from a keen sense of "it's now or never!"; now is the time for doing metaphysics, that is:

> [...] for inventing (as one "invents" a treasure);[32] for discovering positive modes of existence, coming to meet us with their palm branches, ready to receive our hopes, our intentions, or our problematic speculations, in order to take them in and comfort them. All other research is metaphysical famine. (162-163)

31. Souriau, (1925), p.xiii. The quotation occurs in a text titled "Thirty Years Afterwards," written by Souriau in 1952, on the occasion of the re-edition of the book.

32. See fn.9. [TN]

THE FIRST CHAPTER, IN WHICH WE FIND A PLAN THAT WE MUST BY NO MEANS FOLLOW....

To begin with everything seems easy. It rises on a gentle incline. So why have all these preliminaries been imposed upon us? The first chapter is the first chapter. There's a plan. And summaries. And transitions. We might think we've found ourselves in an *agrégation* in philosophy; we're going to be reading a thesis. It is truncated, technical and allusive, but the essential argument is clear: we're going to get on with *counting* the modes of existence. There is no Sphinx at the gates of this book.

And yet, as it so happens, Souriau isn't going to follow his plan. The first chapter announces a project that he's going to transform into a journey … and things are quickly going to get complicated. Everything proceeds as though his approach is torn between two logics. On the one hand, there's the project of a view of the whole, a synoptic view of existence in its totality (87, §16), and, on the other hand, there's an entirely different problem that powers up the whole argument. Hence the terribly jerky character of a book which, initially presenting itself under the guise of rigorous organization, then returns by stealth to the original question of instauration. Chapters I and III, and the first part of chapter IV, correspond with the first logic; chapter II and the remainder of chapter IV are examples of the second. The two logics are original, but not in the same way. A compounding difficulty: Souriau acts as if nothing was up, multiplying titles, sub-titles and transitions[33] as if he were advancing at the same pace on the same path—while simultaneously being engaged in modifying the path itself.…

Rather like mountain-guides who will lead their clients right up to the summit so as not to be accused later of deceiving them, let us show the reader the culminating point. Here are the final three sentences of the book:

> It is by Amphion's song that the City's walls are raised. It is by Orpheus" lyre that the Symplegades are stopped and transfixed, allowing the Argo to pass. Each inflection of our voice, which here is the very accent of existence, is a support for these higher realities.

---

33. Multiplying *anaphors*, this time taking the word as understood within literary criticism: everything that ensures the continuity of parts of a text by means of cross-reference, emphasis and repetition.

With just a few moments of existing, lodged between abysses of nothingness, we can tell of a song, which sounds beyond existence with the power of supernatural speech, and which may be able to cause even the Gods in their interworlds to feel a yearning for the "to exist"—as well as the longing to come down here by our sides, as our companions and our guides. (193)

That is what we must get to. Heavens, what a sheer climb seems to be before us. How has counting the modes of existence passed over to this formidable and by all appearances very obscure decentering that allows existence to be shared with many other beings, to such an extent that the gods begin to long for us? At the beginning of the book the philosopher at the wheel decides upon and arranges the modes of existence; at the end, he is not the one deciding upon anything at all. Clearly it's no longer a Sphinx but a whole alleyway of Sphinxes that will have to be confronted.

Let's begin, in the first chapter, with what seems to present itself as a treatise classifying in systematic fashion the impressive array of conflicting answers proposed by more recent philosophers, as well as by the *philosophia perennis* to the same problem: how many ways are there of grasping existence?

First of all, let's clarify the word "mode" in this apparently banal expression "mode of existence." The notion is as old as philosophy, but, until this point, in speech, the *modus* has been considered as a modification of the *dictum*, which has precisely the advantage of remaining identical to itself. In the series of phrases: "he dances," "he wants to dance," "he would really like to be able to dance," "he would so like to know how to dance," the "to dance" [*le dancer*] doesn't change despite the sometimes vertiginous encasing of this series of modalizations.[34] It is according to this very model of speech that the modalization of being was first conceived, for example by causing the degree of existence to vary on a scale from potency to act, but without even going as far as modalizing "what it was" that became actual. However numerous and dispersed they might have been, predicates always came back to nestle like doves in the same old dovecote of substance....

---

34. "Thus, we have to assume that modality procures for the predicate it modifies another mode of existence" in Fontanille, (1998), p.168.

And so at the beginning of the book, Souriau sets up his project in contrast to the venerable act of collecting categories, a schema that dates back at least to Aristotle: if there are indeed several ways of saying something about something, the fact remains that this is always a *saying*. In this way, we remain in the same key, precisely that of the categories, which consists in "speaking publicly about or against something," as the etymology of the Greek word *cata-agoureuo* suggests. To say it another way, the old Thomist phrase "*quot modis praedicatio fit, tot modis ens dicitur*" doesn't manage to escape the narrow strictures of the *to mean to say* [*vouloir dire*]. Now multi-realism, to speak like William James, would like to explore many other modes of existence than simply this single action of saying many things about the same being. In fact, it would like for there to be many ways of being.[35]

Perhaps this is what it would like, but as soon as philosophy admits the plurality of modes of existence it risks being swamped by a mob of candidates:

> After all, the world as a whole becomes quite vast if there is more than one kind of existence; if it is true that we have not exhausted it once we have covered all that exists according to one of its modes (for example, that of physical or psychical existence); if it is true that to understand it we need to include it in all that bestows upon it its meanings or its values; if it is true that, at each of its points, intersections of a network determined by constitutive relations (for example, spatio-temporal relations), it is necessary to enter into relation, like a basement window opening out onto another world, with an entirely novel ensemble of determinations of being—non-temporal, non-spatial, perhaps subjective, or qualitative, or virtual, or transcendent (101).

This is why Souriau can claim at the same time that philosophy has never ceased interrogating itself on the question of the plurality of modes of existence—with Plotinus, for example—but that it has never truly counted beyond a single mode. It has never been able to let go of Ariadne's thread that prevents it

35. According to Souriau the same problem arises in Spinoza: "than that of substance, but of the fact of being in the existence of the latter. The meaning of the little word *in* as it is found in this proposition is the key to all of Spinozism, that effort not to go beyond, but to annul the existential specificities with an apparatus borrowed entirely from, and only effective in, the ontic order." (169).

from getting lost in the labyrinth of worlds opening out, one onto another: the identity of substance to itself that obsesses the tradition ever since the challenge of Parmenides. Of course, non-being had to be added to being—this begins with Plato and every philosophy since has been characterized by the addition of non-being in one form or another—but all these additions are more like epicycles of sorts which do not contest the central privilege afforded to substance. If nobody before Souriau was interested in instauration, this was because the pathway from outline to completion was in the end only ever the filling-in of a dotted line in full. What would happen if there was no dotted line at all and if we were suddenly deprived of substance?

A key question, as we said a moment ago; a crucial point at which the most significant problems converge. Which beings will we take charge of in our minds? Will knowledge have to sacrifice entire populations of beings to Truth, stripping them of all their existential positivity; or, in order to admit them, will it have to divide the world into two, into three?

A practical question, as well. It is certainly of great consequence for every one of us that we should know whether the beings we posit or suppose, that we dream up or desire, exist with the existence of dream or of reality, and of which reality; which kind of existence is prepared to receive them, such that if present, it will maintain them, or if absent, annihilate them; or if, in wrongly considering only a single kind, vast riches of existential possibilities are left uncultivated by our thought and unclaimed by our lives.

On the other hand, a remarkably restricted question. As we can see, it is delimited by the question of knowing whether or not the verb "to exist" has the same sense in all of its uses; whether the different modes of existence that philosophers have been able to highlight and distinguish all deserve the title of "existence" in full and equal measure.

Finally, a positive question. One of the most important, by virtue of its consequences, that philosophy can propose, it presents itself in the form of precise propositions, each susceptible to methodical critique. Making an inventory of the most important of these propositions in the history of human thought; putting the chart in order; seeking the kind of critique to which they are accountable—all this is a substantial task, indeed (103).

The crucial point, perhaps, but how are we to articulate the problems which, according to Souriau, converge at this point? Can the task, substantial perhaps, but on the whole a rather classical one, of making an inventory of the propositions produced in the history of human thought, of drawing up the chart, of critiquing or arbitrating, fit with the terrible responsibility of determining which beings to take responsibility for and which beings to strip of all existential positivity? Of course, one possibility exists for making these two distinct tasks converge, tasks which in both cases are those of a justice of the peace, albeit one arbitrating between different claims, those of beings and those of philosophers. The trick would be to line up these discordant propositions in the form of a royal highway, taking us up to a vantage-point, one that would allow us to deduce which beings have the citizenship rights in the midst of the empirical pell-mell. And yet this is a temptation that Souriau, at the end of the third chapter, fiercely repudiates. "A deceptive attempt, a false clarity" (182), he argues:

> [...] we must vigorously resist the temptation to explain or deduce the modes of existence that have already been discovered. Let us be wary of dialectical infatuation. It would certainly be easy, with a little ingenuity, to improvise and, in broad strokes, to outline a dialectic of existence, in order to demonstrate that there can be no modes of existence but those, and that they engender one another in a certain order. But in doing so, we would subvert all that could be of any importance in the observations made here. (161)

In fact, the necessity of resistance is announced even in the first chapter. To order discord into a royal highway is to suppose that this highway exists as a dotted line; that is to say, the one doing the ordering would be doing nothing more than taking cognizance of a convergence that no-one before him had seen. Now, as Souriau stresses, there is no such pacification: the question of existence has always been open and it remains so (we will even add that today it has become a veritable battle-field). But it gets worse. Regarding existence "the philosophers" responses are tendentious. "For while they affirm, they also desire" (97), and desire here has the power of "doors of bronze swinging with a fateful pulse—now open, now shut—within the philosophy of great hopes, in the universe of vast domains" (101-102).

In this way, the meaning of synoptic vision shifts. Now, it's no longer a matter of classifying theories bearing upon what "might really exist" in opposition to what "might only be a construction," a mere illusion that the philosopher revels in dismantling. That would entail classifying desires and tendentious answers—deconstruction, not at all instauration. It would be to assume the role of "justice of the peace," seated well above the fray, but for the weakest of justifications. For the one who classifies the desires of others can only escape being classified himself by claiming to be without desire, perfectly indifferent to the question at hand. This is not, of course, what Souriau claims.

As we read in his 1956 lecture, we are "implicated" (213) in the problem, and by this Souriau didn't mean merely that the question is addressed to us, but rather that we are enlisted by it, whether we want to be or not. The question of modes of existence is well and truly a practical one, even a pragmatic one, in the sense given to this word by William James when he asked what is required for a life worthy of being lived. This, in any case, is the reading we propose: synoptic vision renders the diverse modes of existence in their full force as a questioning situation, where it's not simply a matter of responding, but of instauring, of succeeding in the journey required by way of response. The outcome of this journey is none other than the determination of "how" we are implicated by the modes of existence—for which we might once again refer to the closing sentences of the book as summation of the whole "enquiry."

This reading meets with an objection, a somewhat knee-jerk one, as is the case whenever critique becomes a conditioned reflex. Since Souriau is not neutral, since he is in fact engaged in the audacious construction of a problem that has been imposed by his own "desire," that of securing metaphysical acclaim for the concept of instauration—thus, he is "like everyone else." Synoptic vision is nothing but a trick, but we won't be fooled. Which also means: not only will we refuse to be implicated by Souriau's question, but we will be determined to remain so. But it's at this point that the singular power of this little book becomes apparent. For the one who chooses the path of critique it will remain unreadable. Far from functioning as a trick, every stage of the enquiry into the different modes of existence is liable to plunge us into confusion if we take it as concealing tendentiousness under an appearance of impartiality.

The reading we propose takes sides with Souriau; for us, this is the only way to read him. To be more precise, our reading forges a coherence between how Souriau thought the problem had to be constructed and the way in which he actually constructed it. His chart of the modes, the question of "how many" there are, is certainly an artifice, but it shouldn't be taken as a pitiful exposé of Souriau, as if he were portioning out existence in a sovereign manner, conferring honors on beings who pander to the desire of the sovereign. The chart operates like a journey prompted by the question of anaphoric progression (which is a metaphysical question enjoined by the fact of instauration), a journey whose every step necessitates and calls for an experience that is itself anaphoric. Here is an alleyway of Sphinxes, in fact, each one demanding that we should "work it out"—that is, that we should perform the necessary anaphoric transformation.

A journey, in Souriau's terms, is not cumulative: the resolution of one riddle does not necessarily put us in a position to answer those that follow. But there is something common to them all. If we are to succeed each time, it will come via the experience of the philosopher losing his place as judge, such that beings instead gain the ability to define their truth, their own mode of existence. *We* have to situate ourselves in relation to these modes of existence, what they require, their own, unique perfection, their "own success in the art of existing." Then adding what they might need in order to be supported in existence (abaliety) if they're not able to exist in themselves or by themselves (aseity). It's therefore in relation to them that *we,* we who pose the question of existence, find ourselves situated and implicated.

CHAPTER TWO: IN WHICH WE
ENCOUNTER A STRANGE GHOST STORY

The reader will thus find herself faced with two routes in quincunx: one bearing on *how many* modes there are; the other on *how* to render oneself worthy of responding to a mode, whichever it may be. To complicate things, Souriau will describe the second question (which, as we know, is primary, although it comes after) by the misleading term *surexistence*, which should not at all be taken as a kind of appeal to transcendence. Let's be patient, we're not out of the woods yet!

It's with the "intensive modes" that Souriau begins what he himself calls the "inquiry." Recall the reprimand he made to those "children" who thought they existed: "you only exist weakly!" Is existence susceptible to a more or a less? This would be an initial question well worth entering into the chart of philosophical propositions. But its direction leads instead to a trial: what happens when, instead of the world responding *for us*, we are put in a situation of having to respond *for the world*? Roquentin reckoned on the tree-root without his perceiving it: it proceeded "of itself." Now, suddenly, it fails or ceases to exist unless he himself has the strength to maintain it in existence—this would truly induce nausea. Faced with the same tree-root, Souriau's Roquentin, vacillates. What's at stake is his existence in relation to the tree-root and the tree-root's own existence as reprised or continuous—continuous *because* reprised. Paradoxically, it's by not following existentialism that Souriau is going to define existence.

How does Souriau carry this out? The reprimand ("you only exist weakly!") addressed to those "children" immediately orientates us toward a distinction between what they are and what they might become, from the point of view of the possible, of what is in them as potential, ready to emerge. Who would not desire for such children a developing intensity of life, and an ever-richer experience? And yet that is a point of view that Souriau dismisses as "obliging" (112) and the first trial is to refuse it. For to accept it would be to kill the question, to pose the problem in terms which provide its solution. Emergence, isn't this the notion that discerns in the present a future that is already half determined, a dotted line indicating where it is to be filled-in? Souriau will just as much reject the alternative, rival explanation, according to which existence would be that which we possess entirely or not at all. In both cases, he writes, we are in the realm of *doxa*, that is, of answers that seem satisfactory only because the problem to which they appear to correspond was never constructed. Such answers are free to fight endlessly with each other.

And here we have the beginning of the construction of the problem: the question of existence, framed in terms of strength or weakness, must, to avoid lapsing into *doxa*, go through an "existential affirmation" (113). Let us recall that for every being we must be able to specify "on what plane of existence we have, in a manner of speaking, sounded the kill."[36] And yet, it's only from an actual experience of dissolution in nothingness that the question of strength or weakness finds a way of becoming that actual, terrible interrogation:

> Let us insist. We must not reduce the question "am I?" to the question "what am I?" We must not allow the response "I am not," or "I hardly am," to mean "I am not myself," or even "it is not I who am, but something is, and I am merely participating in it." For example, it is God who is, or (transposing *Ich denke* to *Es denkt in mir*) it is thinking [*Denken*] that is. The response "no" or "hardly" must mean: there, where I am looking, there, where I am testing existence, there is only a little bit of existence or none at all. In other places and for other things, it is of no concern. (121)

This is precisely why Descartes, for example, failed the trial that Souriau has set up. The *Cogito* "has not been jeopardized, not even by the hypothesis of the evil genius" (114). Descartes, a thinking being, never conceded that the response to the question "am I?" might be "no!" For him, strength and weakness are not immanent to the one who says "I" and to his thought. He has not vacillated. All he wanted to do was situate the thinking being along the length of a scale rising from the least to the greatest perfection. It's a bit like confusing the measurement of the height of a child who is in the process of growing with the question of whether that child will continue to exist forever. The same objection can be made to Heidegger. He gives the impression of being a little too sure about "Being as being" for us to believe he has passed the trial. He relies on Being. But what if

---

36. Souriau, (1938), p.23.

he turned out to have longed for Being? What if Heidegger set out to answer for it and defaulted? He never did think it. He has not passed the trial.

It's at this point that Souriau takes leave of the history of philosophy (§27), for this chapter at least, and sets about creating a series of conceptual personae which, unlike Descartes and Heidegger, will submit themselves to the trial of transition [*basculement*]: "I take it upon myself to answer for what makes me exist, but I may find myself without support." Each one of these personae undergoes an experience of vacillation, indeed of annihilation: the ghost vanishes; the shipwrecked sailor allows himself to flounder; the man with a religious vocation confronts the question: "am I able to bear my mission?" In each of the three cases, the persona is not convicted of weakness by dint of the example of another, one more strong, more lucid, more sincere than him. There is no point of comparison, no psychology, no past, no future. The ghost exists as emissary, summoned to avenge; the shipwrecked sailor swims because he knows how to swim and because, his vessel having overturned in the middle of the ocean, he has to swim; and the man with the missionary vocation is existentially constituted by the call of God to which he responds. In each of the three cases, there is first of all a support. A world—whether it be the summons, the habitual practice, or the religious institution— is to be found there that confers reason and meaning. But in each of the three cases this support might begin to go missing—"why, am I doing this?" Suddenly each persona finds himself deprived of the reasons that had carried and reassured him. This is what happens, Souriau insists, to anyone who *seriously* interrogates himself concerning his being. To respond to the trial Souriau puts before us, to follow the journey, we must have hesitated, we must have trembled, at the thought that anaphoric experience could very well, as we have said, have no *respondent*.[37] How are we to trust one who speaks of being if he has not risked being devoured by the Sphinx?

Be careful: when Souriau speaks of God here, that is to say, when he treats the example of the believer, he's not dealing with

37. The phrase *avoir du répondant* ("to have money to pay") implies the idea of "guarantor, warrantor, underwriter, etc." The same nuance would apply to all expressions derived from *répondre pour* which are here translated with variations on "answer for" or "respond for." [TN]

transcendence—and this is confirmed in what is without doubt his most accomplished book, *L'ombre de Dieu*.[38] The man with the religious vocation does not "lose his faith," as if suddenly concluding that "God does not exist"—a little like a child who one day realizes that his presents come from his parents, not from Santa Claus. It is not an "other" world, without God, that offers itself to him; nor is it the discovery of an existential freedom that the self-evident facts of the world [*les évidences du monde*] had obscured. The interrogation is serious, it is even terrible, and yet for Souriau it doesn't consist in a pathway toward freedom, but in an approach to what a "pure" mode of experience signifies, to which the conceptual persona must bear witness. The man of faith hasn't lost faith, he is having an experience of this faith as "pure," stripped of the self-evident facts of religious reality. No longer lodged in a world that answers for him and supports him, he is supported only by the call of God, to which he is the response, an instrument of the God who gave him his mission. God, in this sense, answers for him, gives him his *raison d'être*, supports him, to the extent of judging him and casting him into the abyss if he responds badly or weakly. But who assures him of this? For it is also accurate to say—and this is the true transition [*la vraie bascule*] of existential responsibility—that God needs him for this mission, that is to say that He depends on him. "The terrible power of reversing the question!" (124). God, who was his *raison d'être*, who was answering for him, is now *that for which he himself must answer*. The question is no longer to know whether he will be able to complete his mission, but whether he has the strength to support that mission, given that he has only himself to support himself. It's up to him to answer. Is he strong or weak?

---

38. Souriau, (1955). "Shadow": because this must be clarified for the benefit of those who might laugh precipitously, Souriau's question is not at all that of the existence of God, nor that of the experience of guidance received in the anaphoric variations of a life. Fervor and lucidity are not the privilege of the believer, nor are they specifically nourished by faith. The difference is that the believer requests and seeks a relationship of reciprocity that is active and perceptible. The spiritual vow of the believer is that "everything that takes place in him and that engages his spiritual life […] corresponds immediately to something, no doubt entirely different, perhaps love, perhaps mercy, perhaps anger, that is at least immediate, correlative and certainly of the same order; that, if one may use such inadequate words, everything that takes place in him that is spiritual immediately 'interests' the one who is at the other extreme of this infinite diameter, and vice versa" (p.308).

[…] Both at the same time. I have this strength. Is it really strength or is it weakness? Who is to say? Does it even make sense to speak this way? I am this strength such as it is, this strength itself in itself. (124)

Whenever it's a question of pure existence, existence will not be measured by what is more intense, more strong or more weak—these terms only apply to reality. When the missionary was assured that he was answering to God, when the world and his own religious customs supported him and corroborated the well-foundedness of his mission, all that had to be done to define it was to point a finger at this solid and consistent assemblage. We might even have been tempted to explain the vocation by means of the world that stabilizes and sustains it, in the same way as the sight of the shoreline in the distance was able to stir the effort of the swimmer. But the moment of the terrible interrogation belongs to a pure type of faith: answering to God or answering for God, that is, being strong enough, by himself, to support this mission.

Once again let's not be mistaken here: it's anaphoric experience that leads Souriau to the trial that shakes a man's faith or to the sense of futility that besets the swimmer, and not at all some sort of Romantic fascination or tendentious privilege conferred upon existential vacillation. These experiences are the signature of pure existence, of the tenuity to which it reduces us when we reduce ourselves to it. Therefore anaphoric experience does not translate a lapse into existentialism; nor does it convey disdain for reality and the support it provides. It merely asks that we do not confuse "factors of reality (which must be analyzed for each mode of existence) with so-called factors of existence" (127). A pure type of existence has no factors and, such as it is, delivers no message.

What is crucial, then, is the distinction between reality and the pure type of existence. This is what causes the distinction between the Souriau who thinks of instauration as a "fact" because it links reality and success, and the Souriau who problematizes instauration on account of the question of the modes of existence. And it's precisely at this point that the original illustration of the lump of clay and *its* sculptor intervenes, the one that was considered above.[39] Souriau warns us: the problem

39. See p.15.

has shifted. "Do not look at the chisel, look at the statue" (128): the statue that moves toward existence provided that the sculptor answers for it and that it answers, or not, for him.

We are reaching the end of the transformation of the problem presented by the intensive modes: anaphoric experience is redistributing its terms. The *doxa* pitched those who affirm that one exists either entirely or not at all against those wanting to think in terms of an existence becoming more rich, more perfect, more true. No, the intensive variations do not affect pure existence, which "is sufficient unto itself, despite the appearance of vacillation and tenuity to which it reduces us when we reduce ourselves to it" (131). By contrast, the intensive variations become distinct in the anaphoric movement, for it's in relation to their completion that the stages of the journey, each one full and whole, are shown as being nothing more than an outline and a preparation. Yes, we can say that we exist more or less, but only in light of this anaphoric progression which renders a life into a veritable work. Let he who doesn't submit himself to the work to-be-made not ask whether his life does or doesn't have reality.

With that we return to the plan in quincunx because the work, by definition, requires the putting-together of many modes of existence: there's the clay, of course, but also the soul of the artist, without forgetting the statue in search of its form— all three in great danger of failing. As that already makes three modes, we must pass from the question "how?" to the question "how many?"

THE START OF CHAPTER THREE AND
THE FIVE PRIMARY MODES OF PURE EXISTENCE

"Each mode is an art of existing unto itself" (131). "Unto itself": such is the challenge that energizes the third chapter. It's not a matter of opposing pure existence to reality, but of enquiring of each mode what is its own way of "making reality." From mode to mode, therefore, the comparison should not be made by passing through the intermediary of a substance common to them all and of which each would be a mere variation, but by granting to each the capacity to produce, in its own way, the assemblage of ontological categories that are specific to it. It's a as though each mode possessed a specific *pattern* (in the sense of this word as it is used in needlework), an ontological pattern that cannot be superimposed onto other modes or that, if we insisted all the same in doing so, would result in distortions, folds, discomforts and, in short, innumerable category mistakes.

The third chapter is the longest in the book and the one that seems to be the most logically organized, even if that organization is quite misleading. Since the work to-be-made requires, in one way or another, the crossing of a number of modes, it is paramount that we now consider the differences that exist between them (after all, such is the title of the book!). On this depends the quality of existence, a key point that will be revisited in the fourth chapter. The organization of this chapter is in fact double (not to say duplicitous): we will encounter an array of modes (be alert for the strange terms): first, the "phenomenon"; next, the "*réiques*" (which will include both concepts and souls!); then, the "solicitudinaries" (in fact the beings of fiction); then the "virtuals"; before finally getting to the "synaptics." But all the while, the scales on which these modes are successively measured is their relationship with instauration: each one represents a particular degree of risk, a risk in which the success or failure of anaphoric experience is demonstrated with more and more clarity. We don't feel the risk run by the existence of the phenomenon; with the virtual, we feel it absolutely; whereas for the intermediary elements, we begin to distinguish something. In passing from one mode to another the risk of failing the sketch increases because we are passing little by little from aseity (existence in itself) to abaleity (existence in dependence on another).

Phenomena in Patuity

The first mode taken up by Souriau, that of the phenomenon, never stood a chance with philosophers. Either they over-promoted it by giving it the dubious status of being the only legitimate source of all possible knowledge; or they reduced it too much, rendering the phenomenon into merely a deceptive façade obscuring what was truly real—secondary qualities from which we must turn away if we are to attain to primary ones, which alone are real. But Souriau, just like Whitehead, isn't maneuvering in a nature that is supposed to have bifurcated into primary and secondary qualities.[40] And so in his eyes the phenomenon warrants neither this excess of honor, nor this indignity. No, Souriau wants to capture the phenomenon *independently* of the poorly formulated notion of matter, without immediately enlisting it in the interminable debate over what belongs to the object and what belongs to the subject. He's not going to exploit it as if it were something that was belched out from the chimney of subjectivity. In other words, there is no beyond or below the phenomenon. It possesses its own mode:

> [...] in order to grasp phenomenal existence, we must above all avoid conceiving of the phenomenon as a phenomenon of something or *for* someone. That is the aspect the phenomenon assumes when, having begun to consider existence by way of some other modality, we encounter it after the fact, for example, in its role as manifestation. [...] We only truly conceive of the phenomenon in its own existential tenor when we feel it to be maintaining and positing all that can be supported and consolidated in it, with it, and through it to itself alone. And it is in this capacity that it appears as a model and a standard of existence. It is under this aspect that we have attempted to show it. (139)

In fact, the experience offered by the pure phenomenon is entirely different from what the first empiricists called sensation: "in sensation, the phenomenal characteristic is very intense, but also very mixed. Sensations are the din of the phenomenon, as it were" (137). For the first time since the earlier sort of empiricism, we find ourselves in the presence of a vector, or a "vection" as Souriau calls it, finally delivered from the question of knowledge or even from the obligation of being nothing but the respondent to intentionality. The phenomenon as Souriau defines it no longer finds itself caught in a pincer grip between what is supposedly *behind* it—the primary qualities—and what is supposedly *in front of* it—the secondary qualities. What will characterize this mode, a completely original one and rarely understood as such by philosophy, is its patuity:

---

40. Whitehead, (1998, 1920); Stengers, (2002).

It is presence, a radiance, a given that cannot be repelled. It is and it claims to be just what it is.

We can, without a doubt, work to exorcize it of that irritating quality of presence through itself. We can denounce it as tenuous, labile, and fleeting. Is that not simply to admit that we are unsettled when faced with a pure existence, of one sole mode? (133)

The pure phenomenon, constituting just one mode, "unsettles" us! Why? Because we are rarely arrested by it; we rarely conceive of it as anything other than a phenomenon *of* something or *for* somebody, a means of access to a support or a respondent to intentionality. But we shouldn't set about beating our breasts, rather, we should acknowledge what we owe to it. For "such is the generosity of the phenomenon" (134): it gives itself to all the other modes and receives nothing from them. In what circumstances, then, might we be able to capture it in all its purity? The phrase "let ourselves be captured" might say it better, encapsulating the phenomenon, its "vectors of appetition, its tendencies toward the other," that can be followed, Souriau clarifies, "in their fanning out, for as long as they remain of the same stuff as the phenomenon itself" (136). Of course, for Souriau, it is the privilege of the work, and even of the object of art, to confer upon the phenomenal this power to arrest the existential slippage from what is manifest toward what it is a manifestation *of*, and to impose itself in its true existential tenor.

If the phenomenon appears "as a standard of existence" for all the others, it is on account of its generosity, not because it arraigns the other modes of existence for being weak. Souriau is not a romantic, nor a mystic, extolling an ineffable truth adulterated by human affairs. Or if he is a mystic, it is a mysticism of the monumental. A perceptible scene [*spectacle sensible*] possesses a quality that is entirely different from that of ineffability: it claims to be just what it is. Hence its aseity: it takes its mode of being only from itself; it is the viewer who is presented in it, with it and through it. If a walker finds himself savoring a vernal scene, it is the composition of the scene to which he becomes sensitive [*sensible*]: this scene captivates in the manner of a work of art, even though it is not the product of the labor of any compositor.

We might object by saying that a scene must have a spectator and that without a spectator there would be no scene. But this would be to misunderstand Souriau: it's not the spectator who projects the meaning of the scene onto a blank screen, available for any such meaning, it is the scene that *supports* its spectator. We recall that in his thesis Souriau insisted that if the spectator wishes to retain a memory of what he experienced (were he a phenomenologist, via the phenomenological reduction), he will have to remake it, to conquer the form—or the soul, as he puts it here. And in doing so, it becomes just as much a matter of conquering his own soul. We can see that Souriau is not going to concede any more to phenomenology than he did to existentialism. What is important here is to proceed with an existential reduction, not a phenomenological one. The phenomenon is here located at the maximum distance away from phenomenology, of which Souriau writes with wicked humor, citing Kipling: "so much so that, in this sense, phenomenology is the place where we are least likely to find the phenomenon. As Kim says, *the darkest place is under the lamp*" (136).[41]

THE RÉIQUE MODES: WHAT IS A THING?

It's when Souriau moves on to the second pure mode, the one he calls *réique* (from the Latin *res*), that the reader begins to appreciate the vertiginous character of this inquiry. To exist is to practice the art of existing. The phenomenon was able to support the existence of a soul responding to it—do we not say of the countryside that it "has a soul" or of a scene that it is "captivating?" If there was an art of existing that pertains to a soul, understood in the sense of the "phenomenal I," we are now going to discover that there is also an art of existing for the *réique*, supplied by a different mode of being, that is going to produce both reason and things [*la chose*], both of which can now be defined as that which is in search of permanence and identity. Indeed, since each mode of existence has a way of developing on a particular plane, each one has a different way of undergoing the trial of anaphor. Thus, there will be as many types of forms—it would be better to say formation of forms—as there will be modes.

From his thesis, as we know, it's in science that Souriau found the first example of the work of the forms: the

41. English in the original. [TN]

48

knowing mind will find itself instituted, instaured, by the effort of *réique* beings to earn their right to exist. He's not enquiring into a theory of knowledge. He's not bringing onto stage a knowing subject: this subject never finds himself face-to-face with pure existence anyway, since he is always encountering a plurimodal reality ("this flower, with its smell and coloration; but also this thing, that I can pluck, squash or tear into pieces, and know it by so doing"). It's as though every form leaves in its wake a different way of "having a soul" [*avoir une âme*]. The phenomenon leaves one in its wake, the *thing* leaves another.

But what is a thing, if reduced to its pure existential tenor? It is what *maintains itself* throughout its manifestations—by contrast with the phenomenon, which was *nothing but* its manifestations (all of them). When reason learns to respond to this we leave behind the mode of the phenomenon. If the perceptible scene, the phenomenal, imposed itself upon the spectator, the pure mode of *réique* existence is that which imposes itself as:

> […] presence that is indifferent to its specific situation in a universe that is unfolded and organized according to space and time. That is the basis of its existence. As an art of existing, it is the conquest and realization, the effective possession of this presence that is indifferent to its situation. (143)

This time, the work required to assure the continued existence of things is vividly felt: instauration becomes much more present and with it the risk that everything might fail. In fact, the thing, in contrast with phenomena, does not exist in patuity, it does not captivate, and it takes a great effort to conquer the distinction between that which maintains itself and that which manifests itself:

> […] the thing is defined and constituted by its identity across its diverse appearances. There is agreement concerning the systematic character of the thing, as well as the fact that what specifically characterizes it is its way of remaining numerically one across its noetic appearances or utilizations. (140)

"Numerically one," it's all there. Phenomena formed a composition, one that the work of art had the privilege of making clearly seen. As for things, they form a system, but only when this system is made to exist in the mode of "noetic utilization." Does this mean we have finally arrived at "true reality," the one studied by scientists in their laboratories, the one that belongs to the stone that falls wherever it falls, even if it cracks the skull of a passer-by? Are we finally going to encounter what the scientists describe in terms of movement and energy, the sequence of cause and effect? Certainly not! The sciences are institutions that are too complex and practices that are too plurimodal to yield a pure mode of existence. Galileo needs much more than his inclined plane for his achievement, the noetic association of a physico-mathematical relation that is numerically one with the balls that he caused to roll down it, to become synonymous with "the foundation of modern science."[42]

What Souriau is looking for is not a reality that is "independent" of the human mind, but the thing that manages to stay identical across space and time and which produces *because of this*, and as if by extension, the *res cogitans*. All by itself? No, thanks to another work by which instauration is becoming more visible each time. What an effort it takes to become indifferent to the situation! The point is crucial, especially when we remember that, since his thesis, Souriau has insisted that one of the aspects of this identity—being able to retain for example the thought of an equilateral triangle—is the ability to *re-make* it. What is in play with the *réique* mode of existence is not a non-human reality, foreign to thought. On the contrary, *réique* status *comprises* thought, and in a three-fold way no less: as relation, as consciousness and as agent.[43] Which explains why Souriau doesn't waste a second trying to understand by what miracle thought and the external world might agree: these are two aspects of the same thing, in other words, it is the world taken up again according to the mode of existence of the thing.[44]

Instead of beginning with space and time to define things—primary qualities—of which phenomena would be merely appearances—secondary qualities—Souriau will make the pure

42. Stengers, (2006).

43. We can see here how Souriau's wild metaphysics might connect with the much more down-to-earth studies offered by *Science Studies* and how the link might be made between the thing defined here and the "immutable mobiles" tracked by the history of the sciences. For example, see Netz, (2003).

44. He will use the notion of "correspondence," but in the last pages of the book and as an alternative name for the agreement between the sketch and the work, shattering definitively the metaphor of the mirror and all *mimesis*.

mode of existence of things into that which produces a particular form of space and time. But without forgetting here the generosity of the phenomenon. The signature of the pure mode of existence of *réiques* is to produce a time and a space with reticence and difficulty.

In order to define the specific achievement of the *réique* mode, Souriau proposes a thought-experiment: he asks us to imagine crumpling a large piece of paper, or folding a long ribbon back on itself; and then piercing them with a needle; when this is done, and when the paper or ribbon are unfolded, they will show themselves (their phenomenal appearance) to be riddled with holes—randomly in the case of the paper, along a whole length in the case of the ribbon; each hole representing phenomenal evidence of a "here and now." Souriau then goes on to apply this whimsical illustration to two apparently unrelated examples: a theorem and a certain M. Durand,[45] that is, on the one hand a Platonic object, and on the other hand a particular individual! But to both he poses the same question: how can we understand them as "numerically one" if there is no substance and no spatio-temporal framework to support them in existence?

In both cases, we have to be able to think that there is only a single hole, just as we know there was only a single needle. "*Réique* existence is like the unity of the hole or the needle. As a pure mode of existing, the *réique* mode is possessive self-presence in this undivided state," (143). If we have to concede that the theorem is indifferent to its situation, just like the piece of paper that was pierced, then the same thing must be conceded not for M. Durand, but for the pure mode of existence whose conquest ensures that there is "a Durand-ity" (144). However we can only say that the theorem and M. Durand are "numerically one" with respect to the distinct conditions that correspond to the specific cases of the crumpled paper and the ribbon.

The case of the ribbon corresponds to the ubiquity of singular things whose phenomenal manifestations must connect with each other in a way that conforms with certain laws. And this is the case whether it concerns M. Durand or his pipe. Their ubiquity is circumscribed by time, and then again by the requirement that their appearances respect a certain order—which we might

45. This is indicating a generic name, the equivalent of the English "Mr. Smith" or "Mrs. Jones." [TN]

describe in terms of aging or depreciation. There is a history of things. But they do not benefit from spatial ubiquity: if M. Durand or his pipe have their phenomenal appearance "here," neither of them could at the very same moment be elsewhere. They have "an alibi" (144), as Souriau puts it. Additionally, if a singular thing exists, it is never nowhere. That which we tend to specify as the very definition of the state of "real existence" is in fact the sole lot of things, of which the human condition bespeaks its exacting character: "It is a shame that we can never be in two places at once. But to always be in just one place, how much more stringent a demand is that!" (144)

But what corresponds to the case of the crumpled paper, what corresponds to the case of "singular" entities that are not subject to such conditions?

> The equilateral triangle in itself is the singular essence of diverse phenomenal appearances, of concrete triangles that can be distributed randomly throughout the world and separated, each from the others, just as people are distributed randomly while nevertheless participating communally in a humanity that is identical in them all. (144)

It's not at all as if, with the *réique* mode, we have finally discovered the real world. "Equilaterality" had to be instaured, and the instauration of humanity (a *leitmotif* of Souriau's), we might say, has hardly begun. As for singular things, the strictly anaphoric experience of the needle-hole prevents us from mistaking this pure mode of existence for some kind of "a temporal subsistence that would be guaranteed in a lazy and ponderous manner" (148). If indifference can be transversal to orders we prefer to keep separate, it is because this indifference has to be obtained without the guarantee of space-time that would serve as a frame for known things as well as the knowing mind. Neither must we ever confer upon things the power to act, that is, to explain what is produced over the course of time. Time, here, has an order, that's all. Farewell to those tiny bodies whose collisions are required to explain transformations and events. Farewell to the ever so comfortable opposition between objective reality and knowing subject.

The turn that Souriau gives to epistemology is quite extraordinary: since we have to enquire into the unique factors of reality pertaining to each mode of existence, it's as if every new scene enlists a new type of spectator. Previously the soul of a walker, captivated by a vernal scene, testified to the "vectors of appetition" of a phenomenal reality understood as a harmonious assemblage, which delivers the reality of this world. But when it's a matter of thought as the liaison of the system and of consciousness of singular existence in identity, the two vectors, things and thoughts, are co-produced. Thus we must take care not to make thought into that which is caused or authored by a psychic being. Cohesion and liaison are *implied by réique* beings, as a function of their very constitution:

> Indeed, let us be careful to note that thought cannot be conceived of as the product or result of the activity of a psychical being, which is itself conceived in a *réique* manner, distinct from the assembled thing, and which might be thought's subject or its separate support. Thought has no other support than the very thing that it assembles and feels. In certain respects it is purely impersonal, and we must keep ourselves from conceiving of it as it effectively is in the *réique* status by introducing into it everything we otherwise understand and know about thought. As it is implied by this status, thought is purely and simply liaison and communication. It is also consciousness, though only if that word is understood in the sense of a phenomenal glow. [...] In the final analysis, it is above all the systematic cohesion, the liaison, which is essential and constitutive here for the role of thought. We should even ask ourselves whether it is not a matter of a *factor*, rather than an *effect*, of thought. (147)

This is a decisive innovation: the known object and the knowing subject *do not pre-exist* this mode of existence. It's not that there is first a thought which then turns toward an object in order to extract from it the form. There is first of all "liaison and communication" and "systematic cohesion," what Souriau in a previous passage called the capacity to "remain numerically one," and *only then*, as a consequence, a particular capacity for thought, which he has the audacity to call "a phenomenal glow" … objective thought only glows when things pass by! In other words, it is not objective thought that is first: there are objects, or rather things whose circulation in the world supplies souls with their rational tonality, which will find itself amplified and deepened by this offer. Thought "has no other support than the very thing that it assembles and feels" (147). This is why Souriau inverts the normal order by making cohesion and liaison "factors" of thought, not that which is referred back to thought as its "cause." The soul of the *réiques* leaves behind it a consciousness *more geometrico*.

THE RÉIQUE MODES: WHAT TO DO TO ACQUIRE A SOUL?

We might object that what is thinkable for reason cannot be for souls. If we must accept that *res cogitans* and *res extensa* come into being together and through the same movement that brings into being a somewhat continuous spatio-temporal framework, then in what way might this apply to our consciousness? It doesn't stand up to scrutiny. We can do all the metaphysics we wish, but we won't be able to conceive the universality of mathematical theorems and the continuity of M. Durand in one and the same breath! But this is to forget that the indifference of *réiques* to their situation has been conquered. Or rather, what has been conquered is a form of *monumentality*. Souls, souls to be obtained, to be formed, to be tried out, these too, in this sense, are things. Precisely because they are wanting to *stand upright....*

> If the word réique status seems shocking, and if "chosalité" seems inapplicable to the soul, let us reserve the word réité for the specific cosmoses of physical or practical experience; let us speak more generally of an ontic mode of existence that will be suited to psyches and also to réismes. All that we affirm of psyches, in noting them as a part of this same mode of existing, is that they have a sort of monumentality that makes of their organization and form the law of a permanence, of an identity. Far from compromising its life by conceiving of it in this way, we fail life to a much greater extent if we do not conceive of the soul as architectonic, as a harmonic system susceptible of modifications, enlargements, occasional corruptions, and even wounds.... In a word, as a being. (147-148)

What of these psychic beings in themselves, then? What of M. Durand is identical to himself throughout his various phenomenal appearances? Not at all a Durandian "phenomenal I" captivated by the countryside; nor a M. Durant radiating happiness on the occasion of a new romance, stirred up with the pain of a love lost or the fear of love betrayed. We are dealing here with a "Durand-ity" that gives out these various appearances, that translates the "monumentality" proper to M. Durand and makes of his organization and form "the law of a permanence, of an identity." This Durand-ity is what Souriau calls a soul, or a "psychism."

It is possible that Étienne Souriau had an experience of what he would call his own "Souriau-ity," an experience of "self-possession in the indivisibility of personal identity" (148). We will recall the way in which, at the end of his thesis, the question of form was linked with the necessity of "taking cognizance of oneself." But it would fall to the philosopher of the work to show how this noble aspiration could be brought about in association with the basic ubiquity of the "ontic mode of existence," incorporating *réismes* and *psychisms*, and with the possibility of a positive psychology:

> What is absurd and crude in our thing-centrism [*le chosalisme*] is the way we consider the soul as being analogous to a physical and material thing—particularly with regard to the conditions according to which it persists. It is certainly more admissible, though still inadequate, to conceive of it on the ontic model of living beings and according to the ways in which they are conditioned. But it is up to psychology—to a psychology unafraid of all that is ontic in the soul (let it say psyche if it is wary of that word)—to say how they are specifically conditioned—which would include the plurality, the assemblage, and the counterpoint of souls; that entire interpsychics [*interpsychique*] that makes their ways of coming together into a cosmos. (148)

Étienne Souriau was the sort of psychologist who had no fear of the ontic, he was one for whom "having a soul" [*avoir une âme*] meant first of all being exposed to it "failing," to seeing it wither, to being mistaken about what might enlarge or diminish it, as well as being ready to respond to a wound inflicted on that soul by another. Whereas the art of existing proper to the phenomenon required a lucid radiance, without reference to what was other than itself, the soul of M. Durand does not boil down to a pleroma of moments of lucidity: it requires a cosmos. If the experience of love can have "the discrete and self-enclosed, stellar and microcosmically limited character

55

of the phenomenon" (138), the situation of M. Durand being in love, for that it is necessary that the object of love has not arisen suddenly and unexpectedly as if out of nowhere. And as Souriau drolly remarks, the same is true for the pipe he smokes, which he confidently reckons upon finding exactly where he left it. The psychologist who would set out to understand what remains the same throughout the phenomenal manifestations of M. Durand cannot abstract from a parallel and coherent grouping of other histories, from "a pleroma of specified *réique* existences, their histories harmonized in a common canon" (146). We're dealing here with an agentive thought [*la pensée agent*] (and not with a thinker who acts!) that implies and fashions cosmoses according to the different modes. According to the ontic mode there is a contrast, because things do not act....

We can see how Souriau is extricating himself wholesale from the subject-object pincer grip. It's impossible to continue all the tug-of-war games played out by Kantian philosophy. Object and subject come into being together. Before him, if something had to be added to matter, it was in the direction of mind that one would have to turn, there was no other outlet. And if this mind was able to furnish all sorts of values, dimensions and magnitudes, these were absolutely cut off from any access to being itself—just as we might say of a country that it has, that it is looking for, or that it lacks "access to the sea." Kant illustrates this deficiency perfectly: he lines up the *Critiques* one after another, adding morality to religion to aesthetics to politics, but without being able for all that to bestow upon them being, which finds itself entirely monopolized by knowledge, which in turn is totally at a loss to understand how it is supposed to have objective knowledge of a world from which it is obliged, ultimately, to withdraw. In this book, however, things and psyches are two aspects of the same thing, at least insofar as they obtain to a spatio-temporal continuity—and "thing" must be taken literally here.

With this extraordinary definition of *réiques* we can begin to understand why classical philosophy was never able to cash in on multiplicity except by predicating it as one and the same substance: it never realized that it could grasp "objective" knowledge according to a highly specific mode of existence, to which it is advisable to settle all that is owed to it—and Souriau settles a great deal, as we have just seen—but *no more* than what is owed to it. It's because he failed to respect this discipline that Aristotle, for example, believes he's speaking of different categories of being, while never extracting himself from a single mode of interrogation, that is, of knowledge. This is also why Kant, some centuries later, when setting up his own table of categories, does not envisage for a moment that they might all be in the same "key," such that his various approaches actually coalesce into a single *libido sciendi*. We have always exaggerated the mode of existence of things (moreover distinguishing it from the mode of psyches), acting as if it defined *all* the modes of being, when it actually provides one mode of being that subsists side-by-side with the others. This does not challenge the dignity, the originality or the truthfulness of knowledge, but it does assuredly challenge its right to wrest away the originality, the dignity or the truthfulness of other modes of existence.

With Souriau, the Kantian amalgam is well and truly unraveled. We have phenomena (in the sense defined above) circulating at last with their own "patuity," without having to respond to a support (behind them) or to an intentional subject (in front of them). On the other hand, above them we also have things whose circulations (if we can put it this way), leave as a trail or as a trace objective thoughts in the heads of those who allow themselves to be informed by them. In addition to this we have psychic beings, posing the question of their architectonic and of who might bring it about or ruin it. We are still in empiricism, but there is more than one dwelling-place in the kingdom of experience.

Souriau is not going to stop there, of that we have no doubt. Other modes of existence are still to come, all of equal ontological dignity. Thanks to him, we're finally in a position to count to three, and even higher than that: ontology can finally celebrate after centuries of forced abstinence! We have an end to the "metaphysical famine" (163)!

The Beings of Fiction are in need of our Solicitude

Do we finally have the right to grant existence to beings hitherto dismissed as belonging to the "purely subjective," for example, to the beings of fiction? To those phantoms, chimeras and imaginaries that are sometimes so inconsistent that we have great difficulty recalling or reconstructing the experience, and yet which sometimes seem endowed with such an insistence that they seem more "real" than the M. Durands, Duponds or Dufours with whom we are summoned to coexist?

> Conversely, there are fragile and inconsistent entities, which, by virtue of that inconsistency, are so different from bodies that we may hesitate to grant them any manner of existing whatsoever. We are not thinking here of souls [...] but of all those phantoms, chimeras, and fairies that are the representations of the imagination, the beings of fiction. Is there an existential status for them? (150)

If they do exist, such beings must have a "positive *to exist*" (152), their own existential tenor. We must then resist the temptation of characterizing them according to what they all have in common, which would constitute a negation, for all of them:

> [...] are fundamentally beings that have been chased, one after the other, from every controlled and conditioned ontic cosmos. This single, shared misfortune brings them together, and yet this does not constitute their gathering as a pleroma, a cosmos. (151)

Souriau is not referring here to "possibles" (not to be confused, as we will see, with "virtuals"), but to the beings of fiction. There is a consistency specific to the beings of fiction, a specific type of objectivity that Souriau describes by the pretty word *syndoxic*. In a certain way, we all share Don Juan, Lucien de Rubempré, Papageno, the Venus de Milo, Madonna or *Friends*. Certainly this is about *doxa*, but a *doxa* that is sufficiently held in common that we can recognize these beings as having a specific form of monumentality. Our tastes can vary, but they focus on elements that are sufficiently apportioned to enable a shared analysis. Has Don Juanism not moved out of the domain of fiction and into that of psychology? But Don Juan himself continues to exist. Paradoxically, while psychisms are able to appear and disappear, the beings of fiction persist:

> When Napoleon reread Richardson on Saint Helena, he carefully established Lovelace's annual budget; and Hugo, when he was preparing *Les Misérables*, tracked Jean Valjean's accounts for the ten years during which he did not appear in the novel. (Think about it: the *remote presence* of a character in a novel in relation to the novel itself; now *that* is a strong dose of the imaginary!) (152)

Incidentally it was in order to better grasp this form of syndoxic continuity specific to fictional narratives that Algirdas J. Greimas, a close friend of Souriau's, borrowed from physics the expression *isotopy*.[46] A narrative can only obtain continuity for its characters by means of repetition, since each page, each moment, each situation is different from another. This is what literary theory correctly calls *anaphor*, that which enables a form to follow the same journey throughout its continual transformations.[47] The same is true for a fictional narrative but in a different way, if anything is to persist it must be remade, and remade continually by way of the forms and their mode of reprise as it was defined early on in his writing by Souriau.

And yet, the beings of fiction lack something crucial, which differentiates them radically from phenomena just as much as from *réiques*:

> Their essential characteristic is always that the magnitude or the intensity of our attention or concern is the basis, the polygon of sustentation of their monument, the bulwark upon which we erect them; without there being any other conditions of reality than that. Completely conditional and subordinate in this respect, many things that we would normally think of as being positive and substantial are revealed, when we examine them closely, as only having a solicitudinary existence! By definition these are precarious existences; they vanish along with the base phenomenon. What are they missing? Ubiquity, consistency, *réique* and ontic poise. These *mock-existences*[48] or pseudo-realities are real; but also counterfeit in that they formally imitate the *réique* status, without having its consistency or, if we want to speak in this way, its matter. (154)

On the one hand the beings of fiction have a syndoxic objectivity, and yet on the other hand they depend on our *solicitude*. Humans do not necessarily produce these beings in the same way they receive them; but they must ensure their welcome and

---

46. Greimas, (1968). In that work, Greimas cites one of Souriau's curious books: *Les deux cent milles situation dramatiques* (1959). "Isotopy" is defined in the *Le Trésor de la Langue Française Informatisé* as follows: "a group of repeated semantic categories that allows for a uniform reading of a narrative, such that it results in partial readings of texts, their ambiguities being resolved by means of the pursuit of a single reading."

47. Cf. Eco, (1979).

48. English in the original. [TN]

serve as their support—yes, as their reception!—by providing their "polygon of sustentation." It's as if works of fiction lean on us; as if, without us, they would fall down—rather like a Gallic chieftain standing on a shield that everyone had stopped carrying.... A strange metaphor that aims to describe an envelope so distinctive that it must enfold within its definition just as much its solidity (it's always the same Don Juan) as its lack of being (without an interpreter, Don Juan disappears).

> But we can also exist through the strength of others. There are certain things—poems, symphonies, or nations—which do not have access to existence through themselves. In order that they should be, man must dedicate himself to them. And perhaps, on the other hand, he might find in this dedication a real existence. (130)

This is a surprising modification of what sociology calls "aesthetic reception theory": the reader supports the work, but for all that he is not at liberty. He is no more at liberty than the artist, or the expert, or the one in search of a soul; he, like them, must dedicate himself. And this dedication has nothing to do with auto-mystification. The one who supports, in giving this support, can discover not a "mock existence," but a real existence. "Mme Bovary is me." And this is the case even if the being of fiction is only imitating "a *réique* status," even if there remains a frontier where this fictive world, this pseudo-cosmos, "dissipates and frays" (152). Indeed, in certain cases, even if the isotopy of the character is in question. What is this character doing here? How has he managed to get himself out of that impossible situation in which we left him?

To give an example, recall the way that Captain Haddock, in *The Land of Black Gold*, will never yield an answer to a question of this sort—a question concerning his crucial and unexpected intervention: we're only told that "it's quite simple really, and at the same time rather complicated."[49] We can imagine the shock felt by a young reader of the Tintin comics upon realizing that, because of that little swine Abdullah, he would never get to the bottom of a mystery over which he had been agonizing for many weeks. But we might also say that Tintin and Captain

---

49. This refers to an episode in the plot of the Hergé comic strip *Tintin au pays de l'or noir*, which first appeared in serial form in the Belgian newspaper *Le Vingtième Siècle* from September 1939. [TN]

Haddock risk their existence as beings of fiction at this point; they run the risk of being spurned by their readers. Hence, the characters of fiction find themselves in a situation of radical abaliety. They depend on us, but we don't know how to alter the balance [*en modifier l'assiette*].

Is this a strange mode of existence? Certainly, but how can we claim to speak of reality, to be faithful to experience, to be empirical, if we are not prepared to define very precisely how these beings exist and how they cause us to exist? What would we be without them? Readers, have you not come to understand who you are by reading about the adventures of Tintin and Snowy? Moreover, up to now, we haven't even alluded to the author, Hergé, for example insofar as he chooses to have Captain Haddock intervene in a way that he knows is inexplicable and will remain unexplained. Hergé, through whom Haddock is granted access to an existence he couldn't have without him; Hergé, who must ask himself whether the trick he's going to play on the reader might put this access at risk. Hergé has to ask himself the question: "is this feasible [*faisable*]?" It is to a question like this that a new mode of pure existence, one of the first degree, responds: the virtual.

VIRTUAL BEINGS

If Tintin, Haddock, Snowy and Abdullah have their existence only in a precarious way, if they are "made of such stuff as dreams are made on" (156), then the virtual consists of no stuff at all, *and yet it exists*. It exists with an existence conditioned by a reality, but without that reality grasping or establishing it. We could say, for example, that Hergé discerned a virtual, dependent on the reality of a readership that was eager to understand what had happened; a virtual that this readership was conditioning, but not bringing to completion. It's not that Hergé devised an imaginary readership, authorizing an imagined possible. He discerned a virtual readership for which the actual readership was the "evocatory formula."

> Virtual existence is thus of an extreme purity, of an extreme spirituality. In certain respects, we might think of it as a purification of the imaginary, though the virtual always retains the

characteristic of *abaliety*, which may depreciate it to some degree; it needs a point of reference. This is even what constitutes and defines it. The virtual is a conditioned conditioning, dependent upon a fragment of reality, which is foreign to its own being, and which is like its evocatory formula. (158)

Because the importance of the virtual, characterized here in just three pages, could easily be missed by the reader, we must make a brief detour to that previous work we have already mentioned and which Souriau references in a footnote: *Avoir une âme: essai sur les existences virtuelles.*[50] To continue with reference to our previous example, what was really at stake there was Hergé's soul, right from the very moment in which he "knew" such a thing was realizable, that sharp and lucid moment, in which the virtual plays out according to its proper patuity:

It would be a grave error to suppose that these sharp peaks, these lucid points, emerge out of being "like the point of a sword emerges out of the sword." On the contrary, we must know the point of the sword as being more real in its acuity (however immaterial it is) than the sword itself, which it draws in some way by means of a reverberating effect.[51]

Hergé's readership, surprised, perhaps disappointed, and yet remaining faithful and attentive to these characters, materializes as if by "a reverberating effect." And the sharp moment in which it materializes is not conditioned by the soul of Hergé. On the contrary, the readership conditions his soul. Be careful: this isn't about the ontic soul, the monumentality specific to the equilateral triangle, the "*more geometrico.*" This is another type of soul, the soul that "fixes us," the singular thoughts that sometimes we have "a great deal of difficulty recalling and reconstructing," but which, when they manifest themselves:

[...] have in them something that makes them ours; a certain individual quality of the "I think," by which my own "I think" can be distinguished from that of my nearest neighbor. But let us be careful not to suppose that in the first place I am; and that this thought is therefore mine because it has received my stamp. The

---

50. Souriau, (1938), p.25.
51. Souriau, (1938), p.114.

fact that it has a certain stamp, a certain *nota personalis*, is what outlines the me into which it can be incorporated. If this thought didn't or couldn't have it, it would never be able to belong to me. It is not the me that existentially and ontologically engenders these singular thoughts; it is all those singular thoughts that integrate this me. [...] It depends on them for its reality. And in fact where there is no such thought, this me is absent.[52]

This is why in *The Different Modes of Existence* Souriau can claim that the most precious treasures of the inner life belong to the world of these presences that are an absence, that are always dependent on a fragment of reality that, foreign to its own being, constitutes its "evocatory formula." Once again, we see the extent to which Souriau is no Bergsonian. The flow of time does not save or retain very much. It fails, it loses, it omits. For the emphasis is not put on the treasure, on those singular thoughts that come to us without our having engendered them. What is dramatized is not the mode of existence specific to the virtual "for us," but rather the flurry of evocations to which we remain deaf:

[...] We live in the midst of a forest of virtuals that are unknown to us, of which some may be admirable, perfectly suited to our fulfillment, and yet we do not even think to glance at them, nor to realize them, except by way of dreams, in the sketchbooks of the imaginary. And so we direct our intentions elsewhere, toward absurd and unattainable ends, toward monsters. (157-158)

We must register the cry contained in that final phrase, the cry of the one who realizes, which sounds again in the 1956 text with the grand theme of existential incompletion:

The bridge that no one thinks to build, of which we have not even conceived the possibility—but for which all the materials are available, and whose nature, span, and form are perfectly determined so as to provide the sole solution to a problem, for which all the data is complete though unrecognized—this bridge exists with a virtual existence that is more positive than the one that was begun, but whose completion was rendered impossible by a flaw or a faulty design. (157)

---

52. Souriau, (1938), pp.116-117.

As we'd expect, Souriau is not referring to the demiurge, to the creator God; the philosopher of the work to-be-made is not preoccupied by some Promethean fantasy. The question is not realization at any cost. Rather, the virtual carries out a dramatization of the "realizable." Souriau is the thinker of instauration, not of an impossible work, a creator seduced by fanciful imagination. The "realizable" is what the agent of instauration must discern at every point in the journey. With Souriau, the arrow and the target of intentionality are continually being reversed. There is no temptation toward phenomenology. There is no anthropocentrism. The question of the "realizable" means that instauration is divorced from the manifestation of the will or intentionality of a creator. There's never an *ex nihilo*, never a "*Fiat*" deciding in a sovereign manner what will come to pass, and neither can we ever say: "it is only a construction."

And yet, we are far from the end of the enquiry. For if it is the case that "the curve of the ogives, broken off above the columns, outlines the absent keystone in the nothingness" (156), the evocatory formula for the keystone constituted by these ogives bending toward each other does not have the efficacy of an appeal in itself (that of the vault that needs restoring). The virtual, as a pure mode of existence, does not have the imperative character that would differentiate the kaleidoscopic play of singular thoughts from the journey of one who is making a work. Virtuality must be endowed with a vector, the broken curve must welcome what will transform the evocation into a "to-be-made." And of course, Souriau will not appeal here to the will of a creator appearing, in the manner of a *deus ex machina*, so as to compensate for the weakness of the scheme. What this is pointing to is what he calls a second-degree problem in relation to pure existence, a problem that all this brings forward, but does not resolve: the problem of anaphoric progression. That's why we're not out of the woods just yet.

And it is here that we discover this strange plan in quincunx. Beginning with phenomena and ending with the virtuals, Souriau has unfolded modes of existence like a hand-held fan that moves from the most complete aseity to the most risky abaliety. It looks as though all that's left is to present the problem of anaphoric progression, for which the virtual provides the evocatory formula. But, as we'll soon see, all the elements of the problem are not yet gathered together. The ontic modes of existence are not sufficient for it to be formulated.

THE END OF CHAPTER THREE
AND THE QUESTION OF SYNAPTICS

As if the trials undertaken weren't already enough, Souriau is now going to attempt another that is even more difficult. It's as if respecting the patuity of phenomena, abandoning an entire epistemology of subject and object, grasping souls in their monumentality, having solicitude for the beings of fiction, and filling up the world with undetectable virtualities wasn't sufficient to define the journey of anaphor. And no, all those things aren't sufficient, for these modes remain unto themselves, whereas experience insists that they must be continually brought together—just as the statue in the sculptor's studio required the conjoining of phenomena, souls and virtuals. If it's therefore true that the work to-be-made requires multimodality, then it must be the case that the journey of anaphor should be defined in terms of its *passage*, the very passage through which the meeting of various modes becomes possible. Count all the ontic modes you like, suggests Souriau, pile them up in pyramids, you still won't have explained how to move from one to another. For moving, passing, tacking, sliding from one mode to another—this constitutes experience itself, and Souriau is first and foremost an empiricist in the manner of William James: he wants nothing but experience, indeed, but he also wants all of experience.

To help us understand transition as a pure mode, Souriau makes use of a comparison that even he agrees is a little dubious: a comparison between words (semantemes) and verbs (morphemes). The first communicate via the formula "it is, and it claims to be just what it is" (133); the second enact a transition. In this form, semantemes, that is the ontic modes, are necessary for instauration, for bringing a work into existence, insofar as success in the art of existing is always played out on a plane of existence determined by one of the pure modes. And yet they are found wanting insofar as they have nothing to say about the transition, the real, active alteration, the modal

65

innovation—about morphemes. Achieving clarity about what this transition requires: this is the trial Souriau submits himself to, leading his reader down an alleyway of Sphinxes whispering: "you shall never pass!"—and all the while we don't know if this intimidation is addressed to him, to the readers, to philosophy, or to this rather truncated book itself (let us hope it is not addressed to its commentators!).

THE SHADOW OF GOD

How will Souriau help us appreciate the necessity of the passage (which he will soon be calling "synaptic")? Let's not count on him to make the job easier for us by taking a straightforward example. No, the example he chooses is: God! He's going to take on, or rather ask us to take on, God himself.... With this he will commence a new cycle of exploration that begins where the semantemes all failed in thinking the passage. If we undertake this trial, perhaps we'll be able to grasp what later on will constitute the journey of instauration.

We might suppose that Souriau is going to approach the question of God just as he did those of the pure modes. The door seems wide open to do so. After all, if the equilateral triangle exists just as much as Don Juan does, then how can God be deprived of existence? And yet, can we specify a type of existence appropriate for that which stands outside all phenomenal presence and benefits from no existential support, not even the "evocatory formula" that hitches the virtual to a fragment of reality? The noumenal God, the God of the philosophers and the learned, the God appended in one way or another to the ontic, can certainly constitute nothing but a pure and simple privation of existence.

However, to suggest that Souriau might conclude that "God does not exist" from this line of reasoning would show that we don't not know him very well. Indeed he draws an entirely different conclusion: that the range of modes of existence detected hitherto by the enquiry, the range of ontics, each defining one way of being, has found its limit. Is this limit involved with how the modes of existence are constrained by the phenomenon, or more precisely, by "the generosity of the phenomenon?" Could we not respond by saying that God presents himself in the order of the transcendent? After all, why might it be the case that the problematic one [*le problématique*][53] should not also be defined by a type of existence—after all, the virtual certainly is?

> God does not manifest himself in his essence; otherwise he would be incarnated in the phenomenon and in the world; he would be of the world. Rather, he surpasses the world, he distinguishes himself from it; his "to exist" develops alongside and outside of it. His "to exist" therefore defines itself as transcendent existence. Whether you want to or not, you define this mode of existence. Even in imagining it, you are positing it (if only problematically) as a definite mode. Therein lies the force, the ineluctability at the heart of the ontological argument. (163-164)

By associating the problematic one with the renowned ontological argument, Souriau, as he so often does, ends up rearranging it. In fact, he's going to merge the question of the existence of God with the idea that was found in chapter II, the vacillation that causes us to pass from what responds for us to that which we must become capable of responding to:

> We can say: by taking responsibility for the ontic universe of representation […] you have taken responsibility for God. For he appears in it. In it, he represents the particular mode of existence that is appropriate to him and that his ontic defines. It is a transcendent, even an absolute mode. Now the onus is on you to prove that this mode must be eliminated, that this existence is really not an existence, that it corresponds to nothing. The burden of proof falls on you. (164)

As Souriau points out, this is precisely the strength of the ontological argument, that which allows it—if not to prove the existence of God—then at least to shift the burden of proof back onto those who deny it. But this strength, which is the strength of a claim of existence, implies that whatever makes this claim, whatever presents itself as an essence, should be capable of making a claim. Hence, its essence cannot be

---

53. The French noun *le problématique* is Souriau's idiosyncratic description of the God that is encountered via this mode of existence and will be rendered as "the problematic one" throughout. [TN]

conceived merely as a verbal construction. We might retort that there are other beings, for example mathematical entities, that seem to be conceived as verbal constructions, but which nevertheless tend to declare their existence, asking to have back that of which we have dispossessed them.

> The same goes for the majority of real essences. Even though we can follow them beyond the world by means of a provisional transcendence that (as we have seen) simultaneously deprives them of their "to exist," it is enough, in order to restore to them that "to exist," to draw them back into the heart of the world, where they are *essentially*. (164)

And yet if the ontological argument is to carry weight effectively, it will not have to do with a passage of this sort, one that passes from essence to existence or from existence to essence, because a passage of that sort only relates to real essences that are *of the world*. This could pertain to a fictional character, even though such a character exists only with a solicitudinary existence. But not to God as transcendent existence. Transcendence does not bespeak another world, but an entirely different way of being in the world, and thus outside it.[54] What *constitutes* the argument, what constitutes its strength, must come down to the insistence that the problem is posed "whether we like it or not." The existence of the problematic one "is in no way a kind of existence, but only the opening up of a problem pertaining to existence" (160). A problem that requires a response. If the ontological argument is to carry weight, then the question "what is the divinity?" must truly, indubitably have "made passage":

> The ontological argument will not, then, be a passage from essence to existence or from existence to essence, but from one mode of existence to another; [...] to whichever mode of existence we wish to affirm in the conclusion: God exists. It is the passage from one mode to the other that *constitutes* the argument. In any case, it implies that a positive response, in the form of a real, concrete proposition, has been given to the question: What is in question

---

54. Let's not forget that, since it is multimodal, there is nothing immanent about this world either, by definition, and that the patuity of phenomena has nothing to do with, for example, the quasi-transcendence of *réiques* which manage to remain identical to themselves like the needle that pierced the ribbon or the folded paper. At the very least we would have to say the "immanences" of the world.

when we ask what the divine is? And that some kind of model, glimpse, conception, or example has at least been articulated for him; that he has been in some manner put in play, in movement, in action, in presence; that he has appeared before the court; that he "stood" [*esté*] in his own defense, just as Job had summoned him to do. (165)

No irony, here, only a "terrible demand" for any philosopher who wields the ontological argument without sufficient care, as if speaking of theories or things.

> A terrible demand. The only ones to respond to it—the only ones, among the philosophers, *to invoke the divine* [*s'object-ent le divin*]—are those who dare to make the Word speak (Saint Augustine, Malebranche, Pascal). In general, we could say that there is no divine taking of the stand [*d'ester du divin*] in the universe of human discourse, except for the twenty-some-odd pages of all the Scriptures of all religions, in which the impression of hearing a God speak in the language of God can be had. And twenty is a lot. Perhaps there are really only five altogether. (165-166)

A hundred million pages of theology, but just five pages where God himself appears after having been addressed *in his language*! Perhaps not even Saint Anselm fully realized what his argument literally *implied*. So why worry about the paltry link between predicates and substance? What we have is the creation of a battleground, a judicial arena, more brutal than the ring in which Jacob wrestled with the angel, in which the addresser and the one being addressed find themselves convoked by the same mode of existence, absolutely specific to them. We must not by any means arraign Souriau for reviving a form of "Christian philosophy" here, since he claims that almost no-one has been able to meet this "burden of proof" and that the majority of words spoken "about God" or "of God" are nothing but deplorable category mistakes, which apply to a specific mode of existence a pattern cut from the cloth of others. Yes, of course, we might *miss* God, but this is not because pathetic humans, engulfed in the mire of immanence, should have believed the religious and finally turn their eyes up to the heavens: we miss God in the same way that we *miss* the phenomenon, that we *miss* knowledge, that we *miss* the soul, or even that we *miss* fiction: because we are incapable of recognizing that each mode of existence possesses its own tonality and produces, by means of a reverberating effect, different each time, a way of having a different type of soul.

But we're not yet done, for might it be the case that wherever the passage is effective a transcendence is being corroborated, in the sense of a veritable existential exteriority? Yes, perhaps so, if the implication is that the divinity that ensues, the one that is given when man invokes the divine, is an agent. It is up for discussion, but this justifies, in any case, the conclusion toward which Souriau now leads us: it is in the passage that "the existence constituting the reality of this transcendence will be invested" (166), and this is the case even if the experience of this passage entails a "for-himself of God" [*un "pour soi de Dieu"*]:

> As individuals, we exist for ourselves. And if we are able to constitute ourselves in this mode of existence, we are cured of all dependence on the other and the elsewhere, of all abaliety. But in a universal view of this mode of existence, we are led to recognize it for other individuals, as well, insofar as we do not think of them as being for-us, but as being for-them. Is that not the way in which love thinks of them? We realize transcendence in our tête-à-tête with God, without ever departing from our own experience, if, in this dialogue, we are able to feel the for-himself of God; or else a for-him of ourselves, which changes the center of gravity of our tête-à-tête, so to speak, from an architectonic point of view. (167)

The originality of Souriau's approach is that he manages to insist that this experience does not entail a transcendent existence, but neither is it reduced to the status of mere illusion, whatever that might be. The fact of existence is situated in an inter-ontic relation—think of the individual who is loved not for us, but for her own sake. He warns us of the peril of this approach in a footnote:

> [The operation] succeeds in positing *its* God, in its reality in relation to itself. It [the soul of the man invoking the divine] takes the personality of *this* God upon itself by sacrificing itself as an individual. Thus, it receives its reward—or its punishment. It gets what it wanted. It gets the God that it deserved. (168)

70

But, whether reward or punishment, we must preside over the architectonic transformation of a mode of existence:

> There is no transcendent existence, in the sense that transcendence is not itself a mode of existing. The problematic transcendence must be coupled with a real existence, summoned to stand before the problematic entity, and that *alone* is what gives it its existence; the fact of transcendence is therefore in no way constitutive and modal. (168)

The fact that transcendence shows itself where existence invests in the modulation itself, that is to say, in a "transcendentalizing architectonic transformation of the mode of existence" (168), is a signpost of the journey we'll need to be following in order to describe anaphoric experience as precisely as possible, a journey that is becoming ever more perilous. We'll have to be able to consider modulations of existence. As for the investment in the modulation itself, this will resurface in chapter IV in an even more demanding guise. For Souriau, God is not added as a layer of being to other layers of beings, according to the ways of thinking of rationalistic theology. This adds an altogether more risky dimension to what it means to live and, indeed, to what it means to succeed or to fail.

> To live in accordance with a God—as has been said—is to bear witness for that God. But mind also which God you bear witness for: he is judging you. You believe yourself to be answering for God; but which God, in answering for you, situates you within the scope of your action? (212)

Synaptics and Prepositions

But, for the moment, the enquiry must continue. The necessity of the morpheme, the transition or the passage has just been affirmed insofar as they are elements of the problem of anaphoric experience *par excellence*, that is, of "invoking God." Considering philosophy since Kant has not even managed to count up to three, everything will have to be restarted. It's not for nothing that Souriau is the thinker of anaphor, that is, of reprise:

Naturally, the cycle traveled thus far is only that of human knowledge. In any case, whether absolute or relative, this poverty is reason enough for the necessity to conceive of and to try out the Other as a mode of existence. (170)

Now we have to "try out the Other." Here the examination must proceed with the same discipline that was appropriate for the pure modes of existence: henceforth it will be a question of morphemes, no longer of semantemes. Thus, we will have to take great care not to confuse our account of passages with our account of the modes between which there is passage. We will have to take acts of passage as the only reality, as tenuous as every pure mode.

> The only reality would be the immense drama or the ceremony of such acts.... The beings therein would implicitly serve as props, like those in the imagination of a child at play. [...] The man who is dying would be mistaken to think of his death as the temporal conclusion to the cosmic dimension of a being; he would fail to comprehend that the true reality of that moment would be the mystical drama of a death [...] (171)

But how can the passage be grasped without reducing it into a mere combination of modes? Here, just as in the first part of the chapter, what we need is some self-evident fact on which we can lean. Faced with such a prodigious expansion of empiricism, some kind of handhold is needed. While it was the indubitable, sufficient presence specific to the phenomenon and its generosity that directed the initial enquiry concerning the ontic modes, it is the *event* that will fulfill that role for the enquiry concerning modes that Souriau calls "synaptic"—inasmuch as the very nature of a synapse is to "bring together," to make transition. The event is that which has taken place; an absolute of experience, "indubitable and *sui generis*" (172).

> In the having, in the doing, even in the being; in the being born or in the perishing, in the coming or the going, there is something that differs profoundly and fundamentally from the simple idea or meaning of these actions: there is the "what-is-done" [*le fait*]; there is the "this is," the "this is happening." I was holding this glass, I released it, and it shatters. (172-173)

This is precisely what the synaptic modes draw together, as if it were a new patuity, a new indubitability, something irreducible to any attempt to refer it back to the object of a reference. The patuity in view here is not that of a presence, which is specific to the phenomenon. "The connection to the *what-is-done*, to the event, is what is efficacious" (174). As an illustration, take what Robert Musil wrote about the stick which, when in the hands of the bearded man of science, the interlocutor of Ulrich, triggered the malicious temptation to use it to smash into smithereens a large, beautifully-glazed crystal vase.[55] This would have been an "irreparable, insuppressible, unretractable" (173) blow of the stick, a gesture that would have had efficacy only for him as the smashing of an admired vase—"*falsely murder'd!*," as Desdemona would say. But her complaint has no echo in the synaptic world. The patuity of the event deploys an entirely new cosmos separate from those that came before, while nevertheless overlapping with them, insofar as it is a stranger to the work and to the monumentality of the soul, and insofar as their destruction constitutes its occurrence, its only occurrence.

> [...] we know what importance William James attached to what he called "a feeling of *or*, a feeling of *because*," in his description of the stream of consciousness. Here we would be in a world where the *or rather* or the *because of*, the *for* and, above all, the *and so*, *and then*, would be the true existences. [...] This would be a sort of grammar of existence, which we would thus decipher, element by element. (174)

It is significant that Souriau refers us to the attention that radical empiricism pays to prepositions, and that he refers in particular to the stream of consciousness of William James. For James' stream of consciousness bears and handles that which is existent in the ontic mode, never ceasing to carve it up, to complicate it, to cause it to bifurcate, indifferent to all claims of existence. It's no longer a matter of engendering beings in continuity with one another, but of following "The modulations of existence *for*, existence *in front of*, existence *with*," (176) that make up the synaptic world. Hence he posits "divided selves," not captivated ones. The patuity of phenomena and the

---

55. Musil, (2011, 1978), p.327. Also cf. p.325 for a description of the "beard of the scholars." [TN]

patuity of events are woven together like a plait. The complexity of experience is restored, but without abandoning the fine differentiation of the modes.

However, readers believing themselves to be on familiar ground here, perhaps thinking they are re-encountering the grand tradition of pragmatism—having recently been taken up again in France—will find themselves short-changed. As soon as he's shown us the richness of this world, this alternative cosmos given by the synaptics, Souriau once again changes course. He skirts around two dozen enormous philosophical problems, notably problems to do with the passage of time, the status of the future, and the causality that was foreign to the *réiques*, as if he was ever so urgent to get to the real problem, the one he's been at work constructing from the very beginning. We will be less taken aback at the rather hurried nature of these considerations if we realize that above all else Souriau wants to avoid the project of a systematic metaphysics that would cause him to forget that it's the passage, the journey from sketch to work, that he wants to be able to qualify. In unfolding the pure ontic modes, and in throwing himself into the synaptics, his aim was not to say what they are, but rather to lay down an option for existence. We have to choose: being or action, to present (or dream up) a world of beings or to sacrifice this entirely stable ontic situation for a way of life in which connections with all beings will become "exclusively transitive and situated or constituted in the action itself, and according to its mode" (178).[56]

We do not get to side-step this deity, existence; it does not get taken in by our specious words, which cover up a choice unmade. To be, and not to be in some specific manner, is of no value. Cut

---

56. The treatment of causality is typical of this option, for Souriau defines it as "having greater existence insofar as it operates synthetically—in its capacity as a dash—than the measurable elements of phenomena, which depend on it for their reality" (155). When he mocks what he calls the "miserable" Kantian antinomies, Souriau reveals the superiority of his method: the antinomies are not actually contradictory because one bears upon the ontic and the other on the synaptic (§ 103). We should add that Souriau's thesis, according to which the question of causality and of ontic substantiality cannot be associated, as if the fact of being the cause of something other than oneself constituted nothing more than an attribute brought in to complete substantial reality, finds dramatic confirmation in the history of rational mechanics. The dash is here replaced by the "equals sign": this is what sanctions the learned indifference with which the physicist will continually redefine the terms of this equals, depriving them of any possibility of claiming themselves to be real existents (cf. Stengers, (2003), pp.101-158).

yourself from whatever existential cloth you like, but cut you must—and, as a consequence, to have chosen whether to be of silk or of wool. (179)

All we've done, then, is to prepare ourselves for Souriau's real problem, a problem he never stopped referring to throughout his text—the problem of the second-degree, as he puts it, concerning anaphoric progressions, such as when, for example, a perceptible thing progressively comes into existence where previously there lay nothing but a mere lump of clay. With this we come again to the question of risk and failure. Of course the sculptor acts, and the thing that comes into existence belongs to the ontic. But we would be missing the point if we were to suppose that the synaptic and the ontic join forces here in order to form a richer type of existence, such as to transcend the choice. That's not playing by the rules!

But Souriau does not just give up on exploring the synaptic world. So like Penelope he systematically undoes the web he had systematically woven together—or, more accurately, he undoes the temptation of systematizing modes he previously untied. Perhaps Souriau is the philosopher of the architectonic, but he is certainly not the philosopher of the system. For him, completeness does not come from counting the modes and seeking some reason to be sure that the count is complete. This is achieved by way of completely letting emerge what is required for the journey of anaphoric experience, and then being completely faithful to it.

A deceptive attempt, a false clarity. What do you want from me, a metaphysical machine? Such a thing would deceive us all the more in giving us the impression of being in the presence of the elements necessary for a complete discourse. Which would be the most mistaken idea one could have of these modes. (182)

And the enquiry closes in an even more abrupt fashion as all of a sudden we are told that the modes are arbitrary. Clearly chapter I, which claimed to post a plan for the enquiry, did indeed lead us astray! The modes are certainly elements, but their selection has come down to convenience in one way or another:

They must be taken as they are: *arbitrary*. Think about it in this way: a primitive painter can find on his palette the colored soils that furnish him with his base and his technical range: yellow ocher, red ocher, green clay, black soot. (182)

Let us therefore resist any temptation to structure and to hierarchize the modes by explaining them dialectically. If you strip it of the arbitrariness that is one of its absolute characteristics, you will always lack knowledge of existence on its own terms. (183)

The modes are all of equal dignity; equal from the moment they are taken in their own terms. It's the "you must cut" that allows for the problem of the second-degree to appear, which is the problem of their unification. From his first chapter, Souriau has been making use of the analogy of colors, calling for a:

> [...] thought [that is equipped] not only for all the multicolored rays of existence, but even for a new light, for a white light, unifying those rays in the luminosity of a *surexistence* which surpasses all those modes without subverting their reality. (101)

The reader emerges from chapter III somewhat shaken, dazzled by the vertiginous perspectives that have been afforded onto these interwoven cosmoses, but alarmed to see that he's going to have to start all over again in chapter IV. In all this time has he only been taught erroneous responses to the questions of the Sphinx? How many false answers will he be allowed before being devoured? The objective is to decipher the riddle and that, as we've known from the very start, can only come via instauration, which Souriau, employing a neologism, describes as being "at once the action of an ontic and its positing. It is ontagogic" (164). And he adds: "a philosophy of instauration will bring together both the modes of acting and the modes of being in examining how and by what means they might be combined" (164).

CHAPTER FOUR
AND QUESTIONS OF SUREXISTENCE

And here we encounter once again the plan in quincunx. The true anaphoric journey has still only been defined in terms of the pure modes, whether they be ontic or synaptic. The word that designates what we're looking for, as we know, is the word *surexistence*. But only as long as we don't get thrown off course by the prefix *sur*, by referring back to how it is employed in philosophy or in theology. The meaning we should give to *surexistence* is precisely what we're going to have to work out.

We are gradually coming to know Souriau well enough to somewhat anticipate the route he will take. He will require two entirely different ways of thinking about *surexistence*: one in the mode of the "how many?"; the other in the mode of the "how?" The temptation will be that we interpret the general architecture in terms of the coming-together of all the modes in a harmonious whole. A whole which would, by nature, be plurimodal. But to do so would be to betray the injunction: "you must cut," and, even more so, it would be to betray the affirmation of the antitype with its anti-Bergsonian emphasis. Necessarily, then, Souriau will approach the question of *surexistence* according to another mode. As usual, he will pretend to have fallen into the trap of systematization, before demonstrating, with a sudden reversal, how to escape from it.

Surexistence against all Conceptions of Totality

The pure modes of existence must be understood, as Souriau has shown, as "elements," rather like the arbitrary range of colored soils with which the primitive painter created his work—except that here, of course, there is no painter. Or more accurately, we should say that here it is a matter either of the painter's life or of our own—a life that won't have the tenuity that is specific to the pure modes, a life that is requesting to be realized, not to be analyzed. The position of the problem can be defined, then, in terms of a request for realization that is confronted by the plurality of pure modes. Souriau will first of all consider the possibility that *values* might be that which is able to confer a status upon a life that is more than the sum of the elements with which it must work.

Just as we saw in chapter II in relation to the question of the intensity of the modes, Souriau's response calls upon certain conceptual personae, each of whom are attempting to attribute this power to values.

77

[There is the type of existence that] seeks to realize itself according to its highest value, to situate itself with precision on a single plane, in the type of pure existence that will allow it to determine itself best. (195)

And then there is the type of person who seeks:

[…] a manner of being that is so complete, so rich, and so evident on the plane of both the sensible and the intelligible, the present and the atemporal, the abiding and the acting, that it resides—as if of a thousand facets—in all of these domains at once, and yet, surpassing each in assembling them all, does not entirely fit within any one of them. (195)

Here are two resolutions and a double movement: one heading toward existence, the other heading toward reality, toward accumulation, toward the plenitude of an assemblage. The big question, then, is to know whether we can avoid being torn in two [*l'écartèlement*]. Can we take the side of one mode of existence without cutting ourselves off from something more valuable? Can we look in the direction of a superior reality as a remedy for plurimodality without straying from existence? Souriau, however, breaks up the symmetry. Later on he will "cross the t's and dot the i's in a rather rough-handed way" (203). Our feeling that we have to actualize all our virtualities and unify them in one life is an abstraction, lacking the virtual that alone can mark out its feasibility. Who would advise a young man to be both a Don Juan and a saint *at the same time*, on the pretext that this embodies two possibilities instead of just one? (203) Father Charles de Foucault was a pleasure-seeker *and then* an ascetic, but he could never have been both at the same time.... *Surexistence* isn't at all a matter of mere accumulation. Here again it is a question of the difference between good and bad ways of protecting multiplicity from the danger of unification, as much as from the danger of dispersal. And for this to take place we must first of all stop thinking of the plurality of modes as something that needs a remedy!

In fact, values have nothing to do with the question of *surexistence*, because the former constitutes the diversity of types of existence as a problem, whereas, far from being a problem, this diversity is what "poses the problem of *surexistence*, if nothing more: if it does not posit *surexistence* itself" (197). Provisional conclusion: the originality of *surexistence* cannot be assimilated to an axiology.

> It is not at all because it assembles or unites that a totalization entails an increase in reality. What interests us is a totalization, which, beyond the plurality of the kinds of existence, brings about something that not only embraces them, but distinguishes itself from them and surpasses them. If *surexistence* is to be defined, then, this must not be done through any axiological consideration, nor as a higher, more sublime degree of existence (though it can have such sublimity), but through the strict and severe idea of a passage to problems of the second degree, which concern existence, and yet protrude beyond its plane. (197)

But we're not there yet. We still have to address the idea that what is in view here is the realization of that which is possible [*l'idée de possible*], for out of this arose the powerful notion (in Souriau's time) of the most Real Man, next to whom we, by comparison, look like adolescents needing to be exhorted to develop all our "potential" [*potentalités*]. And yet surely a Man like that, who would be Master of all kinds of existence, represents no more than a fantasy? It takes more than merely positing, in a problematic way, the possibility of a complete existence, one that would assemble and surpass all the modes of existence, which renders us into sketches in need of completion; it must also be the case that the problem posed by such an existence should have a positive means of coming about, one that is efficacious in the sense that it should engage us in a journey toward completion.

> We can say [that this man] does not exist, not even with a virtual existence, if those various incipient modes do not, in their harmony, outline a completion, which would be like the mysterious contours of a unique being; and that he does not even exist with an ideal existence, if these mysterious contours remain indeterminate and vacant as regards the essential, which is to say, as regards a definite mode of existential accomplishment. (200)

Then to hell with that fantastical ideal, but just as much as to the notion of a solution proposed in this problematic way, as if from an unknown source. It's precisely this sort of "beyond themselves" (203) that the concept of a mode of existence has allowed us to contest.

Understandably, the reader might wonder about all this. Why this long critical excursus (taking up 16 paragraphs out of the 22 that comprise the chapter) only to arrive at the very question that had already been formulated at the end of the previous chapter? Does this constitute a pedagogical procedure or an efficacious anaphoric progression? Souriau had to determine for himself what *surexistence* could do, without however repudiating the attempt toward full unity from which he dissociates it. In any case, he brings the journey to a close by evoking a question of the third-degree, the question of "the unification of all the possible modes of unification" (205). This question, which he doesn't take up here,[57] is not allowed to intrude because it presupposes that the way in which *surexistence* relates to existence has been resolved, as well as the links that are maintained between one and the other. Be alert: he has just five paragraphs left in which to solve the problem of the entire book.

A New Definition of Correspondence

This is where instauration will begin to play a positive role (finally!), and not only the role of a Sphinx repeating over and over again "work it out!" For instauration in and of itself attests to *surexistence* as a hierarchical and ordered pleroma. It does so because, as Souriau had already made clear when speaking of the anaphoric progression of the work, to produce a work "is also to choose, to select, to discard. And each of these actions *entails a judgment*, which is at once the cause, the reason, and the experience of this anaphor" (129). The book as a whole has sought to expose us to this very experience. And, as we've seen, it's what is conveyed in a dramatic way in the 1956 text where, at every moment in the journey of instauration, the agent is required to "work it out" at the risk of being mistaken, where he is required to make a judgment, but without having any point of comparison or reference. To instaure is not to represent to ourselves where we wish to arrive, and then mobilize the means by which this end might be realized. It is not to follow a plan. If reality is to be conquered, this will not be done in the manner

57. Although this is the question that he will consider in *L'ombre de Dieu*.

of a military operation, but in the manner in which perhaps the trust of a timid animal is won over [*se conquiert*]. One abrupt movement is all it takes for what was being achieved to be entirely squandered. If instauration is ontagogic, realizing the convergence of action and dream, it attests to this convergence as a journey of progressive determinations. It ascends "the Tree of Jesse or Jacob's ladder: the order of *surexistences*" (204). This is also why the work in the course of its accomplishment, despite being perfectly determined as existing at each moment of its journey, is equally a sketch, an evocatory formula for a virtual that is now not only feasible, but felt in the mode of the "to-be-made." Everything that is "to-be-made" "expresses and implies a *surexistence*" (209).

We can see that unification is not the business of a unifying agent. Souriau wants to have a unification that has no other principle or regulator than the demanding insistence that we declare [*qu'on prenne parti*]—for this thing, rather than for a thousand others. Just as the preposition "to" in "to-be-made" indicates, unification implies a synapse, a connection [*un branchement*], a bringing-together [*un abouchement*], what Deleuze would call a "double-capture" [*entre-capture*]:[58] "as they variously come together, the modes of existence bend their branches so as to form places for occupants among the many vaulted arches" (207). And it is vital that Souriau is precise on this point when we consider how tempting the notion of the ideal has been in philosophy just as much as it has been in ethics: these "occupants" are not ideal existences. "There is no ideal existence" (208). Nor does the opening out of existence onto *surexistence* have anything to do with some kind of problematic ideal, one that is eternally insistent, and eternally without reply. If Souriau is a mystic, he is a mystic *of realization*. "What is really at issue is the problem resolved, in the reality of its solution. It is not the ideal, but the reality of this ideal that is in question" (208).

But how does a solution that brings about realization imply *surexistence* if, as with everything that exists, this solution has itself declared for a particular mode of existence? For that which is *surexistant* never declares itself. "At most it might be

---

58. For more on this term cf. the entry by Alberto Toscano, "Capture" in Parr, Adrian, (ed.), *The Deleuze Dictionary* (Edinburgh: Edinburgh University Press, revised 2010), p.45.[TN]

reflected in one of these modes—*per speculum in ænigmate*; and even then it is restricted to an existence that is modal and specular. Yet it is too rich in reality to be able to fit on that plane, or even on the various planes of existence that it assembles" (209).

Let's not be mistaken: what's at issue here is nothing less than the keystone for the whole demonstration or indeed the anaphoric progression proposed by Souriau. If it fails, if no sensible experience, no "fact of existence," can be adduced that attests to this reflection, making itself felt in the mode of the virtual, then Souriau would have been pursuing a fantasy and nothing would remain of his astonishing construction than its ruined columns.

It's toward the venerable idea of true knowledge [*connaissance vraie*] that Souriau will now turn, in asking that we do not rule out too precipitously the characterization of knowledge as the resemblance of thought and its object. For this characterization evokes "the *surexistential* reality, which would unite and coordinate what exists both in the mode of my thought and in the mode of the object (which is hypothetically different)" (211).

Let's recall that, thanks to the discovery of the *réiques*, and the simultaneous production of things and the faculty of reason, Souriau has won the right to make use of that old chestnut: the *adequatio res et intellectus*. He has purged it of what had been contaminating it, that which had rendered it an instrument of epistemological propaganda in the service of a science that was pitted against all human illusions. Correspondence no longer needs to be led astray by the ludicrous idea of a knowing subject that is counterpart to the known thing. It is now available in a fresh way, just as its noble etymology suggests: it responds to that which responds; it is commensurate with what it has instaured. With correspondence, the beginning and the end of the journey coincide; the sketch and the work. And yet it is not a solid line tracing over a dotted line in bold. This is what makes it different from a journey which, as Souriau wrote in 1956, prompts the agent at every moment to "work it out," foisting the question upon him: "what are you going to make of me?," and [what sets it apart from] the coterie of nihilist constructivists who sneer: "this question, it's you who have asked it; and the response is yours, and yours alone."

Here we re-encounter the very definition of instauration and the existential transition [it enacts]: that which answers for us, that "respondent" that is required for true knowledge, can we answer for it? Correspondence is restored to what it always should have been: an anaphor that has succeeded and that defines the successive conditions of its success as it goes along. And this holds true for science, for art and for religion, just as it does for ethics. At last the metaphor of the mirror, the one that has haunted philosophy, is smashed to pieces. Or rather, if instead [we can speak of] the metaphor as having been smashed to pieces, then the mirror can now be used as a synonym for the success of instauration, insofar as model and image are realized together by means of anaphor. Correspondence becomes possible again: "a *response* from the one to the other, forming a couple. The fact of this response (it does not matter if it is right or wrong) is the only existential fact here. There is an echo" (210).

There is an echo. Does this imply that something might be held in common, "a common reality having dominion over both of the two modes which respond to one another, at once" (189)? Could we not object that the involvement of a reality that does not exist, of a dominion to which only the attempt to attain true knowledge testifies, is only a version of the transcendental ideal, in Kant's sense of the term? Does this reality not depend upon the echo as a psychical reality? In other words, is this echo actually a fact of existence, like patuity or efficacy? Or to put it in a different way: is there a synapsis, an effective transformation of the one who attests to [*surexistence*]? At this point Souriau appeals to the nature of the experience alluded to at the end of his thesis, to that coming to awareness of oneself by means of a form that must be kept open to every kind of adventure, every kind of occurrence. The efficacy of a synapsis like that:

> [...] is to feel, as a real passion, as a submission that modifies me without changing me, the fact of being under a gaze, of being illuminated by this vision of myself—and of being truly presented in a new kind of existence, for this being would not be of the same kind as I myself am. The person alluded to here is indeed the one who would participate in both of these modes simultaneously, while also overcoming their constitutive diversity. This *surexistential* being does not exist, but I myself can respond to him through an

undergoing of the same kind as that by which he was defined. Undergoing the *surexistential*, in experiencing a modification that responds to it, and of which it is the reason (in the sense that the reason is the relation), is without a doubt the only way in which we are able to bear witness for it and be in a relation of action-passion with it. (210-211)

Of course, not every response is the response of existence to *surexistence*, just as for Souriau not every life is truly worthy of being lived. But there is no external standard, no reference at work here, as there was for the intensive modes of existence. It is necessary and it is sufficient that the mode of response from one existent to another should be a function of the *surexistential*, that is to say, that it brings it into play or implies it "as reason or as law of response" (211). And evidently this is what the act of instauration attests to:

> What made Michelangelo or Beethoven great, what made them geniuses, was not their own genius, but their attention to the qualities of genius residing not in themselves, but in the work. (211)

A formidable coherence. The keystone holds indeed. The trial has been passed. Perhaps, after all, we won't be devoured. Transcendence has been understood as a passage, as a real, active alteration, showing itself in the modal innovation that constitutes "the investment of existence in the modulation itself" (169).

But evidently all this holds only for those who ratify what Souriau has, since his first work, called a true life [*une vie veritable*]. This doesn't bother him in the slightest, we have no doubt. Success only has meaning if failure is possible. Souriau's aim is not to affirm that transcendence implicates, even if they don't know it, those who are content with the affairs of the body or the virtual riches of their souls. He's addressing those who have had an experience of this action-passion, of this involvement with the work, whatever it might be. Let them not moderate this experience according to what pertains to the modes of existence of the body or the soul. Let them know how to honor what makes them "spiritual" beings, whose mode of existence is nothing less than the investment of existence in the modulation of two others, the action-passion that attests to another form of reason, that is, to a relation with a something else. Let them

84

know that in this way they bear witness to a being that doesn't yet exist, but whose reality is "higher and richer than that of any of those polyphonic voices" (212).

The *surexistence* described by Souriau is completely opposed to any wager on transcendence. Perhaps there is a higher and richer reality, but there cannot be another world, and certainly not a world above this one [*pas de sur-monde*] offering a guarantee. And it's here, for the third time, that the theme of God resurfaces: "you believe yourself to be answering for God; but which God, in answering for you, situates you within the scope of your action?" (212).

We've already emphasized that Souriau's standard is composed of fervor and lucidity. The *surexistants* need us, our fervor, in order to exist, because fervor is a name for the modulation that bears witness to their reality. It's not a "generalized" fervor, a fanatical but confused spirituality. It bears witness to *surexistence* only if it engages in a work, which is always *this* work, the only work bearing witness to this *surexistant*—in a modal, specular way, certainly, and as a riddle. This is where lucidity is important, for assurance is out of place here. *Surexistants* are well and truly without idealistic excess, as if reintroducing in an underhand way a standard of value, a perfection, the fixed-point of a duty. We must dare to interrogate the mirror, to ask the question concerning reality to which we offer a hand-hold in existence.

> One love is annihilation in a communion with a false reality, forged in its depths of nothingness; another is a veritable work, creative and fertile. We can be tricked. We can suffer tragic confusion. To know—through the very nature of the work to which we bear witness when actually working to instaure it, and through the direct experience of the instauration—how to isolate that which *really* is plenitude and richness, is to know that which is most capable, in existence itself, of approaching *surexistence*. (214)

CONCLUSION: IT IS UP TO THE READERS
TO UNDERTAKE THIER OWN JOURNEY

And so, do we not find ourselves back again at the closing words of the book, the ones that in the capacity of attentive and sympathetic guides we had offered to the reader as the summit to be attained? Do the readers now finally understand for themselves how it is that the world deployed by Souriau has become capable of "causing even the Gods in their interworlds to feel a yearning for the 'to exist'—as well as the longing to come down here by our sides, as our companions and our guides" (193)? Were the world to be reduced to two modes—object and subject—what god would be so mad, so masochistic or so ascetic as to yearn for that? But the world given by Souriau, with its pure modes, with its patuity and its efficacity, and with its *surexistence*, is this world not more worthy of being inhabited?

Hence the question we can't resist asking: does Souriau deserve the oblivion into which he has fallen? Is he a failed philosopher? It is legitimate to ask such a question, for Souriau himself never stopped thinking about the very conditions of failure. Did he ever have doubts, he who was in his day a teacher at the Sorbonne, a case-study of institutional success, and representing the self-assurance of a bygone world, with his patrimonial approach, his outdated style and his absorption in the monumental as much as in the idea of the artist at work? Did he feel himself vacillating as the successive blows of existentialism, phenomenology and, later, structuralism set out to eradicate the very idea of a work of art, architectonic projects of any sort, and even, in the end, the institution itself? For all that, sixty years on, it feels like the lay of the land in relation to risk and academicism has shifted in a profound way. It is the iconoclasts who seem passé and this mandarin who seems to have taken all the risks. Precisely because he recognized that an institution was as fragile as a work of art and because, from his first writings, he knew the feeling of how easy it can be to lose one's soul.

We might be tempted to pass before the astonishing conceptual architecture deployed by Étienne Souriau in the same way as Diderot predicted that future generations would pass before the massive edifice of rational mechanics, as provided by the work of Bernoulli, d'Alembert and Euler: contemplating it with fear and admiration in same way as those who, standing at the foot of the pyramids, wondered at the strength and resources of the men who had raised them up.[59] But Diderot's prediction was optimistic, in accordance with his hope for a future in which an alliance would be forged between "those who are intellectually inclined" and "their more active colleagues,"[60] and in accordance with his disdain for those who in terrible solitude took up a body of work made to persist for centuries to follow.[61] We (unfortunately) can't inherit Souriau in this way. His voice really does seem to come to us as if from another world, a world whose inheritance remains to be inventoried.

And yet, for Souriau, to inherit is to re-make. If our reading has indeed tried to "re-make" Souriau, it was not to conserve, to allow what has been "re-made" to secure for itself [conquérir] continuity. There's no doubt about it, continuity has been smashed to pieces. As far as we are concerned, it's been about opening an approach to the question that is perhaps the question of our times, the question that is now pressing down on the majority of people of the Earth. It is the question of an alternative way of inheriting, with special attention placed on the "how?," since a continuity that has been smashed to pieces does not simply put itself back together again. "How are we to inherit?" is the question with which we are confronted when reading Souriau. It is a "questioning situation" to which he himself did not provide a response, but in the face of which he had the strength to show "that it implicates us."

59. Cf. Diderot (1999), IV, p.37. [TN]

60. Citing Diderot (1999), I, p.35, "L'intérêt de la vérité demanderait que ceux qui réfléchissent daignassent enfin s'associer à ceux qui se remuent." [TN]

61. Cf. Diderot (1999), XXI, p.43. [TN]

BIBLIOGRAPHY

Charles, D., et al, (1980), *In memorium: l'art instaurateur* (Paris: Union Générale d'Éditions), special edition of *Revue d'esthétique*, no. 3-4.

De Vitry-Maubrey, Luce, (1974), *La pensée cosmologique d'Étienne Souriau* (Paris: Éditions Klincksieck).

Deleuze, Gilles, (2011, 1968), *Difference and Repetition* (trans. Paul Patton, London: Continuum).

Deleuze, Gilles, and Guattari, Félix, (1994, 1991), *What is Philosophy?* (trans. Graham Burchell and Hugh Tomlinson, London: Verso).

Deleuze, Gilles, and Parnet, Claire, (1987, 1977), *Dialogues II* (trans. Hugh Tomlinson and Barbara Habberjam, New York: Columbia University Press).

Diderot, Denis, (1999), *Thoughts on the Interpretation of Nature and Other Philosophical Works* (trans. Lorna Sandler, ed. David Adams, Manchester: Clinamen Press).

Eco, Umberto, (1979), *The Role of the Reader: Explorations in the Semiotics of Texts* (Bloomington, IN: Indiana University Press).

Fontanille, Jacques, (1998), *Sémiotique du discours* (Limoges: Presses de l'Université de Limoges).

Greimas, Algirdas Julien, (1983, 1968), *Structural Semantics: An Attempt at Method* (trans. Daniele McDowell, Ronald Schleifer and Alan Velie, Lincoln, NE: University of Nebraska Press).

Haumont, Alice, (2002), "L'individuation est-elle une instauration? Autour des pensées de Simondon et de Souriau", in Chabot, Pascal, (ed), *Simondon* (Paris: Vrin), pp.69-88.

Latour, Bruno, (2009), *On the Modern Cult of the Factish Gods* (Durham, NC: Duke University Press).

Musil, Robert, (2011, 1978), *The Man Without Qualities* (trans. Sophie Wilkins and Burton Pike, Picador: London).

Netz, Reviel, (2003), *The Shaping of Deduction in Greek Mathematics: A Study in Cognitive History* (Cambridge: Cambridge University Press).

Péguy, Charles, (1992), *Clio: dialogue de l'histoire et de l'âme païenne* in *Oeuvres en prose complètes, tome III* (ed. Robert Durac, Paris: Gallimard, bibliothèque de la Pléïade, three volumes).

Simondon, Gilbert, (1958), *Du mode d'existence des objets techniques* (Paris, Aubier).

Souriau, Étienne, (1925), *Pensée vivante et perfection formelle* (Paris: Hachette).

(1925), *L'abstraction sentimental,* (Paris, Hachette).

(1938), *Avoir une âme: essai sur les existences virtuelles* (Paris, Les Belles Lettres/ Annales de l'Université de Lyon).

(1939), *L'instauration philosophique (*Paris, Alcan).

(1955), *L'ombre de Dieu* (Paris: Presses Universitaires de France).

(1959), *Les deux cent mille situations dramatiques (*Paris, Flammarion).

Souriau, Étienne, and Souriau, Anne, (eds.), (1999), *Vocabulaire d'esthétique* (Paris: PUF).

Stengers, Isabelle, (2011, 2002), *Thinking with Whitehead: A Free and Wild Creation of Concepts* (trans. Michael Chase, Cambridge, MA: Harvard University Press).

(2010, 2003), *Cosmopolitics I (Posthumanities)* (trans. Robert Bononno, Minneapolis, MN: University of Minnesota Press).

(2006), *La Vierge et le neutrino* (Paris: Les empêcheurs de penser en rond/ Le Seuil).

Whitehead, Alfred North, (1920), *The Concept of Nature: The Tarner Lectures Delivered In Trinity College, November, 1919* (Cambridge: Cambridge University Press).

THE DIFFERENT MODES OF EXISTENCE
ÉTIENNE SOURIAU

First Chapter:
Position of the Problem

§1. Does thought exist, in itself and through itself? Does matter exist and in the same manner? Does God exist? Did Hamlet, the *Primavera*, Peer Gynt exist, do they exist, and in what sense? Do the square roots of negative numbers exist? Does the blue rose exist?

Is it enough to respond to each of these questions (in the affirmative, in the negative, or in whatever way—and already this is not so simple)? Certainly not. By their very accumulation, these questions pose another, vaster question, which contains them all: are there several manners of existing? Is the "to exist" [*l'exister*] multiple, that is, not contained within the individuals in which it is actualized and invested, but rather contained in its types?

§2. Philosophy has always kept this question open. But the responses of the philosophers are tendentious. For while they affirm, they also desire. And, in accordance with what they desire, we see existence sometimes blossom into multiple modes, and at other times, once again become one.

If, when we speak of being, the hope is to see it reign in numerical solitude, all at once the multitude of beings—those supposed beings—that common sense thought it perceived as becoming phantasmal, gathers into tribes, each rallied by the banner of a particular type of existence, so as to be reunited and dissolved in being. It is in this way that we first see all the bodies gather together and then all the ideas. Or what we could call the possibles, the contingents, the necessaries. And, in order to encompass this multitude, the unique being becomes the synthesis of all the types of existence, and unites all of these rays in itself. Spinoza is "intoxicated" by the unicity of substance. But he immediately splits it apart and demonstrates an order, a connection of things, according to the attribute of extension; an order which is redoubled according to the attribute of thought, and then according to an infinity of other attributes, each attribute being eternal and infinite in its kind; none of which suffices to account for the richness of reality possessed by substance, for, "the more reality or being each thing has, the more attributes belong to it."

§3. Eliminate the keystone, take away the pantheistic unity of substance, and it is not the world that is divided into a plurality of parts (since, according to Spinoza, the modes correspond to one another, from one attribute to another), but the "to exist" that irremediably divides into a multiplicity of types. This is the same multiplicity similar to when we, without eliminating the unique, place it above existence. "I pray to God," says Meister Eckhart, "to allow myself to be even with him; for the being without being is beyond God. What could one sacrifice that would be more dear to God than sacrificing God for his own sake?" Plotinus, who does not accept the homonymy of the verb "to be," when it is applied to the One or to the beings that radiate from it, counts nine kinds of existence.

§4. Conversely, far from positing the unicity of being, some philosophers recognize a multitude of really substantial beings. But the more these latter become a multitude, the more their existential status becomes identical and unique. Take for example, the atomists, whether we speak of Epicurus or Gassendi or even, in certain respects, Leibniz. They divide being all the way up to the ultimate limits of division. But these beings are similar, and are founded, for example, upon antitype and indivisibility. And in the end, despite its apparent richness and complexity, the innumerable assemblage of these beings only bears witness to a single type of existence, for which a single atom can be presented as the unique model. At most, two different manners of existing can be recognized from this point of view (as is the case in Leibniz), that of the simples and that of the composites.

§5. Leibniz is quite interesting here. We just saw him cited as an atomist. But far from being that and that alone, he alternates between the two movements that were just in question. After having followed the path of the atomists, after having reduced existence to the monadic kind, and having made even God a monad among monads, he sets out in the opposite direction. Among the monads, he begins to consider a profound difference between those that are created, which only exist through God, and the uncreated monad, the necessary Being. Then, beyond these created beings, which have only a de facto or contingent existence, he perceives essences and truths that are eternal and immutable. And what is their existential status? Taken together, they form the kingdom of the possible, which must also have some reality. For the rest, for the necessary Being, "to be possible is enough to be actual," and possibility grounds existence, which he therefore possesses eminently. By means of the light shed by him upon the world, we distinguish "a moral world in the natural world," a kingdom of efficient causes and a kingdom of final causes, a physical kingdom of nature and a moral kingdom of grace, which proceed like two distinct ontologies resting on different principles. Thus, when he began with the multitude of beings, Leibniz tended to affirm the unicity of their type of existence, for which the single human monad was able to serve as the example. But when, conversely, he begins with the "primitive unity" (*Monadology*, §47), the real immediately begins to split apart according to different kinds of existence. In short, the two movements of thought between which the philosophers are generally divided—some tending to admit existential plurality, others tending to deny it, while at the same time denying or admitting, for inverse reasons, the plurality of existing beings—appear to Leibniz alone as a twofold swaying to and fro.

§6. Thus we see the profound difference that resides between an ontic pluralism (positing the multiplicity of beings) and an existential pluralism (positing the multiplicity of modes of existence). As pantheism shows, ontic monism can accommodate itself to an existential pluralism. And ontic pluralism can endeavor to enhance the value of an existential monism, as in the case of the atomists.

§7. Yet if there appears to be something of an opposition and inversity [*inversité*] between the existential and the ontic plurality, we will immediately confirm that this opposition, though frequent, is not necessary. There can exist—rarely, it is true—an integral monism, which proclaims both the unity of being and the unicity of existence: this is the case with the Eleatics and, above all, with the Megarians.

And, on the other hand, there is a sort of hyperbolic pluralism, recognizing at once, with no connection between them, different beings and different types of existence. This is what we call polyrealism. Such are certain fideisms, like that of Schleiermacher, which posit a sentimental sphere of religion and a rational sphere of science, one being perfectly independent of the other.

§8. Unspoken ideas! Secret aspirations! What do the atomists, those "libertines," hope to do, if not to abolish the beings for which there would no longer be any kind of existence—those beings who only belonged to the purely moral experience or that of an utterly metaphysical hope. And, on the contrary, the adherents of existential pluralism grant themselves a universe of two or three compartments, a universe with a false bottom [*à double fond*], in order to restore the beings thus contested. As for the integral pluralists, the polyrealists, their hope is to show that the things of religion exist, without having to offend the things of science; like the integral monists, the Eleatics want to abolish movement, becoming, without being obliged to deny the world.

§9. Thus we see that our problem is at the center not only of what is most lively, but perhaps also of what is most tendentious, in philosophy. The most divergent conceptions of existence—not only metaphysical conceptions, but practical conceptions, as well—clash over a single proposition, that "there is more than one kind of existence," or conversely that "the word "existence" is univocal." Depending on our answer, the entire universe and all of human destiny will change appearance; especially if we combine those propositions by crossing them with the following: "There is more than one being," or else, "being is unique." Doors of bronze swinging with a fateful pulse—now open, now shut—within the philosophy of great hopes, in the universe of vast domains.

§10. After all, the world as a whole becomes quite vast if there is more than one kind of existence; if it is true that we have not exhausted it once we have covered all that exists according to one of its modes (for example, that of physical or psychical existence); if it is true that to understand it we need to include it in all that bestows upon it its meanings or its values; if it is true that, at each of its points, intersections of a network determined by constitutive relations (for example, spatio-temporal relations), it is necessary to enter into relation, like a basement window opening out onto another world, with an entirely novel ensemble of determinations of being—non-temporal, non-spatial, perhaps subjective, or qualitative, or virtual, or transcendent; perhaps of those determinations of being in which existence is grasped only in fleeting, nearly inexpressible experiences, or which demand of the intelligence an enormous effort in order to grasp that which it has not yet achieved, and which only a greater mind would be able to comprehend; if it is true that, in order to apprehend the universe in all its complexity, it is necessary to equip thought not only for all the multicolored rays of existence, but even for a new light, for a white light, unifying those rays in the luminosity of a *surexistence* which surpasses all those modes without subverting their reality.

§11. And conversely, the world is indeed intelligible and rational if a single mode of existence is able to explain all that it includes, if it is possible to organize it according to a single fundamental determination, or a single relational network. But let there be no mistake: all it takes for this methodical simplification to become illegitimate is a single fissure in the network. If, for instance, all beings have been described in quantitative relations, it is enough for the qualitative to prove indispensable for the explanation of veritable existents, or of variations in the degrees of their existence.

§12. And human reality will also become quite rich if it appears to imply several kinds of existence; if it appears that, in order for a man to fully exist, in order for him to conquer the entire truth of his being, he must (to follow the Biranian analysis) inhabit his biological existence as well as his sensitive, perceptive, and reflective existence, and then, finally, his spiritual existence. On the contrary, human reality will appear quite simple and rationalizable if only one of these types of existence is real; if, for example, a materialist dialectic is sufficient to posit the totality of existence; or if the individual had only to comprise a temporal existence, without concerning himself about the "infinity of points" (so to speak) of his being; if, for him, there is no existence outside of time, which his ignorance, in this respect, might be unaware of or leave vacant. All of which will be decided by a single little phrase: "there is only one manner of existing"; or else, "there are several of them."

§13. I have observed, says the physicist or astronomer, positrons and neutrons, electrons that could be represented according to intermittency and that were dancing the Ballet of the Quanta upon the stage of space and time, sometimes disappearing back into the wings of the Indeterminate; I have seen galaxies expanding, appalling dimensions for my little, human mind. But did all of this have a physical, objective, and cosmic existence; or a rational and representational existence; or, finally, a microscopic and telescopic existence; by which I mean an existence which is substantially bound to that of the thing, microscope, or of the thing, telescope?

I have dreamt of you, says Goethe to Ennoia-Helen or Vigny to Éva. And yet (they will still have to say), is there room for you in the real world, or would the being in whom you would be rendered incarnate not, rather, be unworthy of you in her essential manner of being? Are you, in your substance, a being of dreams, "are you such stuff as dreams are made on," as Shakespeare says, and therefore labile and precarious; or are you, rather, a necessary being, proceeding in me from profound causes and true motives? Is it simply a physiological fermentation that maintains you? Are you the Eternal Feminine, the Eternal Ideal, or the Eternal Lie? Are you a necessary and constant presence, or must one search for you among all that which will never be seen twice?

I have dreamt of me, better than myself, more sublime. And yet, it was me, a more real me. Is this sublime me a true being or an illusory one; a being of objective transcendent life or of contingent and subjective psychical life? An essence, an entelechy; or the illegitimate extrapolation of a tendency? And in what way will I be wisest and most positive: in saying, "this does not exist," or in attaching myself to it in order to live off of it?

§14. Such is the problem. Or rather, such are the questions to which a sound discussion of the problem should allow the philosopher to respond with peace of mind.

A key question, as we said a moment ago; a crucial point at which the most significant problems converge. Which beings will we take charge of in our minds? Will knowledge have to sacrifice entire populations of beings to Truth, stripping them of all their existential positivity; or, in order to admit them, will it have to divide the world into two, into three?

A practical question, as well. It is certainly of great consequence for every one of us that we should know whether the beings we posit or suppose, that we dream up or desire, exist with the existence of dream or of reality, and of which reality; which kind of existence is prepared to receive them, such that if present, it will maintain them, or if absent, annihilate them; or if, in wrongly considering only a single kind, vast riches of existential possibilities are left uncultivated by our thought and unclaimed by our lives.

On the other hand, a remarkably restricted question. As we can see, it is delimited by the question of knowing whether or not the verb "to exist" has the same sense in all of its uses; whether the different modes of existence that philosophers have been able to highlight and distinguish all deserve the title of "existence" in full and equal measure.

Finally, a positive question. One of the most important, by virtue of its consequences, that philosophy can propose, it presents itself in the form of precise propositions, each susceptible to methodical critique. Making an inventory of the most important of these propositions in the history of human thought; putting the chart in order; seeking the kind of critique to which they are accountable—all this is indeed a substantial task.

§15. Is it necessary to introduce this question through the presentation of an exemplary gleaning of existential distinctions, gathered at random: actual being and potential being; explicit, implicit, and complicit existences; modes of aseity and abaliety, of ipseity and alterity; existing formally, objectively, eminently; existence *an sich, für sich, bei sich* (Hegel); primary immediate existence (*Urerlebnis*) or mediate existence of appraised reality (Reininger); cognitive-real existence and emotive-imaginary existence, the latter being divisible into affective and volitional existence (H. Maier); *Dasein, Zuhandensein, Vorhandensein,* etc. (Heidegger)? What do such distinctions matter if we do not know the points of view from which they result, which of them are compatible with the others and which are not, or how exhaustive a scope they can have?

A historical review of the successive ways in which the problem has been posited would be more useful. Yet the proportions of this little book would reduce such a review to an unacceptable abridgment; and we will encounter the essentials of such a review later on. It would at least show us: how the thought of the primitives, or at least the thought anterior to philosophy, was above all sensitive to axiological existential distinctions, which are often recorded in philological evidence (the profane and the sacred; the "strong" and "weak" genera of the Maasai language; the animate and inanimate, the fictive, of the Algonquin; the principles of the *yin* and *yang* of Chinese thought). How, at the philosophical stage, the Ionian distinction between the "to appear" and the "to be" leads (beginning with the existential opposition of phenomenon to substance) to Eleatic monism, based upon the ontological value accorded to the principle of the excluded middle. How Plato renews the problem with this brilliant idea: non-being is not privation of existence; it is, with respect to every determinate mode of existence, being-otherwise. How from this an existential pluralism results, to which Aristotle gave certain essential themes (actual being and potential being; the problem of the status of imaginaries [*des imaginaires*]; of the status of future contingents…), and which develops in the Middle Ages with a unanimous consent in favor of an extreme plurality of modes of existence (let us think only of the importance of the problem of the existence of the singular and the universal), to which the only significant dissidence is that of Duns Scotus, maintaining the univocity of being against the Thomist theory of analogy. How an important move on Plotinus' part is interposed between Aristotle and the Scholastics, proposing, on the one hand, the unification of the modes of existence, beyond existence itself; on the other hand, the idea of intensive degrees of being, which he deems to have been omitted by the Peripatetics—an idea which will be encountered again as much in the Gnostics (Basilides) as in the Christians (Origen, Saint Augustine, Nemesius, Aeneas of Gaza, Dionysius the Areopagite) and up to our day (Bradley or Marvin, degrees or levels) after having taken on a

104

distinctive meaning in the Renaissance with G. Bruno (theory of a minimum and a maximum of each singular existence). How Descartes wanted to reduce the modes of existence as much as possible, and yet had to recognize the non-univocity of created and uncreated substances, the difference between the existential principle of the union of the two substances and that of each of them in isolation. How Berkeley, in particular, opposed the possibility of a "general idea of being," and highlighted certain of its types (souls and ideas, relation and signification) as irreducible and radically heterogeneous; bodies ultimately exist "only in a secondary and relative sense." How Kant not only proposed the theme of phenomenal existence and noumenal existence, but recognized a number of other, more or less traditional, modes.[62] How Hegel transformed the tradition's most important modes into successive dialectical moments. How the continuity of the movement passing through Krause, Lotze, Meinong, and Baldwin finally leads to the phenomenological and existentialist schools, whose principal characteristics are, on the one hand, the postulation of the right to consider existence apart from its investments, the latter being temporarily "bracketed out"; on the other hand, the tendency to multiply its modes almost indefinitely by indissolubly integrating the attribute and the copula; to the extent that: to be human, to be in the world, to be past, to be present, to be future, to be as-belonging-to [être appartenant], to be receptive, to be remote, etc.; as many manners of being, less in the weak sense of the expression (modes of determination of a support) than in its strong sense: means of existing, specific conditions of existence, routes traveled or to be traveled in order to obtain access to being, modes of constitutive intentionality.

§16. Above all, such a historical review would make evident: first, the solidarity of a treasure trove [butin] that unites the most recent instances [instances] with the ineliminable experiences of the philosophia perennis; then, the urgency of

---

62. In the discussion of the paralogisms of pure reason alone, Kant successively introduces the following distinctions: existence as subject and existence as predicate; existence particular to the self and existence of the things outside of the self; a priori existence and determinate existence from the sensible point of view; existence diversified according to modality (existence in fact, or possible, or necessary), distinct from existence as category. Finally, intensive existence, considered as "degree of reality with regard to all that constitutes existence" (farther on: "plurality not of substances, but of realities forming a quantum of existence").

classifying, or organizing it all, of seeing if it arranges itself into complete charts, from which we might be able to obtain some general picture, some synoptic vision of existence in its totality; finally, the division of the problem into three principal questions.

The first is that of the intensive modes of existence. Before asking "does this exist and in what manner?," it is necessary to know if this question can be responded to with a yes or a no, or if it is possible to exist—a little, a lot, passionately, or not at all.…

The second, that of the specific modes, properly speaking, is governed by the opposition between two methods. We can consider invested experience and take responsibility for the total ontic content of human representation so as to classify its modes and evaluate its positive existential content; or rather (considering that existence can be found not only in beings, but between them), begin with as restricted an ontic given as possible and seek the shifts, the connections (representing new modes of existence), by which we can pass from the same to the other.

These two methods lead to different results. Both are equally valid. We will see that it is possible to coordinate their results and gradually recognize, in existence, the manners of being of various beings as well as the various modulations of the fact of existing, their echoes and their calls; thus distinguishing (to make use of a philological comparison) "semantemes" and "morphemes" of existence (see, farther on, §73 and 76).

The final question is that of the search for possible unifications, implicating the notion of *surexistence*.

This triptych will furnish us with the framework for our inquiry's general plan.

Second Chapter:
The Intensive Modes of Existence

§17. To exist fully, intensely, absolutely, what an ideal! To get out from under that incertitude of self, in which one vainly seeks oneself in a fog of unreality, on the banks of nothingness! To reign in the full pomp of the act of being! What an ideal; but also, how completely ideal, perhaps even a dream! Perhaps even an absurdity! Is it true that one can only half exist? Are not all things, this stone as much as this soul, equal in existence as soon as they exist? Are there strong and weak existences? Can the "to exist" be of greater and lesser degrees?[63]

---

63. From a philological point of view we will think of the two "kinds," weak and strong, of the Maasai language, which was just in question (§15). From a logical point of view we will think of the opposition between classifications by class and classifications by type, of which the latter aim, under their logistical aspect, to grasp "the gradable properties of things, which is to say, the qualities which may or may not be proper to a certain object, but which are proper to it at a more or less elevated degree." Cf. C.G. Hempel and P. Oppenheim, *Der Typusbegriff um Lichte der neuen Logik*, Leide, 1936. See their conclusions concerning the substitution of "the dynamic opposition *more* or *less*" for "the static opposition *or–or*"; and its application to the idea of existence as a "gradable property." These speculations go back, principally, to Benno Erdmann.

Yes, respond those who have experienced, or think that they can vividly imagine, this impression of semi-existence; as well as those for whom the word existence represents less a fact than a value; those for whom existence is an act, susceptible to diverse tensions.[64]

No! respond certain rigorous and even rigoristic [*rigoristes*] minds to the contrary, minds trained from childhood in order to found the virtue of veracity upon a strict separation of the thing that is from the thing that is not. Harsh souls, hardly inclined to indulge those intermediary limbos where insincerity and mythomania, as well as melancholia and murky, muddled existential aspirations, confusedly take the stage. Either we have existence or we do not, they will say. We are inside being or outside of it. And were we to straddle the limit, half in being and half outside, it would not be necessary to say that we exist weakly; we would have to say that a part of us exists—fully, really, totally—and that the other part does not.

§18. Let us give the first word to these rigorists.

They will admit that an existence can be more or less rich; that it can assemble a great deal of being in itself. But, they will say, the quantitative, here, is extensive. We can occupy vast or narrow cosmic dimensions, be comprised of many or few ideas or atoms; embrace more or less space or time; enclose a greater or lesser multiplicity. A kind will be rich in existence, which

---

64. In this regard, we observe two strongly opposed attitudes among the philosophers to whom we attribute, a bit too generally, the existentialist label. The first (the more authentic, perhaps, as the existentialism aligned with Kierkegaard), takes existence to be possessed in fact, prior to any effort (perhaps vain, says Jaspers; see, *Reason and Existenz*) to obtain philosophical knowledge of it. Cf. Nikolai Berdyaev, *Cinq Médit. sur l'exist.*, tr. fr. p. 62-64; or Semyon Frank, *La Connais. et L'Être*, tr. fr., p. 127. The other, issued from phenomenology and tinged with romanticism, takes existence to be a fact that may be easy to know, yet always remains to be achieved, to be fulfilled, and to be conquered, and is always remote. This is Heidegger's attitude. We will observe that Gabriel Marcel, who seems to agree with Berdyaev in *Être et Avoir* (p. 227), or in the First Part of the *Journal métaphysique*, where the idea of existence is strictly tied to the corporeal kind of existence, tends toward the second attitude in the Second Part, where the idea of existence is identified with that of salvation [*salut*]. In this author, the opposition of being and existence is so pronounced that it leads him to say that "the expression *being*" is itself detestable and devoid of sense (*ibid.* p. 181; regarding the question of the "to want to be").—As for Louis Lavelle, for whom the situation is more complex, it will be interesting to connect a long note on univocity in a recent article ("De l'insertion du moi dans l'être par la distinction de l'opération de la donnée," *Tijdschrift voor Philos.*, Nov. 1941, p. 728) with a passage from an older work (e.g., *Présence totale*, p. 88). – Finally, see Maurice Blondel, *L'Être et les êtres*, p. 11, 23, 103, etc.

brings together a great number of individuals. Likewise, a mind appears to be intense, which in reality is multiple, since it forms many ideas in a short time.[65]

Or else this richness will be based upon a logical, not an ontological quantity. A biological genus will appear to be richer in existence, more real, when it includes a greater number of species (without taking the number of individuals into account)[66]; a mind will appear existentially full and highly real, when it modulates across a great diversity forms.[67]

Even with regard to values, to the good and the bad (that privileged domain of privation and plenitude, according to a certain tradition), our rigorists will reject the possibility of interpreting them as degrees of being; and will only grant them real existence inasmuch as they can be reduced to a "this is"; for example, in considering them as judgments, having a greater or lesser extension as a social fact.[68]

The same goes for all that concerns becoming. They will refuse, for example, to see the sketch of an adolescent in the child, the sketch of a man in the adolescent, sketches more or less distant from an *acme*, which is to say, from the state of the perfect being that serves as their limit. They will invite us to see in the child of three, of seven, of twelve, so many realities to be taken as such, as sufficient unto themselves; and without anything virtual, without anything midway between nothingness and that perfect being to which they claim to refer it.

---

65. Nothing is more striking than the way in which Spinoza tends to reduce existential intensities to questions of plurality. Cf. *Ethics* I, P9; IV, P38; V, P11, P13, P38, P39; etc.

On the other hand, it is known that Bergson seeks to substitute diversities for intensities, but qualitative diversities, in which plurality only plays a part in an almost indefinable way. In certain respects it may be regrettable for his philosophy that his initial critique of the notion of intensive quantity led him to turn away from the problems of intensive existence. In short, there are two modes of existence for him, existence "in condensed position" and existence "in dispersed position" (as the harmonists say). Otherwise, all "more or less" is extensive.

66. See, e.g., É. Rabaud, "Adaptation et statistique," *Rev. phq.*, 1937, II, p. 28f.

67. Cf. texts, particularly by Amiel, assembled in C. Saulnier, *Le Dilettentisme*, p. 123, etc.

68. It is in this way that the question of existence—in the form of the assertoric, as opposed to the optative or imperative, modality of judgment—is at the foundation of Lucien Lévy-Bruhl's ideas concerning *Ethics and Moral Science*. As for the problem of knowing if morality *is*, particularly as a natural fact, we might bring him together with certain of Callicles' or Thrasymachus' ideas in Plato.

A point of view, which, denying the gradual advance from nothingness to existence, more or less posits the total accomplishment of all being, the impossibility of a stop midway. "It is not in the power of non-being to prevent being from constituting itself in its entirety; it is not in the power of being to be in such a way that there would be more or less existence in one place than in another" (Parmenides, see 103f).

A law of All or Nothing then requires that all the problems of existence be posed in the form of the *oppositio medio carens*. Thus Pascal urges us: God is or he is not. In vain will the libertine, a contemporary of Pascal or a future Renanist, hope to escape toward the idea of a more or less existing God, or something of the sort; for example, God as an ideal[69]; or as an immanent, reflexive given; or because one will identify his dubitable existence with a kind of weakness of existence. No, says Pascal, one must wager. Heads or Tails.

§19. Those philosophers who admit intermediaries between being and non-being are certainly more supple, more nuanced, more obliging; those for whom the possible, the potential, and even the infinite (as in Aristotle)[70] only resemble being and create a middle between it and non-being; or those men of science who, in studying an evolution, already perceive, in the present, the future of the being, midway through its journey, only needing a bit of maturation to emerge.[71]

---

69. We are thinking of Renan because that tender, ironic, elusive soul has expressly risen up against the idea of making the religious problem fit within the existential All or Nothing. Cf. *Drames philosophiques*, p. 78: "All that is ideal, non-substantial, does not exist for the people. When they say, 'this does not exist,' all is lost. I tremble at the thought of the day when this dreadful way of reasoning reaches God."

70. "Thus, since we cannot do without the infinite, and since it cannot exist in the full sense, it is necessary to recognize it as an existence inferior to full existence, and yet distinct from nothingness. This intermediary mode of existence, which Aristotle recognized in a general manner, and only a particular application of which is given in the solution to the problem of infinity, is potentiality" (Hamelin, *Système d'Aristote*, p. 284).

71. On the notion of emergence, see, in connection with the idea of development: Newman; with degrees of reality: Bradley; from a realist point of view: Whitehead, Hobhouse, Broad. Consider the "emergent evolution" of Lloyd Morgan; and the role it plays in the construction of the universe, according to Alexander. From the point of view of biology and experimental psychology, consult, e.g., the documents found collected in the *Année psychologique*, e.g., 1926, n. 576f.; 1931, n. 269f.; etc.; studies by Coghill, Carmichael, Shephard, and Breed on maturing behavior patterns and on their successive and spontaneous emergence at diverse stages of development.—Bergson made us of the notion of maturation

So be it. But are we not faced here with an unsatisfactory compromise, an indistinct idea evoking two ideas at once, in a bastard state, between which we would have to be able to choose? On the one hand, there is the idea of different kinds of existence—the possible, the potential, and the ready-to-emerge being *beside* the actual, the real, and seen through it, as if in rear projection, in another order of reality. On the other hand, there is the idea of a sort of weak existence, stammered out beneath the integral threshold of being.[72]

The truth is that there is certainly something implex in these ideas of possibility, of futurity ready for emergence, with which the problem of degrees of existence is easily contaminated. But this is not at all to say that the latter is a false problem. The real difficulty is that of finding the ground [*terrain*] from which the problem properly arises, and of clearing that ground of all manners of parasitic vegetation. To do so, we must follow the dialectical movement that engenders it, beginning with an existential affirmation.

Thus far, in opposing the two extreme, clashing theses, we have above all found two spontaneous attitudes of thought, perhaps similar to the opposition between tough and tender minds that was dear to James. We are still in the domain of opinion, of *doxa*.

(cf. *Creative Evolution*, pp. 15-23).

72. It is known that the Bergsonian critique of the idea of the possible (*The Creative Mind*, pp. 73-86)—as well as the idea of a practical non-impossibility, to which we will return—consists, above all, in pointing out an illusion, stemming from the retrojection, into the past, of an already accomplished present, which, having been accomplished in fact, then appears retrospectively as having previously been possible. Spinoza had presented the idea of the possible as relative to our ignorance of the determination of the causes to produce or not produce a thing (see, e.g., *Ethics*, I.P33.S1, IV.D4, and IV.P11-12). For a recent study connecting the idea of the possible with the plurality of the genera of existence, in particular, see Vol. XVII (*Possibility*) of the *University of California Publications in Philosophy*, particularly the study by G.P. Adams.—On what can be positive in the idea of the possible, without, however, making it a veritable mode of existence, see below, §60.

§20. I think, I exist. This can be immediately considered as a given, as indissoluble and ready-made. But as soon as existence is distinguished, by however little, from the thought that serves as its evidence and testimony, the possibility of doubt and the necessity of intensive modulations are introduced with the idea of measure: I exist to the extent that I think.

Descartes hesitates. If, without deferring to the reflective attitude, he takes thought and existence to be given together (I am, I think, I am thinking—it is all one), existence appears to be sufficient to him and the very problem of all or nothing does not arise: only the all is given. I am in existence, initially and completely. Can I even conceive of my nothingness? In fact, no effort has been made in that direction. The Cogito is not a truth that is re-established, that is instaured, after a tragic instant of total dissolution into universal doubt. It has not been compromised, not even by the hypothesis of the evil genius. It is a truth that we simply find persisting, alone untouched by doubt. A marble pillar intact after the blaze; not a column to be erected.

The correlative conceptions of nothingness and of integral existence, and of my intermediary status between the two, arise from a reflection upon the relations between existence and thought—a reflection which, in grasping their relation, separates the two terms. I am thinking. But what am I? What is this I? It is a thing that thinks. And what is it to think? For this I exists, thinking, only if this is a true thought.

As a result, my existence is no longer absolute; it is referred to something else.[73] The essence of thought becomes the origin of an abscissa, its complete existence is that of an ordinate. My actual thought is as far from the absolute perfection of thought as I am from the absolute perfection of existence. The one is a function of the other.

---

73. On this point, there is agreement between Cartesianism and the phenomenological-existentialist thesis briefly recalled above (§15): inseparability of the predicate and the copula in subsumptive judgments. To be human is to exist to the extent that one is really human. To be brought together with the Thomist theory of the *veritas in essendo*.

An entire construction results. Existence is measured. It has its zero and its infinity; and I occupy a position in between. It is a magnitude, and this magnitude is measurable.

Measurable? Surely this is lacking in precision. What exactly does this distance between my thought and the archetype signify? Is it a matter of a difference in nature or in value? Is it a matter of a greater or lesser resemblance? And is this archetype itself an abstract, notional standard; a pure essence of thought; or is it a matter of another kind of thought, serving as a model; a thought substantially different from my own, but equally actual? Or is it a matter of other moments of my own thought, compared to itself in its various instants, more or less lucid, more or less complete? Finally, does this double distance, from myself to the archetype of thought and from myself to complete existence, respond to two distinct orders of facts, or is it a matter of a single and self-same fact, considered from two different points of view?

So many questions that can be responded to in a variety of ways; that have historically been responded to in a variety of ways. When Kant takes up the question, when, in his important discussion of Mendelssohn's *Phaedon*, he introduces the idea that for a conscious being, degrees of consciousness imply degrees of existence, he conceives of these degrees of consciousness as being introspectively graspable through observation. The remove of thought from its perfection is conceived on the basis of a comparison between the various moments of an identical thought, between the various lucid states of an identical monad. When phenomenological existentialism refers this distance to that of a mundane thought in relation to a transcendental thought, it is a matter of an inactual archetype, situated in a different kind of existence other than that which is measured against it, despite its not being substantially distinct from it.

But Descartes himself had also taken a stance. For him, the archetype is transcendent, but also substantial and actual. It is God who serves as the referential term. As for my distance from him, it is a question of resemblance. In terms of my will, I am made in his image and truly his equal; in terms of my intelligence, the image is imperfect. There are degrees of resemblance. My intellectual resemblance to God is at once positive and mediocre. Correlatively, my situation between the zero and the infinity of existence is intermediary. It is a function of that imperfect resemblance and is measured against it. However, even though my distance from God and my distance from being are—insofar as the one determines the other—distinct in reason, in other respects they represent one and the same fact, since it is through God that I have being and that I am substantially dependent upon him.[74]

In certain respects, this last point restores the degree of existence to the subject himself, as he now finds within himself a certain degree of aseity, a strong or weak power of maintaining himself in being and of existing in and through himself. Ultimately, though, Descartes denies this aseity and establishes that, by myself, I have no power of maintaining myself. Thus, we can abstract, at least provisionally, from this immanentist point of view—pushed ajar only to be immediately shut again—and consider the two distances, in Descartes, as if they were two distinct orders of facts.

§21. What would result from this?

Something quite important.

Indeed, we can ask ourselves if Descartes overshoots the mark, so to speak; if intensive degrees of existence still actually subsist in the construction at which he stops.

The degrees of resemblance with God are akin to that great vision of the world of hierarchical degrees which generally

---

74. "[W]hen I consider the fact that I have doubts, of that I am a thing that is incomplete and dependent, then there arises in me a clear and distinct idea of a being who is independent and complete, that is, an idea of God…. I am, as it were, something intermediate between God and nothingness … insofar as I participate in nothingness or non-being, that is, in so far as I am not myself the supreme being and am lacking in countless respects" Descartes, *Meditations*, IV, in *The Philosophical Writings of Descartes*, vol. II, tr. Cottingham, Stoothoff, and Murdoch, pp. 37-38. See also, *Replies to the First Set of Objections*. The interpretation of this participation as effectively constitutive of the "degrees of reality" is formally affirmed in the *Replies to the Second Set of Objections*, ax. IV and VI.

It is interesting to bring this together with the ideas Pascal expresses in the fragment of the "Two Infinites" (*Pensées*, tr. W. F. Trotter, §72). There, Pascal presents the "sphere" [*milieu*] between being and nothingness as having "fallen to us as our lot." The position of our intellect in the order of [intelligible] things is the same as the position "our body occupies in the expanse of nature." For nature, nothingness is the limit of the infinitesimally small and being is the infinite in greatness. The necessity of considering these relations as existential is clearly affirmed. "The nature of our existence hides from us the knowledge of first beginnings which are born of nothingness." But, for us, the infinite above amounts to a nothingness, the extremes being in the same position with regard to us: "We are not within their notice." Only in God do these two extremes meet and reunite.

belongs to the Platonic movement, and which remains, at bottom, quite distinct from the idea of a world of degrees of existence. In Basilides, Aeneas of Gaza, Saint Augustine, Origen, and Dionysius the Areopagite (cf. above §15) we likewise find a world of gradations, with degrees of remove in relation to God. For example, this remove will be indicated by a progressive diminution of the effects of divine goodness (*Bonum sui diffusivum*), the result of its distributive justice.[75]

The good and the bad will thus be allocated quantitatively and each creature will participate in them to a greater or lesser degree, receiving an evaluable share of each. Correlatively, being and non-being will be quantitatively measured and meted out for them. As the cupbearer measures wine and water in the krater; as the potter measures sand and clay to make his clay body; so the Demiurge will measure out for each the share of being and non-being that falls to it. Recipe (if we dare to say it) for a stone: three quarters non-being, one quarter being. For a steer: *half and half.*[76] For a man, one quarter non-being, three quarters being. *Homo duplex.* A double nature is imparted to him in the proper proportion. There is nothing intensive about this; it is purely of the domain of arithmetic and therefore extensive quantity. According to the true Platonic tradition, this non-being is always the Other. The quantity of non-being that human nature contains is the quantity of the Other that it includes. Instead of first bringing together the all and the zero, and then bringing man into existence proportionally, we can simply set ourselves before man in the first place, as Nemesius and then Pascal will do, and take the measure of his being. If he appears to be empty and hollow, lacking in density of being, this is because we have only momentarily considered the being he contains. But reason is always proportional. It makes Man with some of himself and some of the other, each contributing to his nature, to the total plenitude achieved through the two principles.

Descartes clearly expresses his thought in this form in the text cited above. And to the extent that, as an algebraist and geometer, he thinks somewhat differently, to the extent that he instead conceives of the human situation between being and

---

75. Dionysius the Areopagite, *De div. nom.*, IV, 20.

76. In English in the original. [TN]

nothingness as a distance on an axis, his evaluation, for being geometric, belongs no less to the domain of extensive quantity.

§22. And let us not forget that all of this remains valid for the Kantian, Husserlian, or Heideggerian conceptions, insofar as they evaluate the degrees of existence of the conscious being, the thinking being, or the human being as distances in relation to a lucid consciousness, an essence of thought, or a fulfillment of intentions; and thus, insofar as they conceive of the distance between the being that is examined and the being that exists fully as that being's remove in relation to itself; a metaphysical, gnoseological, or even simply temporal remove. How long must I try, or what attempts must I make, and which dialectical aporiae must I overcome, in order to find and instaure myself in my plenary existence? According to Maine de Biran, the three degrees that man must traverse (the passage from biological existence to psychical existence, and then to spiritual existence) are a passage across three planes, across three existential ranks, which are, at once, three kinds of existence and three hierarchical degrees; for a Hegelian, they will be three dialectical moments. But no one is any more or less real in itself than another. And the intensity of existence only appears as an effect of perspective, so to speak, as the remove of a being, given in one existential status, in relation to that same being in a different existential status to which it is referred. A remove that is either qualitative (this is an aerial perspective) or quantitative and even measurable; capable of being counted by the dialectical moments or the different kinds of existence that must be traversed in order to attain it.

* *
*

§23. This analysis has just placed us in the presence of facts whose significance is hard to deny. For the most part, if not always, the philosophical theories that reveal intensive modes of existence do not find them immanent to an existence considered in itself. They make them appear through an effect of perspective, which situates them between different modes. They are relative not to *pure existence* (in a given kind), but to the order of *compared existence*. They are beyond pure existence, for which the Eleatic instance remains valid. They are in the

118

interval between two planes or modes of existence. In fact, it is precisely the passage from the one to the other that makes them appear. Each taken on its own, or in their static relation, that which was actualized as intensive in the dynamic stage can resolve itself in extensive considerations.

For if the two kinds under comparison can ultimately appear as fully real, the stage of passage, the transitive link is also real; and expresses itself through the positive experience of existential intensity.

§24. Yet we are hesitant to annul, so to speak, every parameter of intensity in a solitary mode of existence; to refuse a pure existence any possibility of a more or a less. Must we fully accept the Eleatic instance in this domain? And if so, where would such a difference in our treatments of pure existence and of compared existence come from? Would one of them deserve the name "existence" more than the other? Problems worth pursuing.

§25. One means of lending consistency to pure modal intensity still presents itself, however, and we must say at least a word about it: it is the thesis of the ontic population of the interval.[77]

The distance between myself and God would be concrete and substantial not through the number of nights of asceticism and purification, but through the reality of a "celestial hierarchy," through the presence, at each degree, of spiritual or mystical beings which would be the paradigms of those degrees (the Leibnizian thesis). Between me and the original cell, beyond which there would be nothing but biological nothingness, a positive series of living beings supports me and lends a

---

77. It is known that Louis Lavelle has strongly insisted upon this notion of the interval (cf., in particular, *L'Acte pur*, p. 200f.). As for us, we insist upon the impossibility of conceiving it otherwise than as a metaphysical interval between two modes of existence. For Mr. Lavelle, "the absolute interval would be the very interval separating nothingness and being" (*ibid.*, p. 202). But if the preceding is true, there is no interval between being and nothingness except in those constructions that bring the same and the other into play as modes of existence.

On the other hand, we know the effort that Heidegger has made to existentialize nothingness (cf. "What is Metaphysics?" in *Pathmarks*, ed. McNeill, p. 86): "the nothing is more originary than the 'not' and negation." Anxiety is its unveiling. All of this is interesting to compare, in French literature, with the precise declarations of the poet of nothingness, Leconte de Lisle: "The anxiety of nothingness will fill your heart… / … That which is no longer is such only for having been, / And the ultimate nothingness of beings and things / Is the sole reason for their reality…," etc.

plenitude and consistency to the interval that separates me from nothingness (the biological and evolutionist thesis).[78]

These positions are historically quite important, though—it is hardly necessary to mention this—they in no way modify the positions already established. To illustrate perspectival degrees and theoretical intervals, to render them concrete through the consideration of the concrete beings (imaginary or real) that serve as their paradigms is still to pass from one mode to another; it is to substitute for my own intensity a sort of external ladder, a stairway whose steps are populated with creatures, whether angels or animals, of an existential status absolutely different from that which makes me, myself, fully or halfway existent. It is not my own existence, it is the existence of those beings that I thus bring into the discussion, and that illusorily lend their consistency to my own. Thought always travels a circuit through other modes, as is characterized here in a pure and exemplary manner.

§26. Therefore, in order to truly test what is intrinsic to the existential plenitude at the heart of a single mode of existence, we would have to be able to rid ourselves, once and for all, of all those systems of reference, of all those circuits through other planes. We would have to place ourselves before, or at the heart of the specific existence of a being [*étant*]; to test it, so as to know up to what point, in this isolated state, it maintains itself by itself and shows itself to be intensive.

But we cannot achieve such existential purity without a sufficiently difficult asceticism of thought.

As we said a moment ago, the Cogito itself, having never discovered a true motive for existential doubt, has never achieved such an asceticism. Instead, we would have to place ourselves in the perspective opened by G. Bruno when he speaks of a being's oscillation between its maximum and its minimum. But therein lies the entire problem: how will the mean mode, taken as

---

78. Note the tendency of various minds to consider either the interval below or the interval above (and also, through contamination, the past and the future) as *more* real, depending on the kind of reality attributed to the beings that constitute its population and *Erfüllung*. Consult Bergson's important pages (*Creative Evolution*, pp. 304-329) on the Greek philosophers, for whom every position of reality implies the reality of inferior (or anterior) degrees. Compare those pages with H. G. Wells' strange discussion of the reality of beings of the future (*The Discovery of the Future*, conference of the Royal Institution, Jan. 1902). Bring this together with the problem of the existential relations between the large and the small, touched upon below (§95).

the point of departure, be assured of not being a fully realized given; how will we feel real oscillations around this middle? We would have to grasp them in a real doubt on the part of man concerning his own existence, a doubt founded upon the direct examination of the latter; upon an interrogation so unsteady, so shot through with perplexity, that in posing the question "am I?," the possibility of responding in the negative is not excluded.

Let us insist. We must not reduce the question "am I?" to the question "what am I?" We must not allow the response "I am not," or "I hardly am," to mean "I am not myself," or even "it is not I who am, but something is, and I am merely participating in it." For example, it is God who is, or (transposing *Ich denke* to *Es denkt in mir*) it is thinking [*Denken*] that is. The response "no" or "hardly" must mean: there, where I am looking, there, where I am testing existence, there is only a little bit of existence or none at all. In other places and for other things, it is of no concern.

In order to fully understand this terrible interrogation, which truly calls existence into question, will we have to evoke a man dying on a battlefield, regaining consciousness for an instant and asking himself if he really exists? Tolstoy was haunted, literarily, by this figure. Yet it is either too literary or it is ineffable and far too tragic in its reality. It will suit us better to borrow a less remarkable and more accommodating fairy tale from folklore.

§27. "One year later, the dead man returned to Earth so as to once again see what he had loved so much. He returned thirsting for revenge."

There he is, existing anew; and, let us say, walking down a twilit road that follows the seashore. He is like a man recovering from amnesia. He has vague memories, as if from a previous existence. "Did I really exist?" He asks himself questions: "Where am I? What am I like?" Can these questions not wait until later? All of this will become clearer, more organized, more certain. But there are hints. That sunken road. It leads somewhere … Premonitions.[79]

---

79. Naturally, the reader who is embarrassed by phantasmagoria can imagine that this is really the story of an amnesiac. But if the latter really poses his problem thus, it amounts to the same thing and to what we are looking for: the question is posed according to the concrete varieties of a real doubt.

Could this not be a dream?—a poorly posed question. If it was a dream, somewhere there would be a man in a bed, sleeping. It seems to me, he says, that I am a man who is walking. The toil of my feet in the sand. Lights flickering on the horizon. Tepid, aimless winds. It is the arbitrariness of the given which overwhelms my mind, and yet which establishes me and keeps me from believing in nothingness…. There is something. A world barely determined by several imperfect and precarious hints. I am not contained in—so as to be buttressed by—some enormous and indubitable ensemble, which I might know, and which might answer for me [*réponde pour moi*]. However weak and worn down I feel myself to be, I must answer to myself alone, in order for this world to gradually be installed around me. And what is there within me? That love, that desire for revenge. A mission. I have been sent here for something. I am a man headed toward some work, still to be accomplished…. I am, insofar as I am this Emissary. I am an instrument in the hands of a God who has granted me life in giving me this mission; but that God also needed me—he needed such an Emissary. If I find that the will that legitimates my presence here is sufficiently strong in me, then I am that Emissary, walking toward a house I see, that I must have seen….

Let us not take the fable too far. Following the legend, let us imagine the ghost inside the house, invisible, watching as his wife and the very young child of another man dine, feeling his desire for revenge vanish before this sight, little by little until extinguished completely, and, at the cock's crow, as his desire for revenge finally vanishes, vanishing himself, since it was, at once, his *raison d'être* and his being.

§28. Why tell this ghost story? Because each of us more or less—as soon as we *seriously* question ourselves about our being—is this ghost. Because, instead of feeling included and engaged in a world, which answers for and supports him, which, as is usually the case, prevents him from posing the question "am I?," he too is only led to ask this question for some reason. What reason? The fact that, for a moment, he agreed to answer for the world, instead of the world answering for him. And his strength fails him immediately. It is like the shipwrecked sailor, who has swum for a very long time—furiously, peacefully, with great, rhythmic efforts of his arms and legs, instinctively or with training—for he was seized and held by the momentum and

122

reality of the catastrophe. Then, suddenly, it dawns on him that he is alone, swimming in the vast ocean. And so he loses all his strength at the very moment he becomes conscious; and can only let himself founder.[80]

All the drama resides in this reversal of perspective—*de jure* always possible, *de facto* always effectible and at every moment. It is not a question of man in the world (let us avoid sending the reader down a wrong path) or outside of the world. Nor is it a question of the objective or the subjective, of idealism or realism. Those are only partial or technically specific aspects of the general and fundamental problem. It is a question (to speak like the scholastics) of aseity or abaliety, as two kinds of existence; to be in and through oneself or to be in and through some other thing. In this relation between the self and the other, which we can perceive in every being and which I can perceive in myself, the existential responsibility can be borne either by the one or by the other, and can be transposed entirely to one side or the other, changing the being's equilibrium.

What is this other? With aseity, it is a matter of existence proper, independent, absolute in its mode; with abaliety, a matter of referred existence.

Our ghost of a moment ago existed as the missionary of a revenge mission, as emissary. Such a man will feel himself to be existentially constituted and buttressed by an appeal, a vocation. Sent by a God, this God answers for him, in certain respects; or else it is the world that answers for him, the world about which he feels himself called to deliver his testimony. But who assures us that God answers for us? Who will answer for him, in order to ensure that I am not usurping this mission and that he sanctions it? Is it not true that, at bottom, it will always remain the case that, in certain respects, it is up to me and me alone, examining myself, to know if I answer for God

---

80. Let us make note of a point whose importance will be confirmed in what follows: the fact that part of this feeling of vacillation, this feeling of a decrease in being, results from precisely that paring down, that reduction to a kind of existence. We will encounter this feeling again, since each mode of being, reduced to what it intrinsically is, will appear tenuous and fragile to those who are for the most part accustomed to considering complexes of existence; beings established in several modes simultaneously, making each commensurate with all the others and assembling them all within itself.

or if God answers for me.[81] To answer for God or to answer to God? I answer to God if I answer the appeal and the external vocation with an internal vocation, with an interior reality of the vocation. And if I answer to it poorly and feebly, God, for his part, ceases to answer for me, for my existence. He abandons me—and the ghost, proving to be a flimsy and unsuitable instrument—vanishes once more. If he fails completely, he is annihilated completely, for that is all he was.

But, on the other hand, I answer for God, or for the world, or for the object of my thought, insofar as God needed me for this mission; insofar as he needed not a weakling, but someone with the strength for the task; insofar as I could deceive him or not as regards my personal strength or weakness. And brought back to myself in this way, I have only myself for support. Is that enough? In any case, that alone will have to rise to the task— that which is here, it hardly matters whether or not I call it me, will have to rise to the task as best it can; or nothing will.

Under the first aspect, of course, I was judged and supported at the same time. But that did not spare me from the terrible power of reversing the question, of considering myself to be solely responsible for my own quiddity, and in certain respects of supporting, of maintaining God, insofar as God needs me. Am I strong enough, by myself, to bear my mission? When referred to my *raison d'être*, I was weak in comparison with the accomplishment, with the perfection in itself of the reason with respect to which I was judged. When I weigh my strength—the strength with which I answer to that reason—am I strong or am I weak? Both at the same time. I have this strength. Is it really strength or is it weakness? Who is to say? Does it even make sense to speak this way? I am this strength such as it is, this strength itself in itself.

Will I assure myself of my being on the basis of the intensity of my joy or my sorrow? I feel this sorrow; it assures me of my being. I can (like that madman Gerolamo Cardano) take

81. Think of the problem of prayer. Cf. Fernand Ménégoz, for example: from a certain point of view, the believer attaches himself to and suspends himself from God by means of prayer; he believes in God. From another point of view, he posits the Divine by means of his prayer; he believes in God. The same goes for Husserlian intentionality. From a certain point of view, the intentionality of a thought refers that thought to its transcendent, the fulfilled intention. From another point of view, the thought posits and includes the intention, as immanent to the act of thinking.

pleasure in making myself suffer in order to assure myself of my being. I exist; I know so on account of my extreme sorrow. *O vos omnes qui transitis per viam, attendite et videte si est dolor sicut dolor meus!*—What do you call sorrow, you senseless child? That you put your puerile sufferings on display for us? Have you lost dearly beloved children, do you refuse all consolation, like Rachel or Niobe? Have you seen all hope vanish and all your pride fall to pieces? Have you seen Jerusalem razed forevermore? Do you cry the tears of all humanity, for all humanity, like Jesus in the Garden of Olives? Your sorrow will always be weak if you compare it to Sorrow itself, to the limit and very essence of all sorrow. Yes, but this sorrow is mine, for me and at this very moment it is the entirety of suffering. What will sorrow be if this is not an instance of it? However weak my own sorrow may be, do I not bear witness to sorrow itself, in its essence? Even if it is no more than a child's grief, it is, with its strength or its weakness; its strength or weakness resides in it and constitutes it.

*
* *

§29. Perhaps we know enough to respond, now definitively, to the question at hand.

When referred to the essence of sorrow, a real sorrow will always be weak. But considered in itself, after that still relative, existential vacillation, which comes to it from its detachment from the other, from its reduction to itself; its intrinsic strengths or weaknesses become constitutive. They are no longer strengths or weaknesses of existence, they are existing strengths or weaknesses, and are so at the interior of an existence, which they accomplish or perfect for what it is. As integral or analyzable elements of this existence, they do not divide existence, which only results from their assemblage in a single presence. Existence is not analyzable. Let us call what appear to be elements of existence by another name. Let us call them, for example, reality.

§30. Yonder, on the horizon, a thin, slightly rosy vapor stands out upon the bluish evening sky. Must we see in this the weak existence of a rose-colored cloud, or the existence of a cloud, faintly tinged with rose?

Let us remark that therein lies the entire problem of perception. Whether it be a tree seen through fog, or a landscape through a steamy windowpane, or ill-adjusted eyeglasses. "What then!" Cournot exclaims, naively enough,[82] "according to Bacon's excellent comparison, between our eye and the visible objects, we interpose glasses that contort the lines, deform the images; and what was clear, regular, and well ordered becomes muddled and confused: how can the interposition of the glasses call to mind a participation in nothingness?" If we are given the tree, our retina, and the glasses in an objective ontology, a diminished existence clearly never intervenes in the relations between them. It is our percept, referred to a typical, clear and distinct vision, which is made to participate in nothingness. And this participation is something positive, insofar as our confused perception does not proceed without embarrassment, without appetition for an optimum vision—without an appeal to the archetype. But, in its turn, this percept ceases to participate in nothingness if it is taken in itself, seen as constitutively out of focus and indistinct, accompanied by such an appetition. At most, we will say that, as a percept, it is not very real, in the sense that it is constituted by poorly ordered elements and in a poorly defined relation with an objectivizing [*objectivante*] intention. Thus, three pictures or three givens: the pure existence of the percept itself; an undecomposable existence, to be taken as such, whose greater or lesser reality is all there is for us to examine. Beyond that, on the side of the archetype or the ideal, a model of distinct perception, for which another perception (that which one would have with well-adjusted glasses) can serve as an example. And below it, on the side of objective, physical existence, the things—eye, glasses, tree—whose reality as physical existents we can moreover assess (it will be nothing to the tree, for example, if, all corrections having been made, it was nothing but an illusion, or a mirage, etc.). Without such a strict, exhaustive analysis, there is nothing in all of this besides idols of confusion and poorly posed problems.

§31. But let us return to our cloud. Weak existence of a rose-colored cloud, we said; or existence of a cloud, faintly tinged with rose?

In the first case, we are in the domain of referred, compared existence. We call to mind, in the usual fashion, the solid and

82. *Considérations*, 2nd ed., t. I, p. 260.

illuminated fullness of a superb and perfect cloud, the glory of a lovely evening, to which we then compare our cloud, now no more than an inceptive sketch or a hint of the first. In the other case, it is a question, rather, of what is, not of an ideal and representative archetype. But also, what is, is; and fully occupies its pure existence. If we can discern in it weaknesses, lacks, and delicate gray vaguenesses, all of this determines it and accomplishes it for what it is. What I can speak of, then, is this tenuousness or vagueness as constituting a barely consistent "reality" (here, specifically, a *chosalité* [*a thing-reality*]) for it. Now hardly real, it will become more so when it is concretized, strengthened, and constituted as an effective reflector of light. But the modification of these conditions of reality will not make it exist more. Let us not confuse factors of reality (which must be analyzed for each mode of existence) with so-called factors of existence.

Let us add that the instability and brevity of certain existences, quickly constructed and almost immediately destroyed (notably in the psychical order), easily create the illusion of a weak existence; while we readily bestow a superior level upon durable and stable existences. And quite incorrectly.[83]

§32. It would not be useful to insist upon this further. We will have to consider the specific factors of reality for each mode of the "to exist." Nor is it the right moment to discuss the greater or lesser suitability of this vocabulary. In conformity with the usage of certain thinkers, though not all (nothing fluctuates more than the use of the words existence and reality),[84] let this vocabulary only serve to distinguish the plane of the integral elements from the integration, which alone certifies the indivisible possession of existence—we ask nothing more of it. All that we require is that we have the words to describe this essential fact, the fundamental object at this point in our study being the anaphoric variations of a being, rising, little by little, toward its maximum of presence.

---

83. We will return to these ideas, and also to the error of attributing a stronger existence to that which is simply greater, spatially more vast, in §53 and §95. This higher value, which often creates the illusion of a more intense "to exist," will be treated in §93.

84. The usage we employ therefore conforms sufficiently enough with the Kantian vocabulary. We will have occasion to return to the difference between existence and reality for MacTaggart. Cf. *Nature of Existence*, Book I, Ch. I, Section 4: *Reality does not admit of degrees?*

§33. A lump of clay on the sculptor's bench. A *réique* existence—undeniable, total, accomplished. But nothing yet exists of the aesthetic being, which has still to bloom.

Each application of the hands and thumbs, each action of the chisel accomplishes the work. Do not look at the chisel, look at the statue.[85] With each new action of the demiurge, the statue gradually emerges from its limbo. It moves toward existence—toward an existence, which in the end will burst forth in an intense and accomplished, actual presence. It is only insofar as this heap of earth is consecrated to being this work that it is a statue. Existing only weakly, at first, through its distant relation with the final object that gives it its soul, the statue gradually frees itself, takes shape, exists. The sculptor, who at first only senses it, accomplishes it, little by little, with each of the determinations he gives to the clay. When will it be finished? When the convergence is complete, when the physical reality of the material thing meets the spiritual reality of the work to-be-made [*l'œuvre à faire*], and the two coincide perfectly; to such an extent that in both its physical existence and its spiritual existence, the statue now communes intimately with itself, the one existence being the lucid mirror of the other; when the spiritual dialectic of the work of art permeates and informs the mass of clay such that it is made to burst forth in spirit; when the physical configuration in the material reality of the clay integrates the work of art into the world of things and gives it presence, *hic et nunc*, in the world of sensible things.

§34. Let us insist still more; for we are at the very key of the problem and will have to return, in what follows, to this important experience of the anaphoric movement, the peak of which is an intense, existential presence, in relation to which prior beings or states are only preliminary sketches and preparations.

To instaure, to build, to construct—to make a bridge, a book, or a statue—is not simply the gradual intensification of an initially weak existence. It is carrying stone after stone, writing one page after another.... To create a work of thought is to give birth to a thousand ideas and to submit them to rela-

---

85. It is not for nothing that when Spinoza wants to teach the philosopher the distinction between two of the four senses of *being* [*des quatre être*] that are distinct in creatures, he sends him "to some sculptor or woodcarver" (*Metaphysical Thoughts*, Part I, Ch. II *in calce*).

tions, to proportions; it is to invent great, dominant themes and to impose their control over the ideas, those monstrous rebels that need to be subdued time and again. It is also to choose, to select, to discard. And each of these actions *entails a judgment*, which is at once the cause, the reason, and the experience of this anaphor, of each moment in the progressive coming together of two modes of existence. Each new informing [*information*] is the law of an anaphoric stage. Each anaphoric gain is the reason behind a newly proposed informing. For, at each stage, the succession of the instaurative dialectic's operations entails the involvement of a new formal determination. But, if this latter concretely modifies the physical mass in its reality, it is obvious that it in no way intensifies its physical existence. Nor does it in any way intensify the existence of that purely ideal or virtual being: the work, ideally determined by this dialectic's ensemble of laws. And yet, that which arranges itself over the course of this anaphoric progression is the progression in the direction of an intense presence, in the direction of that triumphant existence that the completed work will manifest. As we have seen, though, this rising existence is ultimately made up of a coinciding, double modality in the unity of a single being, which is progressively *invented* over the course of the labor. Often without any foresight: up to a certain point, the resultant work is always a novelty, a discovery, a surprise. *So this is what I was looking for, what I was destined to do!* Joy or deception, compensation or punishment for attempts or errors, for efforts, for true or false judgments. In no way, then, is it a simple blossoming or intensification of existence. This is well known to the true creators, who know all the judgments, all the willful decisions, and also all the reprises that make up this progression in the direction of the terminal being, the resting point and reward of creation. It is in relation to this terminal being, whose plurimodal existence is gradually realized through the mutual approach of those two modes, and is only real, only existent in the end (since its instauration is invention), that each preliminary stage, perfectly real and existent in itself, becomes a sketch and a herald.[86]

---

86. Hence the regret sometimes felt for the style of the sketch, which can manifest in the desire to regard the sketch as a completed work. Hence Rodin or van Dongen. Hence also, perhaps, the regret certain of Pascal's commentators have shown: would the completed *Apologétique* have measured up, in intensity and incision, to the sketches presented in the *Pensées*?

Conclusion: the anaphoric experience, in which we actually observe intensive, existential variations, is entirely relative to an architectonic construction, in which several pure modes of existence take an active part in their relation. With respect to pure existence, it is *of the second degree.*

Later on we will have to see whether the problems of the second degree can be reduced to problems of existence, or if, rather, they require that a notion of *surexistence* be brought into play. In any case, at the first degree, where we find pure and specifically different existences, we are well within the perfectly delineated domain of existence. It corresponds to the positioning of a being upon a determinate plane of existence; without which, as we will confirm farther along, there is truly no existence. And in the domain of pure existence, the Eleatic instance is perfectly valid.

And this answers our difficulty: from which the need arises to treat existence, enclosed in its first degree, and the *sous-existences* or *surexistences*, which we can imagine below or above it, differently: the latter implicate plurimodal existence (which defines the second degree); the complex combination that relates different and distinct modes of existence. The second degree presupposes and necessitates the first, not the other way around. And that is what we wanted to show.

§35. This validity of the Eleatic instance explains something else still: that we grasped neither the entrance into nor the exit from pure existence. At bottom, though, this is fortunate. It implies that for a being, for us humans in particular, the effort toward intensity of reality fits within the limits of what concerns us, without requiring that we linger over the following difficulty: to exist, it is necessary to act, but to act, it is necessary to exist. As Paul Valéry says, the gods give us the first verse for free. Herein lies the truth of that great fact: every being initially finds itself within a given situation, which does not depend upon that being's refusal or acceptance. This is constitutive of existence. Yet there still remains something to be done.

§36. If you want to have being, says Mephistopheles to the Homunculus, exist by means of your own strengths.

So be it. But we can also exist through the strength of others. There are certain things—poems, symphonies, or nations—which do not have access to existence through themselves. In order that they should be, man must dedicate himself to them. And perhaps, on the other hand, he might find in this dedication a real existence. Whatever it may be, the "to exist" designates and certifies this success (of the being or of its support), inasmuch as it is achieved.

Later on we will have to deal with problems pertaining to the region in which problems regarding the second degree of existence, beyond existence itself, arise, and in which the prevailing question asks, "how is it that a being can be the same and correspond to itself across the different modes of existence, across the different planes upon which, if it is to exist, it must be positioned and realized?" At present, we must identify and study those different planes, those different modes of existence, without which there would be no existence at all—no more than there would be pure Art without statues, paintings, symphonies, and poems. For art is all the arts. And existence is each of the modes of existence. Each mode is an art of existing unto itself. And the same goes for them as for the different arts of the aesthetic order. It is not out of the question that there would be syntheses among them (theater can bring poetry, dance and mime, and, with the set design, even painting into collaboration). Nor do the existential "purisms" disprove the attempts at synthesis. But pure existence is sufficient unto itself, despite the appearance of vacillation and tenuity to which it reduces us when we reduce ourselves to it. As for the experience of intensive variations itself, it ineluctably attests, by implication, to the plurality of the modes of existence.

Third Chapter:
The Specific Modes of Existence

Section I

§37. Of all the existential statuses, the phenomenal status is certainly the most obvious, the most manifest. As manifest in its existence as it is in its essence (the two being inseparable), it may just be the manifest in itself.

It is presence, a radiance, a given that cannot be repelled. It is and it claims to be just what it is.

We can, without a doubt, work to exorcize it of that irritating quality of presence through itself. We can denounce it as tenuous, labile, and fleeting. Is that not simply to admit that we are unsettled when faced with a pure existence, of one sole mode? With respect to it, behind it, we can postulate something stable, something subsistent, some support. And yet it is the pure existence that serves as the confirmation of that support. Not only as its confirmation, but as its coronation, its reward. It is an existential sanction; and the most sought after of them all. A technique of making-appear, such as that which dialectically informs the experience of both the physicist and the mystic, is an art of bringing any ontic whatsoever into relation with the phenomenon. Initially manifest, the phenomenon thus becomes manifestation; initially appearance, it becomes apparition. But this occurs as it shares itself with its support, as it gives to it what indubitable patuity it has. Such is the generosity of the phenomenon.

Is it actually even a matter of a relation, of an encounter? We can insist that phenomenal existence is existence in patuity, existence in the lucid, resplendent, or manifest state. The supposed encounter with the phenomenon would then be the passage from obscure existence to manifest existence—the blazing, spiritual incandescence of being. And let us even be on our guard against the prejudice that would grasp the obscure existence as bathic and necessarily prior to the luminous existence. Let us not forget that this obscure being is only inferred; that between the two, only the being that is adorned or woven with the light of the present (for that is what the phenomenon is) can be considered to be immediately incontestable.

Does such an observation bind us to so-called phenomenism? Not at all. Whether we are dealing with David Hume or Renouvier, phenomenists or phenomenalists[87] all maintain that there is no true or certain existence outside of the phenomenon. We are therefore a long way from that. The existence of the phenomenon does not exclude the possibility of other modes. And besides, has there ever been a philosophy that denied existence to the phenomenon? Even Platonism is keen on "saving" it. Even Mr. Maurice Blondel, for whom "existence" is "only an extrinsic aspect of the inviolable being," refuses to believe that "the phenomenon is found on one side, and everything else on the other," and to deny that "the universe of appearances would not itself be real, solid, good." "It constitutes," he says, "a reality."[88]

---

87. The meaning of the word phenomenist seems to be, above all, existential; that of phenomenalist, critical (see the *Vocab. hist. et crit.,* s. v.). René Berthelot attributes the first use of the word phenomenism in French to Renouvier; but that does not appear to be correct. To our knowledge, the first use would be that of Mérian: *Sur le phénoménisme de D. Hume,* in *Mémoires de l'Acad. de Berlin* (in French), 1793. Moreover, Mérian repudiates phenomenism and borrows from Lambert his use of the word phenomenology. As for the true instigator of phenomenism, it is, without a doubt, Arthur Collier in his *Clavis Universalis* (1713, reprinted in 1837). But he does not employ the term, nor does he exert any serious influence. – Francesco Olgiati, in his *Cartesio* (Milan, 1934) makes phenomenism one of the three cardinal attitudes of philosophy; to the point of ranging Descartes among the phenomenists—simply because he does not fall into any of the other theses; a mode of reasoning that may not be fully satisfactory.

88. *L'Être et les êtres,* p. 18, 30, and 53. Saint Augustine, whom Mr. Maurice Blondel has studied very closely, said this. See, *Contra Acad.,* III, 24-26; and *de Vera Rel.,* 62.

§38. Where then do the difficulties begin?

Some are theoretical. Is the phenomenon not truly sufficient unto itself? Can it be isolated? Does it not imply something other than itself; and not only the substance or support, as in the Ionian tradition; but even intentionality and essence, on the one hand; subjectivity and the witnessing I, on the other?

Others are practical (by which I mean to say, as regards the effective practice of thought). It is not easy to completely isolate the phenomenon, to reduce it to itself alone so as to experience it purely.

§39. Trees are flowering before me, bursting forth upon the background of blue sky and green grass. There is a freshness and an authority to the hues; the colors press in upon one another, both in opposition and in harmony; the rosy white radiance of the sun; the poignant picture of a single, little bouquet of flowers at the end of a branch upon the turquoise blue of the sky; does all of this not compel us to admit that there is something real?

Yes, but we have also long known—apart from all that is conceptual in perception, in which every sensation is grasped—how much of the sensory itself is relative and differential. More profoundly, must we not acknowledge, at once, that the key to this spectacle's intensity of presence lay in the harmony, in the structure, in the essential art of that *Dreiklang* in blue, green, and pink—in short, in a spiritual principle, whose very own perfection brings about its present solidity, and ensures this solidity of its reality? The sensible content of the ensemble can be bracketed: it is its architectonic—a pure formal principle—that we can single out and regard as the soul and the key of that indubitable patuity.

Besides, does this luminous and vernal complex not owe its radiance to the contrast that opposes it to the gray hues of winter, still present to my memory? How I have waited for spring! I almost doubted it was still possible that it would come. If now it triumphs, it is a victory over doubt and absence. If it is said that *the beauty of the world* is not a meaningless phrase, this is because the arrival of spring testifies against that doubt. Its testimony therefore appeals to and presupposes the doubt itself. A force finally freed, a being finally come to pass, it is upon the obscure ground of all that absence that it stands out. Another play of relations, now affective and conceptual, which contribute to both its radiance and its meaning. And then, of course, what would that meaning be without me, the one for whom all of that has meaning? Does he who says scene not also say spectator?

§40. To all of this, there is only one indisputable response: to actually carry out the existential reduction that is the exact antithesis of the phenomenological reduction, and that, as we have seen (cf. §28), demands a difficult reversal. That existential shifts and morphematic relations lead from the pure phenomenon toward other realities in other modes, is a different question. Conversely, we can make the pure phenomenon the center of this entire systematics and position ourselves in this center in order to feel it as the support and guarantor [*répondant*] of the rest: that is what it would be to place ourselves in the point of view of the phenomenon.

For the phenomenological dialectic brackets the phenomenon itself in its real presence and immediacy, explicating and accomplishing it separately, from without, in order to preserve and to look only—which is what the phenomenon implies and requires by moving toward something other than itself.[89] So much so that, in this sense, phenomenology is the place where we are least likely to find the phenomenon. As Kim says, *The darkest place is under the lamp.*[90]

We are truly confused when we say: the phenomenon implies … it calls out to… it assumes…. In that case, it does not exist independently of everything surrounding it, informing it, clinging to it—everything without which it would not exist. But that is the result of a bastard thought, in which we seek the phenomenon while simultaneously and unjustifiably leaving it behind. We imagine the phenomenon to be dissected. Bloodless, surrounded by its own organs. Those who grasp it as it lives see that the phenomenon establishes its intentions and other factors of reality in the phenomenal state. Its vections of appetition, its tendencies toward the other can be followed in their fanning out, for as long as they remain of the same stuff as the phenomenon itself. Thus the I is phenomenal not

---

89. This has been highlighted several times by Fritz Heinemann. Cf. his Leonardo da Vinci, *Rev. phq.*, 1936, II, p. 365-366; or again: *Les problèmes et la valeur d'une phénoménologie comme théorie de la réalité; Être et apparaître*, Congr. internat., 1937, t. X, p. 64f.

90. In English in the original. [TN]

because it is still insufficiently adhered to in transcendence [*suivi en transcendance*], but because there is some form of the I in the phenomenon itself. It is a form of egoity [*égoïté*], a signature, so to speak, but only in the sense that the formation [*le faire*] and the intrinsic style of a painting can be called the signature of a master.

§41. The difficulty arising from the relative character of sensation is even less considerable.

In the first place, it proves something: that the pure sensation (to the extent that it could be isolated) would not be phenomenal. Apparent paradox, real clarity. Sensation in general (precisely because it is included in perception), far from being its model and epitome, is quite a bad example of the phenomenon. It is really only a rather impure variety, in which the phenomenon is hard to discern, engaged as it is in a complex construction. There are also phenomena in both the affective, which is perhaps the most distinctive case, and the most abstract or more ineffable experiences of thought, far from any function of the senses.

In sensation, the phenomenal characteristic is very intense, but also very mixed. Sensations are the din of the phenomenon, as it were; while the innumerable and delicate nuances of the sentimental essences, or the somber glimmers, the vague flashes upon the shadowy background of pure thought, of moral or philosophical meditation, or even of mystical experience, are the notes and chords of its music.

§42. It also proves that there is something naive in regarding the pure phenomenon as a necessarily simple being—a qualitative atom. Simplicity and purity are not synonyms. The phenomenon such as we seek it in pure sensation—simultaneously pure and simple—is an extreme case, in which different (though not necessarily connected) demands are met.

We need not even be overly attached to the idea of the qualitative as being definitive of the phenomenon—even though the phenomenon is indeed essentially qualitative. For in doing so we would run the risk of hastily opposing it to the quantitative. Yet there are phenomena of the quantitative, which are the qualitative of the quantitative, so to speak. What is it to have a sense of rhythm, for example, if not to feel it? And it is because what is qualitative in the phenomenon does not exclude the quantitative that it does not exclude plurality, nor any of the architectonics that plurality can entail. Feeling all that is ineffable and unique in the particular quality of a strange musical chord does not at all prevent us from feeling those delicate relations and mathematical ratios [*tout ce nombre*], whose structure completes and expresses itself in, through, and with that quality.

§43. It is possible, then, that the phenomenon owes all its radiance to the art, immanent to the phenomenon, of which we were just speaking, and which is rekindled by the ideas of harmony and architectonics. Yet it owes its radiance not to the abstract art that we can separate from the phenomenon through comparison and generalizing induction, but to the concrete art that is effectively and singularly at work in its present existence. This art is the law of the phenomenon's radiance, the soul of its presence and its existential patuity. To speak of it separately is simply to distinguish (already through some abstraction) the existence and the being of the existing phenomenon; but not to refer it to something other than itself.

If we think less, for example, of those phenomena whose exteriority only leads to impurity and difficulty (as in the case of the sensorial), than of an immanent and intrinsic, interior phenomenality—if we think of what it is for a soul or for a human personality to exist phenomenally, which is to say, in the lucid, resplendent, or dazzling state (oh, how he dazzled human minds! says Pascal), whether for another, or for itself—we will see that the possession of such a "to exist" returns to the effective practice of the art that constitutes a being on the very plane of the lucid and the dazzling; not lacking the dexterity and the knowledge, not lacking the mastery that victory over the shadows presumes, the integral blaze and incandescence of being, which are constitutive facts for such a mode of existence.

§44. If the general orientation of our study permitted it, we could insist upon several interesting points—for example, upon the discrete and self-enclosed, stellar and microcosmically limited character of the phenomenon; upon its relation with the instant (it has immanent, local signs, which are the basis for the determination of the *hic* and the *nunc*); upon the aspect of the phenomenal world (of the pleroma of phenomena: the Maya) as the ensemble of cosmic *points of lucidity*; upon the presence of the I in that ensemble, simply as the signature or personal sign of several of those points, which themselves form an ensemble; upon the possibility of *shared phenomena*, marked by several egoic signatures [*signatures égoïques*] at the same time, which are therefore capable of belonging jointly to several different selves, united with one another under these types; and, more generally, upon the fact that phenomena organize themselves with one another, that their pleroma is harmonious. Yet this last aspect then raises questions pertaining to their mediate organization, in accordance with other entities and other modes of reality.

§45. What is most important for the moment is to have abolished several errors through the provisional suspension of certain habits. Let us repeat that, in order to grasp phenomenal existence, we must above all avoid conceiving of the phenomenon as a phenomenon *of* something or *for* someone. That is the aspect the phenomenon assumes when, having begun to consider existence by way of some other modality, we encounter it after the fact, for example, in its role as manifestation;[91] or rather, when, having taken it as our point of departure, we attempt (as do the phenomenologists) to bring about a shift toward other existences by referring ontological thought and experience to morphematic relations, which are in solidarity with the phenomenon, and which lead from it toward other modes. We only truly conceive of the phenomenon in its own existential tenor when we feel it to be maintaining and positing all that can be supported and consolidated in it, with it, and through it to itself alone. And it is in this capacity that it appears as a model and a standard of existence. It is under this aspect that we have attempted to show it.

Now, what does it become when it is put in relation with other modes? Does it retain its proper essence? Does this essence remain unchanged when it serves as the referential term and final confirmation for a being installed in another mode? Does its existence, which was principal here simply because the study of the "to exist" deliberately began with it, retain any primacy—in the capacity of *ultima ratio* of existence—for the other modes; and must these necessarily be referred to it? Can we conceive of beings without any relation whatsoever to the phenomenon? So many problems to be considered presently. They are approached most easily through the idea of the thing.

---

91. This is what one finds in MacTaggart. Cf. *Nature of Existence*, Book II, Chapter XIII: *Manifestation*.

§46. What exactly is a thing? The approach to this question that begins with the phenomenon has been thoroughly explored in philosophy.[92] And there is agreement on the essential. Whether we consider the thing as a system of phenomena, particularly of phenomena that are sensorial and more or less ranked according to the primacy of a sense (generally the tactile sense); a system that is stable in its essentials and capable of reappearing unchanged; or whether we seek the essential and the stable beyond the phenomenon, the sensible qualities being no more than their variable illustration or approximation, in which nothing remains identical of necessity (in which case the primacy, the keystone of this hierarchy, is established on a plane distinct from that of the phenomenon, unless, for example, it is a question of a phenomenon of form or structure, or even of association and order); in either case, the thing is defined and constituted by its identity across its diverse appearances. There is agreement concerning the systematic character of the thing, as well as the fact that what specifically characterizes it is its way of remaining numerically one across its noetic appearances or utilizations. The disagreement solely concerns the fundamental elements included in the system and the nature of the connection that brings them together, as well as the hierarchy of those elements and the nature of the dominant, pyramidionic element. Whitehead alone maintains that systematization is not at all necessary and that a single *quale* can have the *réique* character if it subsists, identical in each of its different

---

92. See, in particular: Hume, *Treatise on Human Nature*, Book I, Part IV, Ch. II; Kant, *Critique of Pure Reason*, ed. Guyer and Wood, p. 304f.; Meinong, *Ueber die Stellung der Gegenstandstheorie im System der Wissenschaften*, §15; Bradley, *Appearance and Reality*, Second Ed., p. 73; Husserl, Formal and Transcendental Logic, p. 154; and J. Nicod, *La géometrie dans le monde sensible*, p. 99 (interesting applications of the ideas of Russell and Whitehead). See, also, Frege, cited by Brunschvicg, *L'expérience humaine et la causalité*, p. 481. As for Gonseth, *Les mathématiques et la réalité*, it is in relation to the "physics of any object whatsoever" (see, for instance, p. 164) that he enters into this general agreement. But his goals (to which we will return) are different: for him, it is above all a question of different stations (for which reason we could bring him together with Baldwin's geneticism) assuming a sort of successive recommencement of the structural status itself, for the "Aristotelian object," for the "Goethean object," for the "Brouwerian object," etc. But be wary, in all this literature, of the confusion and wavering that takes place, in certain authors, between the two notions, thing and object.

incarnations or appearances. In that case, numerical identity suffices to characterize the *réique* status.

Lotze integrated this identity with the completely subjective identity of the self. But there is a difficulty: the identity of the physical object consists of two aspects, one of immediate presence, and another of remote or inferred presence (Baldwin's *remote presence*[93]), whereas the self is generally supposed to be ever present to itself. Only the unconscious could be and sometimes is considered to be a *remote presence* of the self. Thus, we can re-establish the unity of those two identities by passing through the intermediary of the presumed continuity in foreign or exterior selves, and by subsequently attributing such continuity, by analogy, to non-psychical objects.

There is another difficulty: the *quid* of this remote or nonapparent presence? Is it not sometimes destruction or inexistence between the appearances of the thing, and not nonapparent existence?[94] Perhaps this depends on the nature of the diversity of the thing [*des diverses choses*]. Theories of apocatastasis and of palingenesis admit the possibility of a reconstitution without identity. The idea of a reconstitution with identity, though without existence in the interval, is put into practice in the Catholic dogma of the resurrection of the flesh. Milton applied this idea to souls themselves, between death and the final judgment (see *Traité de la doctrine chrétienne* [*A Treatise on Christian Doctrine*], p. 280, cf. Saurat, *La Pensée de Milton*, p. 153). Ordinary theories of the physical thing deny that the thing ever vanishes temporarily, admitting inexistence only *a parte post* and *a parte ante*: things have a beginning and an end. The ideas of maturation and potentiality partially deny inexistence *a parte ante* by presupposing a state of latent existence, prior to emergence, for a period of a duration, which itself is, for that matter, quite insufficiently defined. Leibniz absolutely denied the possibility of any temporary existence of beings, and reduced the idea of

---

93. In English in the original. Souriau uses the English phrase "remote presence" many times throughout this chapter. The reader will be able to distinguish the instances in which Souriau has used the English phrase from those in which he uses the French equivalent, "présence éloignée," by the fact that we have left the former in italics (as they were in the original). [TN]

94. The best example is that of the mode of existence of the musical (or theatrical) work, which has no latent or obscure presence between its theophanies, its performances. The musical work's supposedly inferior status with regard to the other arts upset Leonardo da Vinci. "Ill-fated music," he says, "dies straight away."

latent existence to that of microscopic existence (see, for example, his theory of the preformation of germs). The theory of the fixity of species—which admits no possibility for the appearance of novelty in the order of *réité* between the universal creation and an eschatological terminus, whether those be specific to each species or equally universal—makes *réité*, thus understood, bear upon the species, not the individual. According to the Masoretes, Leviathan exists, now and since the origin of the world, because it will be necessary on the eve of the Judgment for the great communal meal of the elect (see Samuel Bochart in his *Hiérozoïcon*). These divergences correspond less to different philosophies than to attempts at the diversification of a single *réique* status, in accordance with specific cases: physical or psychical beings, animate or inanimate beings, etc. We will soon see the importance of this observation.

§47. From its own perspective, identity is always of the same nature. It is a communion with itself, an indifference to collocation and spatio-temporal distribution; of which the state of latent existence or *remote presence* is a subsequent consequence.

Let us take the most simple case: that in which, of all the appearances of an identical thing, we are able to discourse upon a single, temporal line (this the "chronal order" of Leclère and Michel Souriau, "Introd. au symbolisme mathém.," *Rev. phq.*, 1938, I, p. 366). Let us compare this discourse to a ribbon, along which would be found brocaded ornamental motifs, here and there, all of the same kind. We are able to fold the ribbon in such a way that these motifs will be made to coincide, and even to interpenetrate (if the ribbon is without thickness), so as ultimately to form only a single being. Let us unfold the ribbon and extend it in a straight line: this single being now finds itself separated from itself, distributed in a plurality, here and there, along the ribbon. But our ribbon could remain folded. A perfectly flat observer, who is compelled to travel its length in a straight line, will encounter the motif several times without knowing that it forms one and the same being. Let us imagine that, instead of a motif, there is a needle penetrating the folded ribbon: our discursive observer will believe that he encounters similar needles, or multiple holes, at more or less regular intervals, without knowing that there is only one and the same hole and a single needle.

Instead of a ribbon, let us imagine a vast sheet of paper, crumpled at random and pierced by the needle. Once unfolded, the sheet will be riddled, aimlessly, with holes. Nevertheless, despite this chance dispersion and the intervals on the sheet, there is only one hole, only one needle having pierced the sheet in a straight line.

Réique existence is like the unity of the hole or the needle. As a pure mode of existing, the *réique* mode is possessive self-presence in this undivided state, presence that is indifferent to its specific situation in a universe that is unfolded and organized according to space and time. That is the basis of its existence. As an art of existing, it is the conquest and realization, the effective possession of this presence that is indifferent to its situation. The various aspects, the separated presences of this self-same entity result from a subsequent confrontation with phenomenal diversity. The distension of its unity between those multiple manifestations, the distension that constitutes the state of latent existence or remote presence, results from this subsequent separation. In the case of the identity of the self, to feel such distension is to feel the mode of existence proper to the identical being. Such a being either exists thus, or it does not exist at all.

§48. But as we have said, all of this varies in accordance with different specific ontic characteristics. What follows from this for such specific characteristics: for instance, for rational entities, living beings, physical things, etc.?

Nothing is more simple than the status of rational entities, of abstract beings, of Russellian systems, for instance, this geometric being, that theorem, etc.[95] Indeed, they have only to

---

95. Concerning the case of mathematical existences, consult, in particular, Oskar Becker, *Mathematische Existenz*, Halle, 1927, where the problem is approached from the same point of view as that in which we will encounter the problem here. See also, of course: Pierre Boutroux, "L'Ojectivité intrinsèque des mathématiques," *Rev. de mét. et mor.*, 1903, p. 589; Milhaud, *Condit. et lim. de la cert. log.* (not. p. 150); Brunschvicg, *Étaps de la philos. math.*; Chaslin, *Ess. s. le mécan. psych.: des opér. de la math. pure*, not. p. 176, 234f., 239, 249, 275; B. Russell, *Introduction to Mathematical Philosophy*; Husserl, *Philosophy of Arithmetic*; Meyerson, *Explic. dans les Sc.* (and Lichtenstein, "La Ph. des math. selon E. Meyerson," *Rev. phq.*, March 1923), and then Couturat, H. Poincaré, Winter, Gonseth, etc. The principal difficulties are: 1). Can mathematical existence be reduced to an ensemble of operational conventions (as Couturat tends to do)? 2). Existence being granted to mathematical beings, should these latter be ranged with the *réique* status, tied to a special kind of experience; or rather, 3). Must we conceive of their existence as a transcendent, ideal existence? The considerations that we will encounter farther along will primarily concern the problem of the passage from the second to the

fulfill the conditions we have just stated. The equilateral triangle in itself is the singular essence of diverse phenomenal appearances, of concrete triangles that can be distributed randomly throughout the world and separated, each from the others, just as people are distributed randomly while nevertheless participating communally in a humanity that is identical in them all; without our having to concern ourselves with any *remote presence* or latent existence of humanity between its diverse incarnations. Think of our randomly folded sheet of paper of a moment ago.

§49. Things become more complicated, however, as soon as it is a question of singular things—not, for example, the essence of universal man, but the essence of Socrates or Durand.

In the first place, Socrates or Durand responds completely to the conditions we have just stated. There is a Socrates-ity or a Durand-ity that causes the diversity of phenomenal appearances to link up with one another. These are the phenomenal appearances of a single being, understood according to the mode of existence defined just now.

But, *in addition*, they conform to many other conditions.

Durand does not have spatial ubiquity. His presence on this Parisian sidewalk excludes his presence in Carpentras, or in any other place, at this precise moment. He has an alibi. He is not "repeatable" in the order of coexistences (to speak like Jean Ullmo). His ubiquity is restricted to the chronal order. This is no longer the crumpled sheet of a moment ago, it is the folded, linear ribbon.

Furthermore, these appearances must conform to a certain order, characteristic of living *réités*. Durand's presences must not present him now old, now young, with brown hair and with gray hair, in no particular order. They must form a history in conformity with certain laws, which are the lot of the human condition. What is more, the *remote presence* itself is determined in a very particular manner. It is a shame that we can never be in two places at once. But to always be in just one place, how much more stringent a demand is that! His remote presences must be subjected to the law of certain practical

---

third of these opinions, and of the legitimacy of this passage; the case of mathematical beings being only a particular case of a general problem. Here, it is only a question of the *réique* status of these entities; the problem of their *rational* or *transcendent* existence being reserved for later.

conditions of verisimilitude: displacement at a plausible speed (he was not in Beijing this morning), etc.

There is more. It is certainly always possible to arrange a being's phenomena in a reasonable fashion; every ensemble can be arranged from the point of view of a single characteristic. Durand as a younger or older man forms the law of a simple chronal order. But the props of this history—Durand's brother, his pipe, and his handkerchief—must not make disorganized, discontinuous, absurd appearances either.[96] All these "histories of things" (as Rignano said) are parallel and mediated by a common order. There is a universe of things.

§50. Moreover, all of this has a distinctly empirical character. Thought, which certainly brings with it the *a priori* need for this order, nevertheless provides neither the solution, nor the knowledge of the kind of history suited to each being, nor, above all, the *a priori* certitude of the success of the nearly total harmonization of the cosmos of things. In fact, the history of Representation (what a shame no one has ever endeavored to write it) is a testament to the slowness of that harmonization; which is most often obtained through the elimination (or relegation to the imaginary) of all that is inconsistent with the ever stricter and more exacting systems of conditions. In this regard, certain facts take on a prerogative meaning in the philosophical or scientific thought of the present. This is particularly the case with those facts concerning microphysical beings. We know that Heisenberg's celebrated "relations of indetermination" signal our entry into a region where certain of the aforementioned conditionings—for instance, that a position can always be assigned—are suddenly no longer capable of being fulfilled. Whatever other philosophical repercussions might result from such facts, their meaning here is quite clear: it is simply that the thing, electron, breaks out of the *réique* status of existence, such as it is defined for the things belonging to the domain shared both by ordinary experience and by the usual techniques of the physicist. That is why the thing "unreluctantly ceases to exist," as Ferdinand Gonseth says (*Les math. et la réal.*, p. 157). We

---

96. There is a special—in truth, rather inferior—art (that of the "illusionist," of the prestidigitator), which aims to create, in the concrete perception of the spectator, histories of things that appear to be contrary to the way in which they are normally conditioned. It sometimes borrows its models from the stylistics of the dream (Cf., for example, David Devant, *Secrets of My Magic*. It remains for the philosopher to reflect upon the conditions and meanings of this art.

sometimes conclude from this—and wrongly—that *réité* is therefore only a "macroscopic prejudice" (*ibid.*, p. 158). In what way is it a prejudice, if by that we mean phantom, error, idol? It is true that we often believe that the small is more real than the large, and that anything is untrue of the large that is not applicable all the way down to the small. But there we see the prejudice. We must simply note, then, that it is here that the *réique* status comes up against the boundaries of its own zone, of its regional ontology. Must we conclude from this (Jean Perrin, Langevin) that the new beings grasped at this ultramicroscopic scale thus become "rational beings"? In any case, we need to take fully into account the remark that Eddington's "universe n° 2," which is theirs, remains suspended in universe n° 1; and that "in the reality of infusoria, of bacteria, of molecular agitation betrayed by Brownian motion, there is also the microscope" (J. Sageret, "La Physique nouvelle," *Rev. Phq.*, I, p. 195).

Let us not, then, forget the empirical and even technical (be it practical or scientific) character of these systems of conditionings and of the cosmos that each defines. When we speak of being-in-the-world, we must hear being-in-a-certain-world[97]; the conditionings correlatively defining (through mutual adaptation and reciprocal accommodation) a cosmos and a class of existents. Such a cosmos is a pleroma of specified *réique* existences, their histories harmonized in a common canon.

§51. Does this important *réique* status imply still something else? Yes, as we have just seen, it indubitably involves thought. But in what way? This demands careful attention.

Thought appears there three times: as liaison of the system; as consciousness of singular existence in identity; and as agent in the accommodations and selections that fashion the cosmos.

The last point is exterior, subsequent, non-resident. It simply shows the effort of human thought to know and to organize a rational ensemble, the greater part of which is objective for it and constitutes an experience: this relational ensemble is a given. But the first two points must be grasped as immanent. Thought does not figure in them as a separate, prior, or subsequent being. *Réique* existence is constituted by thought, and yet thought itself is constituted, resides, and operates in *réique* existence, as well. In such existence, thought is a factor of reality.

---

97. Note that the world is not the universe in phenomenological existentialism. The word is taken in the sense of John 1:10: opposition of Logos and Cosmos.

Indeed, let us be careful to note that thought cannot be conceived of as the product or result of the activity of a psychical being, which is itself conceived in a *réique* manner, distinct from the assembled thing, and which might be thought's subject or its separate support. Thought has no other support than the very thing that it assembles and feels. In certain respects it is purely impersonal, and we must keep ourselves from conceiving of it as it effectively is in the *réique* status by introducing into it everything we otherwise understand and know about thought. As it is implied by this status, thought is purely and simply liaison and communication. It is also consciousness, though only if that word is understood in the sense of a phenomenal glow; the view that would have this singular and identical consciousness of existence reduced to the observation that we only speak of it as existing when it is presented as being lucid and present for itself, may not in fact be constitutive. In the final analysis, it is above all the systematic cohesion, the liaison, which is essential and constitutive here for the role of thought. We should even ask ourselves whether it is not a matter of a *factor*, rather than an *effect*, of thought. Whatever the philosophical importance of this point may be, let us consider only one of its aspects: if there are psychical beings, they are far from being the cause of thought, as it is understood here—they imply it; it is a part of their constitution.

§52. Psychology and even metaphysics easily—even necessarily—conceive of ontic entities of thought: let us name them psyches or souls. It is always a matter of an organized whole, permanent up to a certain point, identical across its manifestations, and (perhaps) not always completely present to itself phenomenally. Yet it is a structure and an existence that is clearly *réique*. We will return to the problem of its spirituality later, as we will to the rational status of mathematical entities. Let us confine ourselves, here, to noting its participation in the very status, whose outlines we just examined. If the word *réique* status seems shocking, and if "*chosalité*" seems inapplicable to the soul, let us reserve the word *réité* for the specific cosmoses of physical or practical experience; let us speak more generally of an ontic mode of existence that will be suited to psyches and also to *réismes*. All that we affirm of psyches, in noting them as a part of this same mode of existing, is that they have a sort of monumentality that makes of their organization and form the law of a permanence, of an identity. Far from compromising its life by conceiving of it in this way, we fail life to a much greater extent if we do not conceive of the soul as architectonic, as a harmonic system susceptible of modifications, enlargements, occasional corruptions, and even wounds…. In a word, as a being. At once systematization of facts, of psychological phenomena, and self-possession in the indivisibility of personal identity. What is absurd and crude in our thing-centrism [*le chosalisme*] is the way we consider the soul as being analogous to a physical and material thing—particularly with regard to the conditions according to which it persists. It is certainly more admissible, though still inadequate, to conceive of it on the ontic model of living beings and according to the ways in which they are conditioned. But it is up to psychology—to a psychology unafraid of all that is ontic in the soul (let it say psyche if it is wary of that word)—to say how they are specifically conditioned—which would include the plurality, the assemblage, and the counterpoint of souls; that entire interpsychics [*interpsychique*] that makes their ways of coming together into a cosmos.

In this cosmos, impersonal thought, or rather its factor—self-assemblage and self-relation, the resident or immanent synthesis—will have a constitutive capacity, in the same way as it does in the other ontic systems. Certainly more susceptible of consciousness and activity; and if not more fragile, then without a doubt more mobile.

§53. Indeed, let us not forget that the ontic status of existence in no way excludes the lability of existence. Its basic ubiquity never implies a temporal subsistence that would be guaranteed in a lazy and ponderous manner—nor in a mechanical or even continuous manner. Moreover, we perpetually observe, particularly in the psychical order, instaurations so quick, so fleeting, that we hardly grasp them. We therefore sometimes posit momentary souls for ourselves (or they posit themselves in us), whose rapidity and kaleidoscopic succession contribute to the illusion of a lesser and weak existence; even though they may be greater and more valuable than those we instaure daily and with the greatest of ease. Souls we rediscover and recreate only with great difficulty, and of whose metaphysical importance we are unaware. The limit case is that of an absolutely ephemeral existence, which would never be seen twice.[98] There would be no possibility whatsoever for such a being to be in full possession of or to make use of its identity. But this brings us to situations of a, so to speak, hyperbolic, practical precariousness, which lead to other considerations.

§54. We would also have to ask ourselves if identity itself is not without a base, if it need not be guaranteed…. That is another question, which departs from the perspective of this inquiry; and which, in all likelihood, could only be responded to through the evocation of that primordial, essential invariance, distinct from practical ubiquity, which is undoubtedly one with a certain perfection. But, once again, that is another story.[99]

⁎
⁎ ⁎

§55. We are led to remark (in order to return to the ontic status, which is best grasped, for now, in its generality) what a great difference there is between beings from the point of view of their stability, and of what we can conceive of as their solidity.

There is one, in particular, whose privileged persistence, whose privileged solidity of being, seems to be eminent: it is the "body itself [*corps propre*]."[100] To such an extent that we sometimes seem to reserve the name of existence for this ontic type alone.

Without a doubt, the body holds a privileged role as the necessary intermediary between ourselves and the world. But what exactly are the reasons for this privilege? They stem from

---

98. We can think, here, of the opposition between "duration-existence" and "idea-existence" that appears in a recent and interesting—and, sadly, much too short—article (Ghéréa, "Existences," *Rev. mét. et mor.*, Oct. 1940).

99. Long ago (see *Pensée vivante et perfection formelle*, 1925), we attempted to show how that identity born of fidelity to oneself requires, as its reason or law, that sort of perfection through which what is actualized, in a certain, somewhat stylized way, cannot vary without being corrupted and cannot be otherwise than it is. *Sint ut sunt, aut non sint.* At the time in which we published that work, it was necessary to react vigorously against certain temporalist and dynamist prejudices, in order to have this way of seeing be accepted. Since then, we believe that this point of view has received many confirmations.

100. Among contemporary philosophers, as we know, Mr. Gabriel Marcel, in particular, has insisted upon its distinctive and intermediary role. Cf. *supra*, §18, and *Journal métaphysique*, particularly p. 130 and 237. In addition, see Plato, Nemesius, Saint Augustine, Malebranche, Whitehead, etc.

the fact that it is possible to deduce the body starting from the basis of the phenomenon. For instance, there is a certain perspectival constancy in the phenomena of our horizon that allows for the determination of an *Ichpunkt* (as V. Schmarsow says), in relation to which they can always be organized. Likewise, we could show that the body is opposed to other bodies (insofar as it is subjectively known), while also being homogeneous with them, through, for example, its antitypical relations. Point of view, mediation, and also dynamic evasion: for, thanks to the body, our selves" boundaries shift by plunging into the world; so many architectonic elements in agreement with phenomena. Through them, the body truly constitutes a *foothold* for the phenomenon in the cosmos of *réique* entities. Whence its privilege. Whence also, without a doubt, the fact that an utterly rudimentary (infantile or even animal) mind is led to begin the process of recognizing *réique* existence through the body and its kind. This is what explains its apparent and empirical existential superiority: it is the first work, the infantile masterpiece of the stage at which we have ceased being simply phenomena.

But to explain that superiority is, in part, to deny it. The existence of the body itself is not, in fact, purely corporeal and physical: it is above all the expression of the obligation of a psychical existence, perpetually constrained to follow a body on its terrestrial adventures. It would almost belong to what we will soon call "solicitudinary" [*sollicitudinaire*] existence, if we could only free ourselves to some extent from that constraint, or emancipate ourselves from that solicitude. But the constraint is too strong for us to be able to contest the objectivity and positivity of this practically privileged ontic.

*
* *

§56. Conversely, there are fragile and inconsistent entities, which, by virtue of that inconsistency, are so different from bodies that we may hesitate to grant them any manner of existing whatsoever. We are not thinking here of souls (which have already been in question), but of all those phantoms, chimeras, and fairies that are the representations of the imagination, the beings of fiction. Is there an existential status for them?

Our body is not a *fata morgana*. In order to perceive, we are obliged to place ourselves in its point of view. It is firmly embedded as a physical thing in the cosmos of such things. But we have fictive bodies in dreams and reveries, bodies incorporated in illusory cosmicities.

This world of imaginaries has for a long time—traditionally in philosophy—held a position of strategic importance for the existential problem.[101]

To consider them to be simply supported by thought, is to regard thought as being capable of positing, arbitrarily and without being conditioned by anything other than its own decree, beings that depend upon it totally. And the resemblance between these beings of representation, these false beings, and certain beings of pure logic, with which we sometimes connect them (think of Aristotle's goat-stag), will risk extending this purely psychological existential status even to logical or rational entities.

On the other hand, is it not rather troublesome, given their spectral character and acosmicity, to grant them a specific existence, to see in them a mode of being? They are fundamentally beings that have been chased, one after the other, from every controlled and conditioned ontic cosmos. This single, shared misfortune brings them together, and yet this does not constitute their gathering as a pleroma, a cosmos.

---

101. On the theory of imaginary existence, see Aristotle, *Metaphysics*, M, 1078b; *Peri Hermeneias*, 1, s.f.; Meinong, *Ueber Annahmen*; and *Unters. zu Gegenstandstheorie*; Baldwin, *Thought and Things*, Ch. 4, which is to say, everything concerning objects of "fantasy," of inferior simulation (the theory of *make-believe*), and of superior simulation (relations between the fictions of play and those of artistic activity); see also *Dictionary of Philos.*, s.v. *Assumption*; Brunschvicg, *Étapes de la philos. math.*, p. 549; Dupré, *Pathologie de l'imagination*; Sartre, *The Imaginary*; Dewey, *Studies in Logical Theory*; Russell, particularly, *Meinong's Theory of Complexes and Assumptions*, Mind, 1904; Ryle, Braithwaite, and G. E. Moore, *Imaginary Objects*, in *Proceedings of Aristotelian Society*, suppl. vol. n° XII, 1933 (important); Reininger, *Metaphysik der Wirklichkeit* (in the logical perspective of the Vienna Circle and the theory of utterances); finally, Heinrich Maier, *Wahrheit und Wirklichkeit*, particularly, I, p. 279 (he strictly opposes cognitive-real existence and emotive-imaginary existence. He connects the theory of imaginaries to the theory of belief). From the aesthetic point of view, consult: Paul Souriau, *L'Imagination de l'artiste*; Witasek, *Allgem. Aesthetik* (particularly, p. 111-112; connections between artistic invention and Meinong's theory of the *Annahmen*); M. Dessoir, *Aesthetik*, p. 36, etc. The word Imaginary does not appear in the *Vocabulaire histor. et crit. de la philosophie*. This lacuna is to be regretted (though they inevitably occur in a monument of such dimensions), above all given the double meaning, philosophical and mathematical, of the term.

To characterize them existentially by the fact that, as representations, they do not correspond to objects or bodies is clearly out of the question. Such a consideration would pertain to a problem of the second degree; and be purely negative, besides.

§57. They only exist—in their fashion—if they have a positive "to exist."

And they do.

How positive they are, from a certain point of view! Even the monsters, even the chimeras, even the beings of dreams. We have been able to study some of them with the same objective spirit as that of natural history, history, or political economy. There are concrete investigations by artists into the anatomy of the angel (how exactly is the wing bone joined to the shoulder blade?), into those of the centaur or the faun (cf. E. Valton, *Les Monstres dans l'art*, p. 54 and 62). When Napoleon reread Richardson on Saint Helena, he carefully established Lovelace's annual budget; and Hugo, when he was preparing *Les Misérables*, tracked Jean Valjean's accounts for the ten years during which he did not appear in the novel. (Think about it: the *remote presence* of a character in a novel in relation to the novel itself; now *that* is a strong dose of the imaginary!) There is a strange question of the reality of imaginary times, which was the object of a controversy between Russell and MacTaggart (cf. *The Nature of Existence*, Book II, p. 16: in what sense can we say that, in *Don Quixote*, the adventure of the windmills is prior to that of the galley slaves?).

Each novel, even each painting, is, in certain respects, a microcosm (create the experience, as in Lovelace's budget: establish what is included, within a radius of 5km, and maybe in the history of several days or years, in the *Mona Lisa* or *Et in Arcadia ego*). Is it necessary to say, in the end, that all these microcosms comprise a sort of great literary and artistic cosmos, in which certain classic [*types*] characters have an innumerable, though nevertheless essential and identical existence (think of Don Juan).

Thus, on one side, this world tends to take on a syndoxic, social, and quite positive existence. There is a literary "universe of discourse," to speak like C. I. Lewis. But on its other frontier, this world dissipates and frays. There is no logic of appearance, there are no laws of identity on this spectral side: think of the chimeras, born in the terror of a tragic wait, which vanish as soon as they take shape. If *poetry*, as an art and a technical branch of literature, fixes Eviradnus or Eloa, the ravine of Ernula or the tent of Samson, with as much solidity as a novel or painting could, does it not, nevertheless, have vague apparitions on its shores, glimpsed for but a moment as they dash through the thicket of *the poetic*, which give the mind [*la pensée*] a sudden start, though without it being possible to arrange them neatly in a stable, definite world, enclosed and solid like a park surrounded with walls?

§58. Imaginaries owe their particular dialectical situation to precisely that transitive and transitory character. In their best regions, their status is roughly ontic; there is no doubt about that. An imagined dog is a dog, since it participates in the ontic of the dog. But in this direction, it tends to escape from the phenomenon to become a purely logical entity, a being of reason. And in the other, it tends to dissipate into pure phenomena, from which it borrows all of its existential reality.

§59. Imaginaries, suspended within a base phenomenon, participate in the conditioning of reality that belongs to the latter, whether those be distinct or vague, intense or weak. And that is one way of defining them. On that account, they are opposed to beings of perception, whose existential consistency in no way depends upon the intensity or clarity of the sensation as base phenomenon, but upon an entire ensemble of cosmic determinations. They are not, then, limited to cases of the faculty of imagination. Their situation expands to embrace all that depends upon the feelings and emotions, as well. In fact, the base phenomenon of imaginaries is often emotional.

In this sense, then, we must arrange them in a much more extensive existential class: namely, beings that are present and exist for us with an existence based in desire, concern, fear, or hope, or even fancy and diversion. We could say of these beings that they exist in proportion to the importance they hold for us—whether many things take part in our mind's disquiet, or whether one alone is enough.

Therefore, just as there are imaginaries, there are also (if we dare say) emotionals [*émotionnels*], pragmatics [*pragmatiques*], attentionals [*attentionnels*]; whatever is important in such and such a care or such and such a qualm; in short, a *solicitudinary* existence (of which we can consider Heidegger to

153

have, in certain respects, made a partial study, without, to our mind, having fully seen that this is not a case of revelation or manifestation, but of existential basis). Their essential characteristic is always that the magnitude or the intensity of our attention or concern is the basis, the polygon of sustentation of their monument, the bulwark upon which we erect them; without there being any other conditions of reality than that. Completely conditional and subordinate in this respect, many things that we would normally think of as being positive and substantial are revealed, when we examine them closely, as only having a solicitudinary existence! By definition these are precarious existences; they vanish along with the base phenomenon. What are they missing? Ubiquity, consistency, *réique* and ontic poise. These *mock-existences*[102] or pseudo-realities are real; but also counterfeit in that they formally imitate the *réique* status, without having its consistency or, if we want to speak in this way, its matter.

And there we can see a second characteristic of ontics of this class: they do not have, but imitate the *réique* status.

§60. In this regard, we will observe that the *possible* is really only a variety of the imaginary (which greatly augments the importance of the latter).

This is clear in the case of those pseudo-possibles, which rely entirely upon the suggestions of fear or hope, upon the typical attempts of foresight.

More subtle is the case of what Bergson calls non-impossibility—the absence of hindrance (*The Creative Mind*, p. 83; cf. *supra*, §19)—which indicates an incorporation into the real, under cosmological species, particularly as regards apparatuses of causality. I can enter into this room if it is unlocked or if I have the key. My imagining this action can be integrated into the real without postulating any modifications (which would themselves be imaginary) of the latter. To become a millionaire from an inheritance left by an American uncle—what a lovely dream! But is it possible? In hoping for this, you imply that your father has a brother who is now in America and a millionaire.… Yet this is no longer a case of the possible, it is either true or false. To win the lottery on the next drawing! Whether or not I bought a ticket, my dream of being a candidate for the millions is absolutely and ontologically the same. It is no more difficult

---

102. In English in the original. [TN]

to imagine that my ticket will win, than to imagine that I have a ticket. But if I do not have one, I know that my dream modifies the real; and I say, "it is impossible." If I have one, my dream modifies nothing—except, perhaps, an unknowable future. Thus I say that there is a possibility. The difference here resides entirely in the implied degree of modification of the actual real; and the possibility expresses nothing more than a certain capacity of the imaginary to adapt to the real.

But the most interesting case is that of what we could call *absolute possibility*. It will be said that such a figure, such a being, such an event is possible in itself, independently of all reference to the actual. I know that there have never been any centaurs or fauns, that there never will have been any. But anatomically (see above), the former (that there have been) is impossible, while the latter (that there will have been) is possible.

What does this mean, if not that the latter broadly conforms with certain morphological laws of life, and that the former does not? An imaginary may or may not—but only gratuitously—be structured in accordance with a given cosmology. Gratuitously, for let it be understood that the law does not reign over the imaginary as it does over its model. Imitative requirements, borrowed from an ontic type that we grasp in a positive cosmology, are all excessive. "Absolute possibility" is, then, the stylistics particular to the imaginary: gratuitous and excessive conformity to a given ontic and cosmic conditioning.

This explains why the possible appears more real or more proximate to existence than the imaginary in general. Naturally, it is neither more nor less proximate to it. It is a sub-variety of the imaginary, which is itself a variety of the ontic mode. But it simulates other varieties well enough that we are accustomed to treating it as if it were more real.

§61. As for the imaginary in general, we see that its specific mode of existence (outside of such simulations) resides in its total dependence upon the base phenomenon. It is true that those simulations can protrude some distance into, and at times even to the forefront of cosmicity; that imaginaries can be organized in such a fashion that they posit a more or less solid discursive universe—for example, a discursive universe of an important, social positivity. Here we do not mean to suggest the literary or artistic universe so much as certain myths, which can even have such a significant effect that they become incorporated into the world of concrete, everyday representation (cf. the theory of myth in G. Sorel's *Reflections on Violence*). But then they cease being pure imaginaries and invest themselves in another kind of existence.

*
* *

§62. Let us go a step further.

Bound to and dependent on phenomenal existence as it is, the imaginary (and its by-product, the possible) is nevertheless formed from a certain positive—namely, psychological—stuff. It is made of such stuff as dreams are made on.

Is there a mode of existence in which (apart from the attachment that subordinates it to another existence) there would be no stuff whatsoever; an existence cut from a stuff of pure nothingness?

Yes: Such is virtual existence.

We will not dwell on this, having dealt with it at length elsewhere.[103] Let us confine ourselves to noting the essential.

Is saying that a thing exists virtually, the same as saying that it does not exist? Not at all. But neither is it saying that the thing is possible. It is saying that some reality conditions it, without thereby including or positing it. Closed in upon itself in the void of a pure nothingness, it completes itself outwardly. The broken or newly begun arch of a bridge virtually outlines the missing section. The curve of the ogives, broken off above the columns, outlines the absent keystone in the nothingness. The inceptive contours of an arabesque virtually posit the arabesque in its entirety. As in the imaginary, there is, in its abaliety, a dependence upon some reality; but completion—whether in representation, perception, or dream—is neither necessary, nor present.

A number of sketches or starts, a number of interrupted indications outline, around an inferior and changing reality, a whole kaleidoscopic interplay of beings or monumentalities that will never exist; that have no other reality than that of being conditioned hypothetically or in advance, and even determined at times with a perfect precision in their stuff of nothingness. It is a particularly rich mode of existence with

---

103. *Avoir une âme: essai sur les existences virtuelles*, Les Belles Lettres, 1938.

a multitude of presences that are absences. It is a particularly economical mode of existence, as well: the lion's claw is sufficient for the virtual existence of the whole animal; the trace "of the lover's bloody, bare foot in the sand" is enough to outline the mysterious passerby in the interworld [*l'intermonde*], on the margins of being.

The interior life, in particular, abounds in presences of this kind. Its most precious riches are made up of them, its treasures are of their world.

And let us not invoke phenomenological "intention," here. That is only a particular case, which moreover is marred with both logicism and psychologism: the case in which the virtuality's attachment materializes in a phenomenal vection, in an impetus in the direction of a completion that either is really underway, or is still expressed in a more or less vague symbolism. But the broken bridge, which no one attempts to rebuild, outlines the interrupted section of the arch just as well as the bridge that is really and currently under construction. The bridge that no one thinks to build, of which we have not even conceived the possibility—but for which all the materials are available, and whose nature, span, and form are perfectly determined so as to provide the sole solution to a problem, for which all the data is complete though unrecognized—this bridge exists with a virtual existence that is more positive than the one that was begun, but whose completion was rendered impossible by a flaw or a faulty design.

For let us not be mistaken: there are intentions that cannot be accomplished, vections that cannot be completed; they do not adjoin any virtual existence. Something besides an impetus and an intention is needed for there to be virtual existence; a law of harmony must close the implied being upon itself, architectonically; launched into the void, those incipient curves must gather together and organize themselves in the void as a virtual, really existing in that mode. And that is, without a doubt, why the soul is, above all else, a harmony. The soul that we do not have, but that we could have, is formed, in its virtuality, from the harmony that arranges whatever it may be, whose interrupted contours were momentarily traced by the sketch of an interior melody, into chords.

And we live in the midst of a forest of virtuals that are unknown to us, of which some may be admirable, perfectly suited to our fulfillment, and yet we do not even think to glance at them, nor to realize them, except by way of dreams, in the sketchbooks of the imaginary. And so we direct our intentions elsewhere, toward absurd and unattainable ends, toward monsters.

The difference—at the heart of intentionality, for example—between what can and cannot be accomplished (and we mean what cannot be accomplished not for lack of strength or ardor, but because the enterprise is absurd or auto-destructive) is where the reality of the virtual resides and is what makes of it a mode of existence.

*
* *

§63. Virtual existence is thus of an extreme purity, of an extreme spirituality. In certain respects, we might think of it as a purification of the imaginary, though the virtual always retains the characteristic of *abaliety*, which may depreciate it to some degree; it needs a point of reference. This is even what constitutes and defines it. The virtual is a conditioned conditioning, dependent upon a fragment of reality, which is foreign to its own being, and which is like its evocatory formula [*formule évocatoire*].[104]

Can we go a step still farther? Can we conceive of an absolutely dematerialized existence, formed from unconditioned

---

104. It might seem as though the three notions of the imaginary, the possible, and the virtual are brought too close together, here. This is what we nevertheless believe appears when these terms are examined from a purely existential point of view. If, of course, with the perspective of critical knowledge, we restore them to the full content of their philosophical significance, the three terms will separate to a greater extent. According to a penetrating remark, which we owe to the first reader of this book (Mr. Émile Bréhier), "the imaginary is referred to an existing real, which is the imagining self; the possible is intrinsic, completely independent of any existing real; the virtual is the existing real itself, only just beginning to show itself. Moreover, they are introduced in quite different ways: the first with a pejorative sense (all of that is only imaginary!), the second in a logical discussion, the third in metaphysics." There are subjective and objective meanings for the possible (see the *Vocab. hist. et crit.*). The former (which Lachelier found abusive) shift it more toward the imaginary, the latter toward the logical *lexis* or even the noumenal. Lastly, once assimilated into the probable of mathematics (meaning B3 of the *Vocab.*), it belongs solely to the order of critical knowledge. The idea of "probable existence" has no properly existential content: it measures certain specific, notional properties of some (most often virtual) existence.

conditionings, freed from all attachment, from all dependence upon a reality that would evoke it; prior to any, even partial, concrete investment?

This is quite an important problem. One will think either of purely rational or logical beings, of immaterial forms, or of essences—or else, and in the first place, of *noumenal existence* (in Kantian fashion).

§64. The expression is paradoxical. Etymologically, it means that we are dealing with things that are known and thought (νοούμενα); which would imply that they are dependent upon psychical realities. In certain respects, then, they would only differ from imaginaries by their abstract and general character. They would be the imaginaries of the understanding, as it were. They would only enter into the universe of discourse under the form of rational representations, beings of ideation, of thought in its psychological actuality.

If, on the other hand, we attempt to free them from this inherence, so as to posit them as absolutely transcendent, we cease to be able to speak of them; with respect to us, they are totally unknown (whatever they may be in their own mode of existence)—since we only posit them separately inasmuch as our thought does not touch them or conceive of them.

It is true that Kant himself has indicated a way of escaping from this dilemma. If our only objection to any discourse addressing the noumena lies in the positive, empirical, and extrinsic fact that they are, for us, unknown, then perhaps they are simply cut off from us by our lack of a suitable faculty for apprehending them (the famous "intellectual intuition"). We would thereby deny the actuality of their connection with a *sui generis* phenomenon, which is characteristic of that intuition. To posit them, though, it would be enough to problematically posit that intuition as potential; or at the very least, short of a direct intuition, to discover indirect evidence of it. The mathematical entity, which eludes our intuition as an existence in itself, would potentially and indirectly reveal itself through the regularity and universality of the constraints exercised either upon our understanding, or upon the figures (or upon both at once, as Plato thought), in the course of arguments and discursive demonstrations. The "beings of reason" (cf. §50 above)—for instance, ultramicroscopic, physical entities—would be situated, in themselves, outside of experience (we cannot detect them experimentally since the very conditions of the experiment modify them); but we would suppose them to be potentially detectable if a new technique of making-appear, touching them delicately enough, brought them into relation with the phenomenon without corrupting them. Besides, they are already related to it in a more or less indirect manner. God himself—the noumenal God of the metaphysicians—would be equal to the felt God of the mystics if indirect evidence explained his presence otherwise, or if, for example, a particular intuition (reserved for certain privileged individuals, endowed with a special sense of the divine) could reach him and render him "sensible to the heart."

In that case, the Kantian "Halt!," prohibiting all discussion of these unknowns, would lose all its value. A more daring seafarer—think of Nietzsche's cry: "Embark, philosophers!" in *The Gay Science* (no. 289)—would always be able to set sail for the Isles of the Blessed (we are thinking of Gaunilo of Marmoutiers), said to be undiscovered, but not therefore undiscoverable. May a new faculty awaken in us....

§65. As seductive as this perspective may be, with its call for an enlargement of thought, for an innovation in knowledge, it nevertheless remains insufficient from where we currently stand. It would certainly allow those noumena to enter profitably into the universe of discourse, though only in the capacity of problematic existences, which is in no way a kind of existence, but only the opening up of a problem pertaining to existence.

The truth is, when we think of the possible isolation of ontic conditionings, grasped outside of all experienced and phenomenal presence, we are thinking of something completely different than problematic existences. We are thinking of essences that are independent of all existence.

We are especially wrong to reproach the ontological argument for an unwarranted passage from essence to existence. At most, it is a question of a return. The truth is that there is passage from existence to essence in every consideration of noumena.

Indeed, we have seen how, having approached existence through the phenomenon, we pass from there to ontic organizations and, in the first place, to the most practical and spontaneous of these, the corporeal ontics; then to the most technical, which rely upon the scientific disciplines that rationalize them by removing a little of their instinctive and sensible solidity; from there, to the imaginaries, and then on to the virtuals. Finally, the representations of the understanding call for a total separation, to be brought about by resolutely pushing off from the coast of the phenomenon. But up to what point, once those moorings have been cut, can we suppose that every existence keeps from failing along with that last existential support? It would certainly be necessary (and this is what is expressed in the commitment to intellectual intuition or problematic experience) to find and assign them a new kind of existence. In the meantime, there is indeed privation of existence, pure and simple.

This privation can present itself in various forms. The nullification of the existential parameter can appear as the suppression (or bracketing) of an attribute. Existence as predicate is Leibniz's thesis (cf. *New Essays*, beginning of Part IV).[105]

When we make existence not a predicate, but the very positing of the thing (this is Kant's thesis: *Critique of Pure Reason*, A598), the suppression of existence is, at the same time, the refusal to posit the thing. We can then certainly set existence to the side and observe it with respect to the thing, as an affirmation that "the universe of discourse is not null."[106] But that is to substitute a logical symbol of existence for existence itself. The thing that is considered, in this way, to be the object of that affirmation is truly a being or a discourse that is considered independently of every affirmation or negation. It is the pure *lexis*.[107] A *lexis*, the utterance of a system of relations that is considered independently of the act capable of affirming or denying the system as existent—such is the final residue to which this approach leads us.

Once again, we would subsequently be able to ask whether a new kind of existence would be able to resurrect these bloodless phantoms, revive them like the blood Ulysses gave

105. We could bring Russell together with this (*The Principles of Mathematics*, 427), inasmuch as he considers existence (which is different than being) as a property of certain classes of individuals.

106. Cf. Couturat, *Algèbre de la logique*, §20. Its symbol is: $1 \lhd 0$.

107. Slight difficulty of vocabulary: These utterances, considered in their contents, independently of every affirmation or negation, have at times (Goblot, *Logique*, §50) been called "virtual judgments," as in the Latin phrase: *sapientem solum esse beatum*. This has nothing in common with the existential virtual as it was described above. The terms *dictum* or *lexis* avoid this equivocation.

the dead to drink. Beyond any annexation to the phenomenon, beyond any actual positing or ideation, beyond even an intention, or an ideal determination in accordance with the properly phenomenological approaches,[108] when every ontic mode finally fails, we can ask whether something new could not arise, which would replenish them with existence. In the meantime, between the moment in which they vanish, stripped of all that had at first maintained them, and the moment of their rebirth, following a transfusion of new blood, it may seem as though they subsist for a moment, in themselves, in the interworld of existence. But that is only the illusion of a limit moment.

What does this mean, if not that we see existence, such as we first took it up, vanish here completely; that we have reached the limits of the world—the ontic world—first explored?[109]

Section II

§66. We cannot—nor, to be sure, do we want to—avoid the problem of transcendent existence. But let it be fully understood: it is not a matter of following the ontic beyond its adherence to the phenomenon and experience, all the way to the void; that is the error of so many metaphysicians—and no doubt of phenomenology, as well. It is a matter of inventing (as one "invents" a treasure) or discovering positive modes of existence, coming to meet us with their palm branches, ready to receive

---

108. On the notion of ideal existence in the phenomenological sense, see, especially: Maximilien Beck, *Ideelle Existenz*, in *Philosophische Hefte*, Berlin, 1929, fasc. (3), 1, p. 151f.; and (4), 2, 197f.

109. It is necessary to mark the properly logical difficulties inherent in this failing (just as physical, or rather, microphysical, difficulties emerge as soon as corporeal existence falters). We will cite one of the strangest of these: the dispute among logicians over the bizarre opinion (maintained by McCall, Venn, J. Jorgensen, etc.), according to which universal propositions would not actually imply the existence of their object; but that particular propositions do. In this regard, Bradley humorously remarks that when we say, "all elves have green shorts," we do not imply the existence of elves; but that we do imply it when we add, "and some of them have a red cap."—In reality, the quibble rests upon a question of verbal expression. In writing, "Every elf has green shorts; some elf has a red cap," as it must, traditional logic avoids all of these difficulties. It is writing "some of them," in the plural, that leads to the phenomenon in question by appealing to the imagination, whose concrete character enables it to realize the plurality of beings. There is therefore a shift from logical existence to imaginary existence. In this respect, we observe some uncertainty in certain logicians, particularly from Cambridge.

our hopes, our intentions, or our problematic speculations, in order to take them in and comfort them. All other research is metaphysical famine.

§67. First hope. It will be said: before attempting a new cycle of exploration, can we not find what we are looking for in the cycle just travelled, simply by changing its order, by freeing ourselves from the unnecessary constraint of beginning with the phenomenon?

Are the thing "man," the thing "flower," the thing "theorem" not, as systems, sufficiently constituted—outside of all phenomenal appearance—to represent existence?

For as skeletal as we ultimately found them to be, those frames, those patterns of relations are not nothing. Do they not, from a certain point of view, possess everything necessary for defining existence—for instance, the local or temporal sign, the intrinsic *hic* and *nunc*, collocative relations, or even *consistency?*[110]

The most striking case will be that of the divine essence in the ontological argument. But we could say as much of every ontology. Is not each ontic sufficient for outlining a manner of being, a particular mode of existence? And if this mode of existence does not accommodate an immanence of the phenomenal and experiential order, it must, then, be regarded as positing itself in the order of the transcendent. Does that not suffice to define transcendent existence?

The case may seem subtle. We need to acknowledge that it has force. One may say, for example, that the divine essence came into play a moment ago (with respect to the noumenal), posited in a problematic manner. But posited in this way, it defines a "to exist," a manner of being—the divine "to exist." And yet, you can neither affirm nor deny this problematic "to exist." And posited hypothetically, it cannot fit back into the frames of experience or the phenomenon—for it is of its essence not to be able to do so. God does not manifest himself in his essence; otherwise he would be incarnated in the phenomenon and in the world; he would be of the world. Rather, he surpasses the world, he distinguishes himself from it; his "to exist" develops alongside and outside of it. His "to exist" therefore defines itself as transcendent existence. Whether you want to or not, you define this mode of existence. Even in imagining it, you are positing it

110. In English in the original. [TN]

(if only problematically) as a definite mode. Therein lies the force, the ineluctability at the heart of the ontological argument.

That much is undeniable. We can examine it in yet another manner. We can say: by taking responsibility for the ontic universe of representation (cf. §16 above, and §82 and 84 below) you have taken responsibility for God. For he appears in it. In it, he represents the particular mode of existence that is appropriate to him and that his ontic defines. It is a transcendent, even an absolute mode. Now the onus is on you to prove that this mode must be eliminated, that this existence is really not an existence, that it corresponds to nothing. The burden of proof falls on you.

It is incontrovertible.

§68. Let us not, however, be mistaken about this. What are we witnessing? A claim to existence. Ontic statuses reduced to the state of *lexis*, pure beings of reason stripped of all that made them *beings* [*étants*], ask that we return what we have taken from them. It is simply a matter of their restitution. The case is the same with mathematical entities.[111] The cycle in which we isolate them as essences, included them as *beings*; and if we really grasp the identity that grounded this existence as being prior in itself (see §47) to all the cosmic collocations of appearance and manifestation, then no transcendent modality is needed for grounding it. The same is the case with the self. At the very heart of phenomenality, in which it is able to appear in the guise of the egoity [*égoïté*] that is one of its aspects, its identity grounds it and forms an existential basis without having recourse to the noumenal and the transcendent.

The same goes for the majority of real essences. Even though we can follow them beyond the world by means of a provisional transcendence that (as we have seen) simultaneously deprives them of their "to exist," it is enough, in order to restore to them that "to exist," to draw them back into the heart of the world, where they are *essentially*. Just like the creation of the scale draws the circle of fifths back into the interior of the octave, even though the structure of that circle seems to depart from it and to stray quite far from the initial position of the tonic.

---

111. It is not surprising to see their fate discussed alongside that of theological entities, their similarity having been thoroughly demonstrated, with regard to Malebranche, by Paul Schrecker, "Le parallélisme théologico-mathématique chez Malebranche," *Rev. phq.*, 1938, I, p. 215f.

The need for transcendence only appears for those existences that either exceed the world's octave in magnitude, or are incapable of coinciding with its content, and so cannot be drawn back into it. This would especially be the case for divine existence; and there may not be many other metaphysical examples to be mentioned.[112] Is the idea valid in this form? Yes, without a doubt. But let us take care that it rests upon the supposition that a *divine "to exist"* is defined. And not merely defined as a verbal construction (I call God the infinite and perfect being…), but really; if only in a completely virtual fashion (the virtual being a kind of reality), through the imperfect idea that we form of him.

The ontological argument will not, then, be a passage from essence to existence or from existence to essence, but from one mode of existence to another; for example, from this virtual existence (or from what Descartes called objective existence) to an actual existence (or formal, in the Cartesian fashion), or to whichever mode of existence we wish to affirm in the conclusion: God exists. It is the passage from one mode to the other that *constitutes* the argument. In any case, it implies that a positive response, in the form of a real, concrete proposition, has been given to the question: What is in question when we ask what the divine is? And that some kind of model, glimpse, conception, or example has at least been articulated for him; that he has been in some manner put in play, in movement, in action, in presence; that he has appeared before the court; that he "stood" [*esté*] in his own defense, just as Job had summoned him to do.

A terrible demand. The only ones to respond to it—the only ones, among the philosophers, *to invoke the divine* [*s'objectent le divin*]—are those who dare to make the Word speak (Saint Augustine, Malebranche, Pascal). In general, we could say that there is no divine taking of the stand [*d'ester du divin*] in the universe of human discourse, except for the twenty-some-odd pages of all the Scriptures of all religions, in which the impression of hearing a God speak in the language of God can be had. And twenty is a lot. Perhaps there are really only five

---

112. We would still be able to ask whether inter-ontic or morphematic investments of existence would allow for a sort of reinsertion of God into the world's octave, without making it coincide with him and with his ontic content. It seems that Bergson sought God in this direction.

altogether. But we would also have to take the *gesta Dei* into account. For instance, let the human clay (the feelings, the thoughts, and above all the events of a life) be mixed and molded in such a way that it recognizes in itself the hand of a God….

For let us remember that the problem is only posed if the subject, whose existence is affirmed, has appeared before the court. How many theological and metaphysical speculations there are in which he has not figured in any way whatsoever!

§69. But let us deepen the problem still more.

In presentations of this sort, there is still no question of a transcendence, in the sense of an existential exteriority. At most, we would be able to speak here of a sort of moral transcendence, of a change in the order of magnitude or value, which belongs to a different group of ideas.[113] If, up to a certain point, there is a passage here from an order of human magnitude to a superior order, this leaves us entirely ignorant with respect to the problem of knowing whether this divine is of a human basis; whether it comes from without or is a matter of man in the process of becoming divine, in his thought or in his experience.

In order to obtain the right to understand the "he exists"— which forms the second member of the proposition—in a transcendent sense, we would require recourse to other speculations.

For instance?

A number of possibilities come to mind.

§70. With respect to this passion, with respect to the divine undergoing of which we just spoke, one of the most simple possibilities would consist in evoking the postulate, sometimes presented as an axiom:[114] that every passion implies an action, every patient an agent—as every valley implies a hill, or every sale a purchase. What does this say if not that the passage we seek will be carried out in the inter-ontic form of the category of community or reciprocity—of *Miteinandersein*. It is in this that the existence constituting the reality of this transcendence will be invested. Naturally, this passage will be worth the same as the axiom; the critique of which must be put into practice. But that is not our concern. The aim of this "thematic test" was to show what kinds of operations would allow us to

---

113. This will be taken up in the final chapter.

114. Cf. Descartes at the beginning of *The Passions of the Soul*; and the scholastic sources in Gilson, *Index scolastico-cartésien*.

problematically attempt outlining transcendences that imply exteriority. They imply—and this is what had to be shown—a change in the very nature of the investment of existence. At which point, we leave the ontic mode behind. It is not, at least not directly, a matter of positing as transcendent the definite, essential ontic, but of passing from it to a different mode of existence; and in this case, especially to the morphematic investments that will be the object of the third section of this chapter.[115]

§71. Another possibility suggests itself on the basis of something still more interesting, as regards the general object of our study. It concerns the idea of existence for itself.

It will be said: it is out of the question to speak of an existence in itself for the divine that is present to our thought in the aforementioned problematic manner. But even without abandoning the cycle we have traveled up to this point, we have the experience of a mode of existence, which, if considered with care, suffices to realize the transcendence we seek.

We encountered this existence in the psychical order. As individuals, we exist for ourselves. And if we are able to constitute ourselves in this mode of existence, we are cured of all dependence on the other and the elsewhere, of all abaliety. But in a universal view of this mode of existence, we are led to recognize it for other individuals, as well, insofar as we do not think of them as being for-us, but as being for-them. Is that not the way in which love thinks of them? We realize transcendence in our tête-à-tête with God, without ever departing from our own experience, if, in this dialogue, we are able to feel the for-himself of God; or else a for-him of ourselves, which changes the center of gravity of our tête-à-tête, so to speak, from an architectonic point of view.[116]

---

115. The argument from the *cause* of the idea in us of God, and from the axiom, "There must be at least as much reality in the efficient and total cause as there is in its effect," such as it figures in Descartes, is another example of the same fact. Here, it is the cause-effect relation that serves as the synapse for the movement of transcendence.

116. We know that the expression "existence-for-itself" is Hegelian, and that it even entails a Germanism, as the *für-sich* implies some idea of separate existence (cf. also, for example, Lotze, *Mikrokosmos*, Book III, p. 535). Whatever the case may be, Renouvier transcribed it as he found it in Hegel and passed it on to Hamelin (cf. *Essai*, ch. V, 2: 2nd ed., p. 356-357), where the difference between existence in itself and existence for itself is posed with respect to the "active system." "We have to discover a mode of existence for him, which does not refer us to another, and

Less than ever is it a matter of argumentation and speculation: it is the effective realization of those acts and dialectical moments that would realize less a transcendence, than (if we dare say it) a transcendentalization of the invoked divine [*divin objecté*]. As we can see, it resides entirely in the architectonic transformation of the system, which substitutes for one couple, in which God depends upon man, another couple, formed from the same semantic elements, but in which, morphologically (to speak precisely), it is man who from now on depends upon God.

We do not have to criticize the legitimacy and the value of these ideas in their ground.[117] What interests us is their present significance. They do not present us with a transcendent existence, but with a transcendentalizing architectonic transformation of the mode of existence. Here again, the fact of existence that is under consideration comes to invest itself in an inter-ontic relation; in the relation of architectonic subordination—we could say, of "composition" (in the aesthetic sense of the term)—that forms the correlative situation of the two elements whose relation changes. Musicians will understand this by thinking of an "enharmonic modulation": the succession of two chords composed substantially of the same notes, but whose succession brings about a key change, since the note that sounds as the tonic in the first, subsequently sounds only as the dominant, or the leading-tone, etc.; and since in this way the entire interior equilibrium shifts kaleidoscopically without changing its constituent parts.

---

which nevertheless would not be existence in itself.... Every free being ... is for itself." In addition, this could be brought together with Maine de Biran's critique of "existence for me" and existence in itself in the Cogito (*Rapports des sciences naturelles avec la Psychologie*). Finally, the problem of God *for me* and *in me* frequently returns in Gabriel Marcel's *Journal métaphysique*.—We would gladly believe that the true faith expresses itself not as "God for me," but as "me for God"; in a for-You or even a for-Him of all being, which remains valid even with a return toward the world. Perhaps the true love, as well.

117. Besides, the critique is easy. *If* the operation is true, if it is carried out in its living reality, a soul thereby succeeds in positing *its* God, in its reality in relation to itself. It takes the personality of *this* God upon itself by sacrificing itself as an individual. Thus, it receives its reward—or its punishment. It gets what it wanted. It gets the God that it deserved. Now, all such Gods—all those of the mystics or of the *real* believers—form a single God, or even God. But on what conditions? That is still a problem of the second degree, a problem of *surexistence*. In any case, it is certainly by some such means that the problem of theodicy is *really* posed, not by the *flatus vocis* of metaphysicians or theologians.

§72. Conclusion: there is no transcendent existence, in the sense that transcendence is not itself a mode of existing. The problematic transcendence must be coupled with a real existence, summoned to stand before the problematic entity, and that *alone* is what gives it its existence; the fact of transcendence is therefore in no way constitutive and modal.

But there are facts of transcendence: passages from one mode of existence to another. And in those that we have just thematically tested, transcendence, as a passage, as an active and real change, shows itself precisely in this modal innovation: the investment of existence in the modulation itself, and, in general, in the passage, in the inter-ontic liaison; in the interworlds of ontic existence.

This is the last group of modes of existence that it remains for us to examine.

Section III

§73. We introduced a philological comparison near the beginning of this study, recalling the opposition made in linguistic discourse between "semantemes" (nouns, adjectives, "elements that express the ideas of representations") and "morphemes" (elements that express the relations between ideas).[118] What we considered in the first section of this chapter constituted the order of existential semantemes, so to speak. And the two "thematic tests" of transcendence in the second section showed us existence passing into what could be considered, by comparison, to constitute morphemes.

This is an important change in the very poise of being. Is it necessary, is it justifiable as fundamentally inherent in a complete conception of existence?

But then again, was what we have seen thus far itself justifiable?

Yes, without a doubt, as long as we have fully grasped the overall meaning of that plurality of existence. Existence is fragmentary because it begins to take shape at many different points at once, and thus remains fundamentally discontinuous and lacunary. We must not lose sight of this if we are to see existence as it really is. And yet, each of those beginnings, each

118. Cf. Vendryès, *Le Langage*, p. 86. See also §76 below.

incipit of the ever new melody of existence represents something surprising and always admirable: the local success of an attempt at the art of existing. As we have seen, this art implies that a precise mode of existence has been found and employed—as when in order for an artistic idea to be, it must be decided that it is going to become a novel or a poem, a painting or a statue, a cathedral or a symphony. We might say that what is most astonishing is that so few of these modes exist. And this is certainly due less to a possibility of unification, than it is to a poverty of resources or to the laziness—if we can call it laziness—of an ontagogic imagination that is endlessly satisfied with two or three kinds of work. Which is not to say that they suffice; this satisfaction results from indigence and perhaps from being's own force of habit. It is true, of course, that we must reckon with the unknown and that only what we know through experience can come into play here…. Naturally, the cycle traveled thus far is only that of human knowledge. In any case, whether absolute or relative, this poverty is reason enough for the necessity to conceive of and to try out the Other as a mode of existence. And that is enough to account for the change of investment that we witness; for those attempts at dynamic evasion, which, so to speak, insert "passing tones" outside of the "chord tones," outside of the tonal notes of the melody; and which, in addition to static, perfect chords, demand the dynamism of the dissonant chord, the principle of movement. Therein lies the necessarily specified confirmation not of the idea of or desire for such evasions, but of their effective realization.

§74. We can form an idea of the general subversion that would result from this, as regards the poise of existence, by alluding to Heraclitism or Bergsonism; or, in another important order of ideas, to those philosophies or physics that place existence in qualitative atoms or *qualia* (Berigard or Whitehead), with respect to which the subjects of those qualities are no more than fortuitous complexes, made and unmade without end. But in all these examples there remains a tendency to conceive of the new existences, thus perceived, on the ontic model, or else to admit that we rediscover the ontic in the consideration of complexes or by making cuts in becoming; or by witnessing simple immobilizations; or finally, because becoming is always the becoming of a being, and thus coincides topically with an ontic (this is said with Bergson, above all, in mind). In order to completely realize both the quartering of beings and the innovation in the status of existence that is represented by the consideration of morphemes alone, we would, for example, have to be carried off by our imaginations as follows.

Let us first imagine a vision detaching being from a determinate, ontic status by transposing it successively into different modes of different levels: a human personality, for example, transposed successively into a physical existence, as a present body in the world of bodies; then into a psychical existence, as a soul among souls; then into a completely spiritual existence, outside of time and the world; lastly, into a divine and mystical existence, in which it would merge with some immense and good being, of which it would be no more than a part. And then, without posing the problem of the correspondence between these beings or of their unity (which would pass to the second degree of existence), let us take these passages themselves as the only realities. Let us evoke a universe of existence wherein the only beings would be these sorts of dynamisms or transitions: deaths, sublimations, spiritualizations, births and rebirths, fusions with the One, and separations from it or individualizations. And perhaps in this way we would conceive of a sort of divine life (perhaps somewhat pantheistic? no, but without beings), in which not even the unique Being, existing by way of the ontic model, would figure: for, at base, only mystical acts would be real in it. The only reality would be the immense drama or the ceremony of such acts.… The beings therein would implicitly serve as props, like those in the imagination of a child at play. It would not be necessary that these shadows should become substances. The man who is dying would be mistaken to think of his death as the temporal conclusion to the cosmic dimension of a being; he would be failing to comprehend that the true reality of that moment would be the mystical drama of a death—with whatever reality he himself may have being based upon and consolidated in it, through his participation in it as a character who, through the drama, is virtually involved in the order of fiction.

§75. In a world thus conceived, the *event*, the occurrence (*das Geschehen, the event*, or *occurrence*[119])—that quite particular kind of "what is done" [*fait*][120]—receives an existential position and value that are comparable enough to the existential position and value that the other vision of the world, to which the first part of this chapter was devoted, identified in the phenomenon.

Just as the phenomenon is, in certain respects, a sufficient and indubitable presence, with which we would be able, if necessary, to construct an entire universe, and yet which is normally taken up and included in the constructions or the various modes that can be assembled into a sort of order or general kingdom of the ontic; so the event is an absolute of experience, indubitable and *sui generis*, with which we are also able to make an entire universe, perhaps the very same as that of the ontic, though with an entirely different existential poise; and upon which a kingdom of transitions, of connections—of the synaptic, if we wish to coin a general term to be opposed to the ontic—depends (as the ontic depends upon the phenomenon).

The grandeur of the event is accounted for neither by its being transitive or dynamic, nor even by its being singular and *hic et nunc*, but by its being the "what is done," by its being that which takes place.

In the having, in the doing, even in the being; in the being born or in the perishing, in the coming or the going, there is something that differs profoundly and fundamentally from the

---

119. Both "the event" and "occurrence" are in English in the original. [TN]

120. *Avoir-lieu* (to take place) translates *Geschehen* into French nicely, provided that this Gallicism's complete suppression of spatiality and even of the temporal topic, suggested by the word "lieu" (place), is taken fully into account. Heidegger, who has insisted upon the importance of the event (of the "historial," as Mr. Corbin translates, questionably enough), has perhaps not sufficiently noted not only its originality, but its autonomy as an existential given, capable of sufficing unto itself; as lending support and consistency to every other reality it has taken up. Whitehead and Alexander also attach great importance to the opposition between being and event. But Lotze is one of the first to have shown the existential characteristic of the event that makes it, in the capacity of *Wirklichkeit*, arrive at the domain of *Realität* (see *Mikrokosmus*, Book III, p. 497-498). Formerly, the sufficiency of the event, recognized by certain philosophers, was often combated on account of a substantialist vision. This is the case for the Stoics, for whom the event, being incorporeal, is only an epiphenomenon of being and implies substance (cf. Bréhier, *Théorie des incorporels dans l'ancien stoïcisme*). For Epicureanism, see also, Lucretius, I, 457f. – On the metaphysical and mystical importance of "events" for Pascal, see the *Mystère de Jésus*.

simple idea or meaning of these actions: there is the "what is done"; there is the "this is," the "this is happening." I was holding this glass, I released it, and it shatters. One could certainly write off the indubitability of this "what is done," reducing it to the consideration of an essence: the entity of the "to shatter," with all that it implies of a fragile ontic, being twice constituted, first according to the idea of the whole glass, then according to the idea of the glass in pieces. But all of that fails to bring us any nearer to the comprehension of the given itself: here, in this moment, *there is* the "to shatter." The having occurred, the fact of the "what is done"—that remains irreducible. One form alone truly expresses this: the verbality of the verb, of the part of speech in which the difference between "to come" and "coming," between "to fall and falling," "fell," or "will fall," is expressed.

That is what Descartes feels confusedly and allows to escape with the *Cogito*. In the Cogito, there is the self, there is thought, there is the existence of the self and of thought. But there is also the "what is done" of the *I* think, in its having happened. This is a mode of existence that is absolutely different than that of the self or of thought. And insofar as you reduce it to an actualization of those entities—of the self and thought—you allow one of its irreplaceable elements to escape, the "this takes place." Later it will have taken place. It is a "what is done" that has happened. The Cogito is not only proof of the existence of the self and of thought, it is an event that declares itself through itself and bursts forth like shattering glass.

A moment ago, there was a whole glass; now there are these pieces. Between the two, there is the irreparable. Irreparable, insuppressible, unretractable even by the most subtle resources available to the mind, which can turn away from it, but cannot contradict it. The patuity of this irreducibility. Such is the existence of the "what is done."[121]

Its patuity being so similar to that of the phenomenon, how many confusions suggest and inscribe themselves in language. The physicist will use "phenomenon" and "fact" interchangeably. This is because there is (though not always) a

---

121. There are some good passages concerning the fact (with a little bit of pathos) in Strada. See *Ultimum organum*, Book II, p. 128: "In making itself an element, the fact is intermediary between being and mind," etc.

phenomenon of the fact, in the same way there is a fact of the phenomenon. But the two are essentially distinct.

The connection to the "what-is-done," to the event, is what is efficacious.

*
* *

§76. As regards the world of the synaptic, the world that is more in contact with the fact than with any other mode of existence, we know what importance William James attached to what he called "a feeling of *or*, a feeling of *because*," in his description of the stream of consciousness. Here we would be in a world where the *or rather* or the *because of*, the *for* and, above all, the *and so*, *and then*, would be the true existences.

On the one hand, let us repeat, there are the semantemes of existence, among which the pure phenomenon would sufficiently represent the pure and now autonomous adjective, separable from every substantive order that the ontic represents.[122] On the other hand, in the order of morphemes, the synaptic would correspond to all that grammatical material (conjunctions, prepositions, articles, etc.) to which we would oppose the event, as corresponding to the very essence of the verb (while still including it in that same morphematic order).

This would be a sort of grammar of existence, which we would thus decipher, element by element.

Of course, it is not a question of making a detailed inventory of the content of this synaptic mode (we will soon see why, §84). A handful of examples will suffice to situate this newly defined order and to evoke it in its richness.

§77. The structure of time will serve as a useful example. Let us conceive of it as a cosmic dimension, as an order of successive attributes, etc. Such conceptions always imply a structure immanent to an ontic ensemble: universe, singular psyche, or psychical cosmos of the pleroma of souls, whichever. And from a certain point of view, this really is a valid conception of time.

But if, from another point of view, we resolve it into that vection, that polarization, that way in which present time flees into a future in the making, then it is this passage, this

---

122. "The final result of the abstract word's evolution toward the concrete is for it to become an adjective," Vendryès, *Le Langage*, p. 155.

transition that is at once the soul of time and the foundation of its subjective reality. The future is not, then, a particular status of existence, neighboring on the possible, the contingent, the potential, or even the veiled, the transcendent unknown (and how many difficulties arise along all those paths!). The future is the virtual accomplishment that completes the movement of this present leaning into the future—of that future falling back into the present.

Thus, it is as if the event to come is called and received, then released and sent back into the past, all by that constant form, by that *and then*, that *and so*, whose essence it is to be situated not in the instant, but between two (think of the expression, the meanwhile), in the interworld, between the departing instant and the one that arrives. And the instant itself, being purely present—and therefore, immobile and dead—is merely a virtual dependency on that constant form, barely more rich than that product of the imagination, the past.

§78. The *reciprocity*, whose significance as a powerful means of transcendence we saw a bit earlier, would of course also appear in this existential order. But we must fully understand the nature of this reciprocity, of which our earlier example presented a representative case.

It is existential in the sense that the liaison to which it bears witness is concerned with the fact of being. There is no passion without action, such is the example that showed us, a bit earlier, a path for passing into transcendence, from the human to the divine. But let it be understood that this is not a matter of passing from the existent man to the existent God along that hypothetical path. It would be a matter of a true investment of existence in that joint action, or in the mystery implied by that action-passion. As "what is done," as event, as existence, it would be the act of that mystery—attesting to its own existence as event, not to that of the two characters the mystery comprises or posits, which would only exist in relation to it.

It is, then, their relation alone that would exist. And we see why Hamelin's project would be definitively impossible, as it is out of this relation that all representation would arise. For no ontic reality would ever be made to arise, existent, out of a world of relations. That would entail two different worlds, or two existential interpretations of the same world; unless, in conversely positing the end as existent, we find the means for a transcendence outside of the relation.

§79. Likewise, causality, that functional connection, which is dynamic insofar as it permits a regression to infinity, will have greater existence insofar as it operates synthetically—in its capacity as a dash—than the measurable elements of the phenomena that depend upon it for their reality (see §103).

§80. And now we see the true meaning of that existence for itself or for something else, which earlier served to characterize the passage from the preceding cycle to the present one. The modulations of existence *for*, existence *in front of*, existence *with*, are so many varieties of this general mode of the synaptic. And by this means we are able to recover from the excess of importance that certain philosophies grant to the celebrated man-in-the-world. For the man-before-the-world and even the man-against-the-world (*adversus*: against it as conflict, as clash and violent collision, as an entirely offensive attempt at gaining the upper hand) are also real. And conversely, there is also the world-in-the-man, the world-before-the-man, the world-against-the-man. What is essential is that we fully appreciate that in all these modulations existence invests itself not in man or in the world, nor even in their ensemble, but in that "for," in that "against," in which the "what is done" of a kind of being resides, and upon which, from this point of view, man and the world both equally depend.

§81. We now see—an important corollary—how the perspective afforded by the "what is done" quite simply resolves (though perhaps with some deception for certain metaphysicians) the ancient problem of knowing if the copula of the judgment, with that little word *is*, really implies existence.

It implies it, no doubt, provided we see that it implies neither the substantive existence of the subject, nor that of the predicate (in whichever way we interpret it), but only that of the synapse, of the copula as the existence of the relation of inherence—which, from this perspective, it is a matter of seeing in its pure existence, belonging to the synaptic mode; an existence upon which the existences of the subject and the attribute depend, in that they are implied in a single "what is done," which is itself the true existent.

§82. It is pointless to insist any further on making an inventory of other species. Let us endeavor to make the weight of thought [*le poids de la pensée*] bear upon the essential, upon the general philosophical meaning of the opposition between the two existential cycles now traveled.

They clearly correspond to the two modes of exploration already highlighted briefly (§16): either to take responsibility for all the ontic content of representation, to divide it up, to split it into existential modes; or to begin with any unique ontic we like and to seek the connections by which we "modulate" (in the musician's sense) from there toward other existential tonalities. It was a question of proposing methods. But here it is no longer a question of method. The opposition thus revealed is real. And in order to fully understand it, we must appreciate the profundity found within the words of the poet who spoke to us.

Of a world where action is not the sister of the dream.

Dream and action are two great examples of the existential option that suggests itself to us as soon as it is a question of effectively bringing about realizations.

Of the second cycle studied here, action—and not the act or activity—is the most distinctive theme. A man can fix upon the ontic setting of his life through either imagination or perception. He can maintain a mode of reality upon which he will rest, in which he will be established, and which will posit a world of beings, of which he will be one. Beings of dreams or beings of a physical and concrete existence, it matters not. What is not in the physical "to exist," he will be able to posit in dream. In each of these cases he will be the demiurge, the creator or support of a kind of reality. But in opting for action, he will plunge into a completely different kind of reality, he will opt for a completely different manner of being. All that is verbal will now be vain, and all that is stable in the ontic will become spectral. Properly speaking, there will no longer be a universe of discourse. There will only be this action, which belongs to the kind of the event. And in order to establish himself in it, in order to situate himself in it, existing in the sense that the action exists, he will have to sacrifice (an enormous, frightening sacrifice) all the ontic solidity and stability belonging to him and even to the world, which, from the other point of view, appeared to be the very model of substantiality. His reward? Simply this plunge into a kind of existence that then offers to him alone, and not without some vertigo, participation in the real, through the very operation of the facts of the action.

We write for philosophers, to whom only the name of action, not action itself, is usually known; and to whom the fact of opting completely and utterly for action, represents a renunciation of all that appears to them to be real life (they will call it the life of the mind), since all ontology, along with the metaphysics that belongs to it, lies in that direction. This is why we have little hope of making them understand what we speak of, other than by making them feel it negatively, in the horror provoked in them by the following idea: to close all the books, to put an end to all discourse, to forget all the theories that maintain the world of the ontic, and to enter into action through a renunciation of their philosophy—of what appears to them to be philosophy; as Pascal renounced mathematics or Rimbaud renounced poetry. To enter into some great adventure, in which the event becomes the true substance, and the connections between all beings become exclusively transitive and situated or constituted in the action itself, and according to its mode.

A kind of life that will assure them an experience of this mode of being; and all the more demanding as the difficulty is not of acting once or twice at random: the difficulty is of always acting, of being included in a "to act" to such a great extent that it encompasses life in its entirety, in each of its moments, in a tyrannical, totalitarian fashion: in short, that it bears witness to the formation of a cosmicity in the pleroma of actions, and to the insertion, into that cosmicity, of life.

What we want to draw our attention to, however, is the obvious significance of the reality of the choice actually made in this manner. It is quite true that action is not the sister of the dream. In such a dreadful subversion as would shatter or disperse our everyday world, we are certainly able to take refuge in dreams and, in them, to re-establish a phantom of that world or of a better one. We are still able to take refuge in the contemplation of all that the real world offers us that is akin to this dream, if only through the beauty of what is offered us in the sky and the trees and the waters. But we are also able to take up arms or tools and act. At first, in the immediacy of being and in the first

178

degree, the two are irreconcilable: they are radically different investitures of life and existence. This is all that we wanted to say.

In a general manner, in order to be, the necessity of choosing between such and such a mode of existence is the sign of the fact that the specificity of the modes of existence does not correspond to an inferior, relative, or secondary point of view, but, on the contrary, to the point of view of existence itself, on its own terrain. The "first degree" of existence, whose content in this chapter we only somewhat begun attempting to explore, is truly the first—not only basic, but direct, exact, and precise—plane of existence. That is what existence is. That is where it reigns, where it resides. And it is demanding.

§83. Of course, it is not necessary to bestow an authoritarian and constitutive importance upon this opposition between the order of ontic existence and that of existence through action. By means of this topical example, we wanted to show living reality and concrete pathos; the experience of those rifts in existence that force a choice, since any existence is a certain mode of existence, and since a side must have been taken for an existence to be real. None of these commitments are temporally definitive, to be sure, unless the cosmic conditions thereby enter into a definitive practice, for example, into the limited dimensions of human life. I can try—"one fruit and then another fruit," as Muhammad says—various kinds of existence; I can constitute that of which I dream, first in the order of dreams, then in that of physical and concrete existence. I can shed my old self and, at my own risk, attempt a new life in a world I have not yet tried—and in every other. But what we must see is that every such attempt is, as an existential approach, an absolute commitment, a metaphysically definitive choice. The being thus instaured is completely and fundamentally what it is, which is to say, of one mode or another. We do not get to side-step this deity, existence; it does not get taken in by our specious words, which cover up a choice unmade. To be, and not to be in some specific manner, is of no value. Cut yourself from whatever existential cloth you like, but cut you must—and, as a consequence, to have chosen whether to be of silk or of wool.

§84. To say it succinctly, *the different modes of existence are the true elements.*

Can we make an exact enumeration of them? Without a doubt: if the philological comparison, already employed here several times, were to be extended a long way, we would be able to flatter ourselves with having constructed the complete chart of the modes of existence according to the type of stature or of compositional symmetry with which it presents us, as soon as we take up this enumeration beginning with the phenomenon, so as to follow it in the forms of the ontic kingdom, and then to take the inquiry up again with the kingdom of the synaptic, which in its turn comes to be concretized in and dependent on the event. To such an extent that a philological chart of the parts of discourse would be able to give us the impression that it has furnished us with the frames for a general table of the modes.

But—apart from the empirical and limited character of this philological expression; apart from the particularly important fact that philological inscription is only an insufficient, approximate attempt at expressing something much more fundamental, however well or poorly it is analyzed by this expression; without taking into account all the space that we must concede to the unnamed and the unexpressed—we must, above all, be wary of the chart's appearance of being closed in upon itself, induced by what may be a superficial symmetry that is based upon the opposition of semantemes and morphemes. This apparent self-enclosedness would mask the essential fact that the table is actually open. The two kingdoms, whose modes are thus empirically inventoried, each comprise modes of an undoubtedly indefinite number, which leave a gap, an abyss in their ensemble, which may never be filled. In the end, the structure obtained depends, above all, on the order adopted for the investigation, for the journey—an order that is not necessary. Indeed, this is symbolized by the methodological duality, marked on several occasions (§16 and §82), which was able to direct us in our investigations. This is enough to assure us that we have without a doubt not omitted anything important, but not enough to assure us that we have grasped the true order of the elements, of the modes of being. Is there even such an order? Is the idea of such an order valid?

§85. When considering the hypothetical plurality of these modes at the beginning of our inquiry, it was the richness of the world multiplied in this manner that struck us, above all else. A short while ago, it was able to strike us with its poverty, as well. The laziness of being, we then said. Yet these lacunae are also propitious, opening their void onto new paths, still to be tried. *Tentanda via est ... Avia Pieridum peragro loca....* For us other men, unswerving hopes. No fresh and new, or more sublime, mode of existence can be refused outright. It is not simply a matter of noting recognized and indubitable modes of existence, but also of conquering them. And the most important ones among them may be those that, in the real human condition, declare themselves so infrequently and thus stubbornly remain in the state of an inferior sketch and a precarious instauration, that they elude consciousness. In order to form an idea of such modes, imagine what the first sketches of spiritual existence might have been for man, when neither morality, nor religious thought, nor science, nor philosophy had yet furnished, distinguished, and concretized the elements of that life; when the first factors of the reality of such existence made the mind of a savage or a barbarian quake in his cave, like an impermanent and unnamed apparition. Without a doubt, it proceeds here as it does in art, where the great instaurators are not so much true inventors, as those who were able to discern, in the childlike stammerings of certain precursors, the outlines of a new style, which they developed, magnified, and justified in great works.

In saying that in order to exist, each being must discover its mode of existence (or else we must discover its mode of existence for it), we are also inevitably saying that there are still unnamed and unexplored modes of existence, yet to be discovered for the instauration of certain things, which will go unheeded until such a time as the necessary mode will have been invented, innovated.

§86. That is why we must vigorously resist the temptation to explain or deduce the modes of existence that have already been discovered. Let us be wary of dialectical infatuation. It would certainly be easy, with a little ingenuity, to improvise and, in broad strokes, to outline a dialectic of existence, in order to demonstrate that there can be no modes of existence but those, and that they engender one another in a certain order. But in doing so, we would subvert all that could be of any importance in the observations made here.

Drawn in by the philological analogy, we would be able to show that there could only be four parts of discourse, to which our groups would really correspond: adjective—the phenomenon, which is to say: evident being as clear manifestation, with instantaneous *quale* at the limit, freed from all substantial ties; noun—identical and permanent being, with eternity at the limit, the substance that abides; verb—real being as event, as action, as fact, with, at the limit, the sufficiency of the act that posits itself and defines itself through its force, and not (like the phenomenon) through its qualitative essence; finally, prepositions, conjunctions, articles—all that is real as correlative or completive determination, which is called synapse.

A deceptive attempt, a false clarity. What do you want from me, a metaphysical machine? Such a thing would deceive us all the more in giving us the impression of being in the presence of the elements necessary for a complete discourse. Which would be the most mistaken idea one could have of these modes.

They must be taken as they are: *arbitrary*. Think about it in this way: a primitive painter can find on his palette the colored soils that furnish him with his base and his technical range: yellow ocher, red ocher, green clay, black soot. He will have to be content with them; it is with this spectrum—which is imposed upon him by the poverty and humility of the given in all its contingency—that he will paint. The same is the case with the scale a rustic musician will find at his disposal, having pierced holes, here and there, in his pipe. From a contingent, initial given, he pushes his modulations, perhaps by necessity, in the direction of that which is *other* with respect to this given. But the initial given is arbitrary.

It is the same with the modes. *The modes of being are contingent*. Each one, taken as the origin, can call for such and such another in a dialectical manner. But each one, taken in turn as the origin, is arbitrary. It is gratuitous. That is what we must not lose from sight. Any attempt to legitimate them, which begins by considering one as having priority over the rest, is therefore a gross mistake and an abyss of error. Each can be subordinated to the others, taken in a certain order. But each taken in itself, *all are equal*; and an indefinite number of unknown others would have the same rights. Let us, then, guard against bringing the cycle to a close by explaining them.

Here again, the comparison with art will be more faithful. Sculpture is worth no more, in itself, than painting, music no more than architecture. It is true that some work to-be-made will be better realized in sculpture than in painting, in bronze than in marble or in clay, etc., as in its favorable environment. It is a particular case (and we will return to it; see also §73). In no way, though, will this establish a general primacy of bronze over marble or over clay. Thus, some human work will function better in dream than in action, some other, better in action than in dream. Some reality will be better instaured in the spiritual than in the corporeal. But do we believe that the spiritual is worth more than the corporeal? We will immediately recall that such a sublime act as the sacrifice of life requires a body, and that the word can gain in grandeur by becoming flesh, since such work requires flesh.

Let us therefore resist any temptation to structure and to hierarchize the modes by explaining them dialectically. If you strip it of the arbitrariness that is one of its absolute characteristics, you will always lack knowledge of existence on its own terms.

§87. We see that it would be vain to want to count the modes of existence on our fingers and to limit their number in advance. Let us be content with having justified the existential plurality in the only possible way. Existence needs this variety as the painter's palette or the elementary pipe of the most rustic musician needs several colors or several notes. And with two or three colors, with four or five notes, fine paintings or beautiful melodies can certainly be made. But without excluding the possibility that it be innovated, that new colors be added to these paints, new notes to that impoverished, rustic scale. Let us imagine what the invention of the *sharp* might have been, opening onto new universes with new tonalities!

§88. And yet attempts at unification are obviously possible—though not, of course, vain totalizations, enclosing the ensemble of those elements within a finite discourse, within a scale admitting of no innovation, within a single universe. But is there not, for instance, the prospect of a single solution, in the form of a single dialectic of existence, valid across all its modalities?

Perhaps. Certainly, even. And it would not seem strange to look for it in the vicinity of something that participates in art, rather than in any other instaurative path that would be fit for providing it with some sort of model—on the condition that it be sufficiently expanded and grasped in its pure principle—a generic art or pure art of existing, common to those different arts of existing, of which we must choose and practice one if we are to have existence. But such a solution would never, in its verisimilitude, abolish the diversity of starting points, of originary roots, or the originality of each of the initial commitments that presided over each realization.

Indeed, it would be a matter of a hypothetical, possible dialectical unity, beyond or below existence.

As for the existential unity itself, as for the real instauration of the Unique, legitimizing the theoretical unicity of the dialectic at work—it raises the major problem, not of an effacement or involutive resolution of the originary diversity, but of its overcoming through the reprise of all those roots in a common bundle, for instaurations that are complex and yet convergent.

This is the last of the questions we have to consider. Perhaps we can now ask ourselves whether it does not participate, up to a certain point, in the hypothesis and the ideal, since the chart of existential specificities is and must remain open, incomplete in that it leaves room either for the unknown or for the as yet uninvented and unrealized.…

§89. In particular, it is certainly not out of the question that we might be able to conceive of a unifying synthesis of those two halves—those two tetrachords—of the semanteme and the morpheme; or from another point of view, of being (ontic) and action. Can the option we sketched out a moment ago between the ontic and action not be surpassed? The idea of instauration can mediate between them. The thetic is at once the action of an ontic and its positing. It is ontagogic. A philosophy of instauration will bring together both the modes of acting and the modes of being in examining how and by what means they might be combined. But those are problems that ineluctably evoke the problems of *surexistence* (let us think of the essentially plurimodal character of the anaphoric experience) and a passage to the plane of the second degree, about which it remains for us to say a word. Let us not forget that, in certain respects, it draws us away from existence. Beyond transcendence simply with respect to such and such a mode, *surexistence* is transcendence with respect to the "to exist" itself in its immediate content, as soon as it is a matter of making its various modes converge beyond the plane upon which they are posited—which is to say, beyond the very plane of existence that they alone legitimately define.

Fourth Chapter:
Of *Surexistence*

§90. Existence is all the existences, it is each mode of existing. It resides and accomplishes itself integrally in them all, in each taken on its own.

Are we to understand that it is irremediably separated from itself, that it is cloven in and through its modal diversity?

The problem is unavoidable. It is difficult to pose it well. Poorly posed, it abounds in false problems and false solutions—which we see, above all, in those who are broadly mindful of the philosophical themes addressed most frequently at the present moment, and who stir them up into an error-laden medley of questions pertaining to being and existence: especially in those concerned with the problem of unification.

To unify can be an effort toward identity. There are scattered beings—scattered in a given mode of existence and seeking their identity. This is a problem we have already encountered and studied here (cf. §47): for instance, the problem of recovering from phenomenal dispersal. From that angle, to manage to be united with oneself is to find one's ontic unity, one's truth of being in the ontic mode.

Being united with others is a problem of the same kind. It implies no change of mode. Through love, through charity, through unanimity, through harmony, through organic correlation, through unifying form—a larger body, a widely vaster soul, a more complex being, microcosm, work, social group, a simple duo of me and you, or some such thing will be instaured. At most, we will distinguish existence unto-oneself-alone and existence together as different modalities. But from the perspective of the part, to conquer this "to exist together" is to see the "to exist unto-itself-alone" that it cedes, transferred to the instaured, global being.

But here we have a different problem. When the part hopes for existence together, it hungers after a different mode; it wants to be transposed into that mode. It wants to recover not from its dispersal in a mode of existence, but from that mode itself. And as we have seen, there are many other forms of this commitment to the other. The original wound: the presence of self, the initial encounter with oneself in an unsatisfactory kind of existence. Effort: to go toward the other, to go elsewhere toward oneself; to find a new plane of existence upon which one is more in tune with oneself, or where that better being, into which one would be incorporated, proves possible—the being that one prefers to oneself and to one's initial isolation.

It is a practical, concrete, and livable problem; and yet, a critical and reflective problem takes shape alongside it: how is it possible to be oneself, but elsewhere; how can a single being reside and find itself, always still itself, in two different modes of existence?

In certain respects, this is still a problem of identity, though now it is a question of plurimodal identity. We were able to and had to compare unimodal identity (cf. §47) to a sort of curvature of the plane of existence, curled or crumpled in such a way that what is separate on the plane makes contact with itself and interpenetrates, integrates into a single ontic existence. But here it would be a matter of bending two planes of existence, of bringing them into contact with one another and making them interpenetrate, such that a single being occupies a place in both at once.

And now the question is raised: is this plurimodal being plural in its identity? Is it the summation and ontic unification of two modes of existence that are simply connected? Or does it outline, in a new manner of being—existence or *surexistence*—a reality that does not simply assemble and add such and such modes, but surpasses their diversity and posits, not through its identity, but through its unity, some other thing in a status that is superior to the double existential specificity that is given?

§91. In this form, the problem may appear to be abstract, constructed, and frivolous. It is nevertheless real: it corresponds to livable, concrete experiences or aspirations.

We left a thread untied above (§55) on this subject. It was a question of our relation to our body. We noted to what a small extent the existence of the body itself is corporeal: above all, it is the expression of a psychical constraint.

Generally speaking, we are souls, or rather (since the word soul evokes virtual riches, harmonies, supposed grandeurs), simply psyches. But let us not linger over the difference.

To pose the question in the terms of Gabriel Marcel, we are souls and we have this body. But can we also be this body?

"What a strange desire!" we will say. Are we not happy to be a soul? If at first we were a body, would we not wish to have a soul, to be that soul? (And as psyches, we are really in need of an asceticism if we are to have a soul.) Let us leave that problem aside, though: let us mix psyche and soul together for the sake of the clarity of our account. Soul is what we are. Is it mad to want to be the body that we have, to want to be it, as well? The Word (we are told) wanted to become flesh. As we have seen, that is because the body is not actually inferior to the soul: it has its own distinctive characteristics. It can suffer pain and death, and it can cause them. The monophysite heretics maintained that the Word had *had* a body, but had not *been* that body—that, in itself, *it* neither suffered, nor died on the cross. This is at least the rejection of a beautiful moral idea. And it is not only pain and sacrifice that are involved in this corporeal existence, but joy and physical participation in nature, as well.

Yet are we our body? We are bound to it, constrained to follow it, enchained to it by the causal synapse. But am I able to be my body with ease? Perhaps I have believed myself to be on the verge of being my body at certain moments when, stretched out on the freshly cut grass, offered up to the sun and the sea's winds, I believed myself to be one with Mother Earth, with the reality of the Great Fetish. For a moment, I believed myself to be matter—a body among bodies. And still, how much fiction, how much imagination was at play in that moment? Could it be possible that Descartes and all the Cartesians after him were concerned with a false problem, and that (we hardly dare to say it)

189

there is no substantial union, after all, not even in God? Perhaps there are only collaborations (I am able to make use of my body, that instrument, and it is also able to make use of me), transitions, correspondences, and a certain habit of being together. But between here and being my body, there lies a distance—and there is also a distance between here and a being that would be both body and soul, not within a mere additive assemblage, but within a surpassing of their duality, without, however, subverting or annihilating their specific existences.

And the problem is posed in exactly the same terms when it is no longer a matter of psyche and corporeal existence, but of daily and concrete psychical existence and existence that is spiritual, sublime, etc.

Here, though, the idea of totality is absolutely ineffective and insufficient. It is of another order, it develops on another philosophical register, it orchestrates completely different problems, always pertaining to the ontic assemblage, and never to the surpassing of the plurimodal, existential heterogeneity. That is the main point to which we must remain attentive in the entire discussion that follows. And in this respect, there are very few systems, especially monist systems, that do not fall into grave errors through the confusion of the ontic and the existential, and through the correlative confusion of totality and unity—a confusion that entails, in its turn, the nullification of the distance (which is noetic, though perhaps also metaphysical and truly ontological) that can exist between a simple, plurimodal assemblage and another, new reality, surpassing that existential plurality where existence fulfills itself completely upon each and every plane.[123] And it is here that the idea of *surexistence* becomes indispensable.

---

123. It is easy to see that, without resolving the problem (far from it), Spinozist monism nevertheless catches sight of it and illustrates it in its vain attempts to escape from it.

   In Spinozism, unity (which is not to be confused with unicity, cf. *Metaphysical Thoughts*, I, vi) is far from simply being totality. But that is what initiates all the difficulties. In any case, we must note—as a means of guarding against those difficulties, and consequently of recognizing them—the attenuation of the existential character of the attributes (only substance and the modes exist, properly speaking), on the one hand, and the preservation of an architectonic relation between the modes and substance, despite a thousand inconveniences, on the other—all of which is mainly accomplished with the help of the theory of *expression*, in opposition to relations of causal dependence, of part to whole, and of grounding existence in essence. From which arises the importance of the fact that there is a distinction, in creatures (and not in God), between essence and existence. See also the distinction between the four senses of *being*, of which existence is one (*ibid.*, I, iii, s.f.). This is what leads Ritter to say that if, in Spinoza, the only distinction

§92. A first—dangerous, but important—approach to the idea of *surexistence* can be attempted in the order of value. We must begin with this precisely because it is dangerous, if only to warn us against the perils it implies.

§93. Although we have not counted out the kinds of existence on our fingers, we hope that we have not omitted anything essential. Do we not risk failing to recognize certain existential aspects, however, when we place all the kinds of existence on the same plane, declaring them all to be equal?

And in the first place, have we even discovered a kind of existence for every reality? For example, in what way do the laws of nature exist? It is clear that, parallel to identity in the order of the ontic, identity in the order of the event grants them the only basic existential support that might be needed in their respect. Even so, does this sufficiently recognize, might we say, the dignity and immensity of their presence? From the same point of view, does not the indefinite dyad of the large and the small diversify not only minuscule existences, which, as we have recalled, escape the normal status of the *réique* ontic on the human scale, but also existences that far surpass that scale in magnitude? And if there are cyclical recommencements, which—between microcosm and macrocosm, perhaps man and God, things and the universe, atoms and sidereal systems—renew certain similarities of status and of structure, can we, who see only analogy in this, nullify the factor of a difference in both sublimity and immensity? Then the questions will gather speed: does the category of modality not present contingent

---

between mode and substance was that of existence in itself, as an arbitrary definition of substance, we would be able to remove that distinction "without altering the system in the development of its consequences, provided that, changing the language employed, we agreed to call substance what Spinoza simply calls mode of being, and that we invented another name for cause of itself or God." But to do so would be absurd if we claimed to attribute to Spinoza, on Alexandrian precedents, some kind of theory of the *surexistence* of substance. Ritter's remark proves that Spinoza's system poses the problem, but as a difficulty, as an unresolved aporia. In the *Metaphysical Thoughts*, where things exist "eminently" in God, as they do for Descartes, there is a distinction, up to a certain point, between the existence of the divine substance and that of creatures. But this is not maintained in the *Ethics*, where existence is certainly univocal, despite Axiom I, in which the *esse in alio* should be understood not of the fact of existing in a manner other than that of substance, but of the fact of being in the existence of the latter. The meaning of the little word *in* as it is found in this proposition is the key to all of Spinozism, that effort not to go beyond, but to annul the existential specificities with an apparatus borrowed entirely from, and only effective in, the ontic order.

existences and necessary existences, of which we might focus on momentary existences and eternal existences?—and although they can and must fit back into the frames already perused, does not a difference of value, which we cannot forget, still remain between them? Was it not also a question of existing formally and of existing eminently, a question which traditionally brings a *less* and a *more* into play—eminent existence including "the same things as … or other more excellent things" than formal existence, and being *at least* equal to it (Descartes, *Meditations*, III, p. 28, n. 2)?

On the other hand, without returning to the questions of intensity, are there not certain manners of existing that are more ardent, more fervent, more gushing or protruding than others? Hugo said of God:

He is, he is, he is;—he is with abandon.…

To exist with abandon (and also to exist lyrically, to exist—if we dare say it—saltatorily, as we take a leap, as we let out a great cry of joy or of love), is that not, perhaps, to exist *more*, quantitatively speaking? But is it not to exist *otherwise* than in a "to exist" formed from drab hues, Sunday rain, apathy, and daily gloom? Finally, if, as we have seen (§86), pure existences are equal among themselves by right, will we not say that a pluri-modal existence, assembling several such existences in itself and unifying them in a rich reality, *will be worth more* than any one of them?

§94. The rather clumsy dualism of the primitives, which divided all things into the two groups of the profane and the sacred,[124] has, without a doubt, been unseated little by little through a series of profanations and secularizations. The physics of Anaxagoras profaned the celestial bodies. Epicurus secularized love.[125] And so on. There nonetheless remains something not only respectable, but considerable in those differences at the level of value. Are there not, in a man's existence, states that are in some way profane, quotidian, and vulgar, as well as noble, extreme, or supreme states, which would always retain something of that dualism in a moral form? And we must ask

---

124. That, for the primitives, this opposition is existential, that the passage from the profane state to the sacred is a transformation *totius substantiæ*, cf., Durkheim, *The Elementary Forms of Religious Life*, p. 37.

125. In daring to say that it was not sent by the gods, οὐδὲ θέopemton εἶναι τὸν ἠρωτα, (Diogenes Laërtius, X, 118).

ourselves if the difference between the sublime and the ignoble does not affect the very mode of existing of that which is distributed in this way. That is of another order, says Pascal. The question of pure, specific existences of the same level would thus be flanked by two problems concerning differences in degree: that of intensive degrees, already studied in Chapter 2, and that of degrees of value, which is different but symmetrical.[126]

§95. Yet there may be—there certainly is—a share of prejudice in certain of these ideas. Nothing is less philosophical than the confusion of degrees of value with the dyad of the large and the small. There is no reason why a great celestial body, a galaxy or a star system, a sort of sidereal Caliban, would be worth more than some minuscule Ariel, some little idea nestled into the pages of a book, some clump of earth molded into a statuette. Is it not said that, in its depths, a grain of sand may contain an atom more lovingly populated than any immense planet. A single act of charity, a moment's work in a humble soul, can be worth more than the vast, blind actions of a great social body. The moral summits of existence have nothing to do with the spatial dimensions of being. And in the same way we could contest the idea that plurimodal existence is necessarily more precious than a pure existence. Will the being that would, at once, be me as body, as soul, as phenomenon, as succession of events or timeless ontic, be worth more than that same being purified, perfected upon a single plane, in a single mode, however spectral that mode may be—even the imaginary? As Calderón's haunted hero says, if *la vida es sueño*, if life is a dream, "the good and bad deeds in the dream remain no less good and bad." And will it not be easier and more effective to realize certain perfections or sublimities in that pure mode than in the density of a heterogeneous existence. Finally, as we have seen, we cannot affirm that psychical existence (for example) is superior to corporeal existence in every instance (an affirmation that has burdened many

_____

126. For Hamelin, in the order in which the *Essai* examines them, each dialectical mode of existence "rests" upon the subsequent and superior mode, such that there is agreement between the dialectical order, the modes, the intensities of being, and the values (see 2nd ed., p. 487f.). For Lachelier, as for Ravaisson, the difference between the inferior and the superior is inscribed in being, to the point that it suffices to justify ontological theories. Whence arises the approval given to Auguste Comte's celebrated definition of materialism as "the doctrine that explains the superior by the inferior."

metaphysicians—for example, Descartes and Spinoza—with a hierarchy of substances that the rest of their system rejects). Each mode of existence has its own distinctive qualities and its flaws (which is why it is certain that none of them are superfluous). Each can receive the sublime (cf. §86 and 91). If the order of value is existential (which is debatable), it interferes with the specific modes of existence as if at random. It is a particular instance. At most we would be led to make moral existence—existence qualified as good or bad—into a specific mode of existence.

In truth, we believe that it is possible to justify the good and the bad differently, as with the beautiful and the ugly or the true and the false. Which is to say that we can respond to the question, "how do they exist?," with, "they exist in something else, they reside in certain conditionings of reality, of which the idea of perfection, in particular, serves as an example." Without taking up this large problem, let us admit that should we be able to say that they exist in themselves, this would only amount to recognizing *morally qualified existence* as a new, pure mode of existence to be added to those we have already recognized.[127]

This mode is certainly preferable to the others (to the neutrality of the event or of action) when it is qualified as good. But it is not preferable to every other mode in every instance, since that would amount to saying that because a crime is morally qualified, it is worth *more* than an indifferent action. Ontologically speaking, the *more* here would result from the addition of this mode to those already recognized—not its substitution for them. Can we attempt such a general substitution by virtue of the ontological theme, "only the good truly exists?" That (along with the famous sophism that error and evil do not exist) would be to re-establish the indifferentism from which we wanted to escape. The assimilation of absolute evil with non-being, and of relative evil with a lesser existence, returns to the imperfect

---

127. It seems that this existence, which is qualified above all with regard to action, and thus also to the event (since it constitutes the moral life), would outline a sort of recommencement of the pleroma of events in a new mode. Would it also recommence the ontic kingdom? It seems that it would not, that it would only *affect* it, with the notions of responsibility and merit appearing as the instrument of their relation. This is the solution that best conforms with the general approaches of the ethics of common sense. This raises problems, particularly because the thesis that connects value to conditionings of reality, especially ontic reality, imply a rather different moral conception. This is not the place to deal with these problems. It is not, however, a matter of indifference to indicate them in passing.

thoughts that are based upon the confusions highlighted in chapter 2. What makes evil evil is the fact that either in itself, or in that which is bad (whether existence or reality), it exists, it is real. It has been noted that we practice evil to feel ourselves exist.

In other words, according to current approaches, the moral problem can be confined within the limits of that addition of a qualified mode of existence. It nonetheless remains the case that, from another, more metaphysical point of view, we cannot conceive of an *existence of value* (thus limited), but only of *values of existence* or of reality. And from that point of view, there would be some agreement between the search for the summits of existence in value and the search for unity, which poses the problem of a pyramiding and mediatizing *surexistence* with respect to these plurimodals.

§96. Yet this agreement (and this is important) can be expressed and understood in two ways.

Sometimes an existence that is complex, implex, and imperfect in its equivocal density seeks to realize itself according to its highest value, to situate itself with precision on a single plane, in the type of pure existence that will allow it to determine itself best. This is an asceticism that both strips down and refines: I will make myself a soul and only a soul, for only in such a crystal can I carve out the resplendence I seek. I will make myself flesh, for in mortifying that flesh I will be the willingly afflicted one that my idea of moral worth demands. I will perform my work through dreams, for its moral splendor and purity will not accommodate the compromises of the real. I will execute it in stone, for I dream of a building that truly receives and shelters wretched bodies, and a hospital of dreams does not really shelter the afflicted. Perhaps we will make it with earth and water, with trees and turf, with paintings and sculptures, with lecture halls and gaming rooms, for we hate utopia and want a benefit for living men, in the complexity of their being. And then sometimes a pure and simple existence—a soul that cannot escape from the solitude of souls, a dream that only sketches an illusory and subjective perfection—seeks a complete and varied manner of being, of finding itself simultaneously on the plane of the dream and on that of action, on the plane of the psychical and on that of the physical. At the ideal limit, we glimpse the idea of a manner of being that is so complete, so rich, and so evident on the plane of both the sensible and the intelligible, the present and the atemporal, the abiding and the acting, that it resides—as if of a thousand facets—in all of these domains at once, and yet, surpassing each in assembling them all, does not entirely fit within any one of them.

Will not such a manner of being be more real than any one of those pure existences onto which it opens? And will not the man who is at once physical, moral and religious, intellectual, acting, and persisting be the more real man, compared to the ghostliness he assumes when reduced to a single one of those modes—those modes which will always call for and require each of the others for the completion of his reality?

§97. Yes, but if this is the case, nothing in this enrichment and plenitude concerns existence, only reality. Perhaps there are three values: an intrinsic value of things, or, if we want a new pure mode of existence, qualified existence, to be added to those we have already recognized. And then those two values, the value of existence and the value of reality. It may be that they are inversely proportional.[128] In any case, they are assuredly separable. From which arises the double movement, sometimes toward reality, sometimes toward existence. We can certainly hope to retain both the "to exist" and that greater reality; to recover from plurimodality without denying ourselves existence. For to exist, from this point of view, to commit to a mode of existence—is that not to tear oneself, to wrest oneself from something of greater value? And conversely, to go toward that superior status of reality—is this not to stray from existence? That is the whole question.

§98. For that matter, though, why use the expression: to recover from plurimodality? Is the diversity of the kinds of existence an ill? Is it not, rather, a relief? Not only is it a consequence, even an expression of the autonomy of existence (to exist, we said, is to opt for, to choose, to take the side of a mode of existence, courageously and deliberately), it is the condition of something else still. Everything takes place as if those notes, those diverse voices, from which the "polyphony" (to take up an expression dear, and rightly so, to M. Lalo) and harmony of existence are formed, were the necessary and admirable

---

128. In chapter 2, they appeared to us (§29 and 31) almost as a distinction of reason at the heart of the sole existence. Here we see the scope of their distinction affirmed, at the same time as its profound meaning.

instruments of something that exceeds their plane and that really is above existence. It is this polyphony that poses the problem of *surexistence*, if nothing more: if it does not posit *surexistence* itself. Hoping to cure ourselves from plurimodality, that inherent condition of existence, let us be wary as well of curing ourselves of existence and *surexistence*; seeking the One, let us be wary of moving toward nothingness.

⁎⁎

§99. One conclusion remains for us from the foregoing. The passage through the notion of value has dispensed with any possible confusion between an increase in reality and an increase in magnitude or extensive richness. And this is enough to exorcise the last phantoms to remain bound up with the idea of totality. It is not at all because it assembles or unites that a totalization entails an increase in reality. What interests us is a totalization, which, beyond the plurality of the kinds of existence, brings about something that not only embraces them, but distinguishes itself from them and surpasses them. If *surexistence* is to be defined, then, this must not be done through any axiological consideration, nor as a higher, more sublime degree of existence (though it can have such sublimity), but through the strict and severe idea of a passage to problems of the second degree, which concern existence, and yet protrude beyond its plane.

§100. From the beginning of this study, we have recalled Meister Eckhart's well-known ideas concerning the Über-*Sein*, the divine *surexistence*. As we know, however, this is not an original thesis of German, speculative mysticism, but an ancient, Neoplatonic tradition, which Christian theology owes, above all, to Dionysius the Areopagite.[129] Its key lies in Plotinus, for whom, if "there are several kinds of being … there is a unity exterior to the kinds, for the One is beyond Being."[130]

---

129. "All thought only rises toward being, and God is above being" (*De div. nom.*, I, 4). On the doctrine of the *Über-Sein* in the 14th century, see, for example: O. Karrer, *Meister Eckart*, 1926, p. 293f. See also *Revue néoscolastique*, 1927, p. 69-83.

130. *Enneads*, VI, 2, 1.—Nevertheless, while the idea of *surexistence* indeed arrives under Plotinian patronage, we must note that the way it figures in the present chapter differs markedly from the idea as Plotinus historically conceived of it.

§101. It is true that Plotinus' One is not the same as everyone else's. But the universality of the problem is evident beyond its strictly Plotinian or generally theological aspects.[131] To consider this fully, it seems possible to maintain, first, that every unity defines an existence; then, to infer from this that every unity of two existences defines an existence of a superior order. But "of a superior order" means a hierarchical and architectonic superiority of the new existence with respect to the two others, not necessarily a status of reality distinct from existence. Thus, if the unity gains in extension at the price of a decrease in comprehension, the existence in which this unity is actualized will be a generic existence; and, at the limit of all the unifications that are possible in this way, "the supreme kind," as a logician, who has put this classic problem in its proper form, rightly says,[132] "will be the abstract idea of being, the most extensive, but the most impoverished of all concepts; so empty that, according to certain metaphysicians, it is indiscernible from its contrary...."

In other words, the unity of the being thus obtained will define, at its hierarchical summit, an existence for the being in question that is abstract, generic, logical, very pure, and very poor. Something has gone wrong [*il y a maldonne*] and it has quite simply been transported to the notional plane.

Historically, the question of the *surexistent* is introduced as a question of the origin of existences, not of their coronation—hence, the consequent distinction between finite and infinite existence, instead of existence and *surexistence*. For Plotinus, if the εἶναι does not pertain to the One, the ὕπαρξις fully does.

131. Among contemporaries, Léon Chestov is perhaps the one who, in the order of theodicy, has most clearly taken up the affirmation that "we cannot say of God that he exists. For, in saying, 'God exists,' we immediately lose him." And he has doubtlessly made an impression on Gabriel Marcel, if it is necessary to interpret his courageous confession, "I do not know what I believe," in that way (cf. Bespaloff, "La métaphysique de G. Marcel," *Rev. phq.*, 1938, II, p. 34).—Against the *surexistential* theory of divinity, the common interpretation of the divine name revealed to Moses (*Exodus*, 3, 13-14) has always argued that it means, "I am he who is." In reality, the true interpretation is, "I am who I am"—a Hebraic manner of speaking, equivalent to an outright refusal of any denomination of the divine. Cf. Adolphe Lods, *Israël, des origins au milieu du VIIIe siècle*, p. 374. The "conventional appellation," Yahweh, "should always recall the phrase of which it is the abridgment: He is who he is; the Being that man would not be able to define." That which, our author adds, "is not lacking in greatness." Certainly. That which let us add, is interesting to bring together with the well-trodden paths of "negative theology," of Alexandrian origin.

132. Goblot, *Traité de Logique*, p. 114.

If we want to avoid this impoverishment, if the being of which we are thinking is not this being with a purely abstract existence—the notional existence of the totality of being—but a being conceived of that is endowed with a supreme plenitude, as rich with all existence, we will conceive of it especially (to remain with this logical aspect) as having "both the greatest extension and the richest comprehension" (*ibid.*).

So be it—but to pose the question in this way is to no longer observe a positive realization of unification, in a precise kind of existence, in the actual operations of thought. It is to posit an ideal and to designate problematically the supreme existence in which this unification would be carried out. Is it still a matter of existence? Is it not a matter of an existence without a determinate kind of existence? I say that it may be determined by the conditions of reality that are problematically imposed on it, but it is not posited as an existence as long as the problem is not positively resolved. It may be that the equation entails a solution; it may also be that this is an "imperfect question" (in the Cartesian sense of the expression; see the *Rules for the Direction of the Mind*) and even a question without any possible solution. Whatever the case may be, the existence defined in this way could only be regarded as having been posited in and through an effective solution to the problem—if such a solution exists (whether it should exist in our thought or in the future, or virtually, or at the universal origin, or in present actuality, whether it be unknown and transcendent or known and participated in by us … it does not matter). In short, posited problematically, it is a reality defined independently of all existence; the fact that it exists constitutes a completely different question and demands a distinct act, a special moment that adds something absolutely *sui generis* (existence, to be precise) to the aforementioned constitution of the conditions of reality.

§102. Other logicians—MacTaggart, for example—take up the problem in the opposite direction. Having first posited reality (which he identifies with *being*[133]), on the one hand, and existence, on the other, he admits (reasonably) that all that exists must be real. But he asks himself if all reality is existent. And forced to acknowledge that there can be non-existent reality (incidentally, his examples revolve, for the most part, around the theme of the possible), he dismisses the gravity of the

---

133. In English in the original. [TN]

problem, remarking that a non-existent reality could not have any practical interest for us, but only a purely speculative interest.[134]

But is this really the case? Without insisting on "the interest of [speculative] interest," without remaining in the cycle of metaphysics or theodicy, will we not say, for example, that the idea or the problem of the most Real Man, such as we encountered it above, is one of the ideas or problems that most indisputably concerns our most fundamental and intense interests? Is it not, perhaps, hidden or latent at the foundation of all our ambitions or desires, though sometimes in a manner that is absolutely secret, even for us?

Yet if there were such a being, we would without a doubt be able to say that it would exist much more so than its fragmentary images, which reveal themselves, here and there, on the different planes of existence where we see it outline something of its reality. But as we know, this is a dangerous manner of speaking, which easily leads to sophisms. What is understood in conceiving of this "to exist more" is, that, in the first place, it is a quantitative increase, since it is actually the assemblage of numerous kinds of existence, and of kinds as diverse as possible. It is also an increase in superiority, in mastery. In this way we dream of a sort of masterpiece of the art of existing. And if Man, who is neither man of the flesh, psychical man, spiritual man, nor moral man, but man as Master of all the kinds of existence, we can say that if man only exists in a single one of these modes, then man does not exist. He would only exist in that plenary existence, which would also be *surexistence*. But we can also say that he does not exist, not even with a virtual existence, if those various incipient modes do not, in their harmony, outline a completion, which would be like the mysterious contours of a unique being; and that he does not even exist with an ideal existence, if these mysterious contours remain indeterminate and vacant as regards the essential, which is to say, as regards a definite mode of existential accomplishment.[135]

---

134. "We can, then, have interest in the real, even though it should not be existent. But it is only that interest which we have in knowledge for its own sake. All our other interests—in happiness; for example, in virtue, or in love—deal exclusively with the existent…." (*The Nature of Existence*, vol. I, p. 8). [Quoted in English in the original. {TN}]

135. This, in particular, is what is so disappointing in the celebrated book by Dr. Alexis Carrel: *L'Homme, cet inconnu*. In it, the unity of man is constantly

Thus, his *surexistence* is not only a situation that is hierarchically highest, it is also a situation outside of existence. It will only return to it in becoming a determinate mode of existence. Thereby losing its *surexistential* character, this determinate mode of existence would return, in turn, to the cycle of the existences of the first degree, and to the architectonic and even hierarchical relations that can assemble them without ascending to the second degree—to that second degree that characterizes a problem, situated by definition outside of the plane of existence, properly speaking.

§103. A third example, no less classic, will situate these questions still better: it is nothing less than that of the Kantian antinomies.

In certain respects, nothing is as unfortunate as those supposed antinomies if we want to see in them an inevitable stumbling block of reason, which necessarily contradicts itself when it seeks to existentially determine the great metaphysical objects within their conditions of reality. Where do we see the contradiction between the theses and the antitheses? Is contradicting oneself affirming A and not-A of a single thing? We read in the "First Conflict," for example, a) that the world has a beginning in time and is also limited in space; and b) that the world has neither beginning, nor limits in space, but is infinite in time as in space. But is having employed the same word, "the world," in one proposition as in the other, enough to have really spoken of the same thing, to have called it into question. On the one hand, we consider a pleroma of events, related by the causal, temporal, or spatial synapse ("an infinite series of successive states of the things of the world," Kant says). On the other hand, we consider an ontic pleroma ("the world will be a given, infinite whole of existing things"). The synaptic pleroma and the ontic pleroma—those two universes, each colligating a particular group of existents, representing two specific modes of existence (for

---

postulated without ever being legitimated. Cf., for example, p. 35: "If we define man as being composed of matter and consciousness, we put forth a proposition devoid of sense, for the relations between corporeal matter and consciousness have not, at present, been brought to the domain of experience. But we can give a functional definition of man by regarding him as an indivisible whole, manifesting physio-chemical, physiological, and psychological activities." See also p. 393, quite optimistically: "Today, science allows us to develop all of the potentialities contained within us." It is a question of "restoring man … following the laws of his nature." But is this nature one?

Kant was right to show that, at work in the antinomy, there is a positing of the object as existent)—those two universes, for they are essentially two, will differ profoundly in their conditioning of reality; what would be more satisfying for reason? The difficulty only begins if we want to make these two universes coincide, if we want, despite their profound difference—the one finite, the other infinite (more likely: the one infinite, the other indefinite); the one static, the other dynamic (more exactly: the one ontic, the other synaptic); the one discontinuous, etc.—if we want, I say, to propose a superior universe, to give ourselves a kind of being that would be the one and the other at the same time, that assembles them into a unique reality. This is certainly a conceptual difficulty, for us (thought was not made for that); it is also an existential difficulty. What will that manner of being be, which brings about not only the assemblage, the "complication" of the two modes of existence in question, but their joint possession of what is original in their "common act" (to speak like Aristotle)?

And Kant is quite right to relate the problem of this "totality" (not "absolute," but strictly in relation to the problem at hand)—the search for which is really a "regulative principle," insofar as it is an undeniable need of thought—to the order of the "transcendental ideal." But the "critical resolution" of the problem is absolutely ineffective. Why accuse the act of hypostasizing this principle of illegitimacy? It is true that in hypostasizing it in this way, we can only posit the idea of a solution problematically. And having named this unknown x, we would be wrong to speak of it as existent, and above all to believe that an equation of the second degree is reduced to the first degree when we write: $x^2 = X$. The real question is that of knowing whether such an unknown, such a plurimodal unity, is capable of existence; and if it is, which manner of existing is there, whether objectively or in thought, to realize it. The right (to be won) of positing a *sur-universe*, of giving ourselves a world as existing, which would assemble those two pleroma and those two modes of existence in a unique reality, is an excellent example of the second degree and of its problems.

§104. Let us not, then, believe that hypothesis to be easy, which would entail a complete and ready-made, pre-established harmony between all the intentions or postulations of convergent accomplishments; through which all the modalities of existence—each bringing with it the need for the other, for a "to exist" in a different modality—would together outline, beyond themselves, a unique and plenary existence that would impart to them their integral reality. Above all, let us feel how that hypothesis, if we want to push it from the side of being—from the side of the idea of a being occupying and maintaining this integral reality—makes being and existence diverge from one another insofar as the being in question is to be sought further and further outside of the plane of existence, with respect to the plurality of which it is defined. For if all of this is correct, we clearly see not only how, but also why the idea of totality is insufficient to define and consolidate the idea of *surexistence* in its value of reality.

With regard to the virtual (§62), we have already seen the importance that must be attached to the possibility or impossibility of accomplishment. To say, for example (in the manner of certain simple personalisms, which align themselves illegitimately enough with Renouvier), that in order to fully exist, a man must realize all his possibilities, must develop and actualize all his virtualities, is to say nothing at all. If we grasp virtuality in a strict and precise sense, then to speak of a *totum potestativum* as virtually existent, is to suppose that a completely satisfactory solution to the problem already exists and simply needs to be transported from the virtual mode to another, as yet undetermined mode (the specific mode is still in question; but it is only a matter of a problem of transposition from mode to mode). But the question is whether or not there even is such a solution, which is to say, such a virtual existence of this unity. Let us cross the t's and dot the i's in a rather rough-handed way with a human example: a kind and handsome young man of seventeen—who dreams and plays, is proud and timid, intelligent and sentimental, sensual enough and a bit of a mystic—has the makings for both a Don Juan and a saint, an army general (he has led this life in his dreams) and a painter (we know he has the gift), a man of letters and a man of action (if he rids himself of his lassitude and hesitations). Were we to tell him, "it is quite simple: be the saint and the Don Juan, the painter, the man of letters, and the general, all at once," would we be speaking wisely? It is not certain that a destiny can be presented through chance, nor that a soul, which would effectively realize all of those characters in a unification, can be constructed and maintained through effort, perseverance, and genius. Such

203

things are not common. In any case, we will not dispute the fact that to imagine this to be realized, or even realizable, is to imagine the invention of something interesting, brilliant, quite important, and completely novel; something of which nothing is given, but which is still to be discovered. What concrete proposal can be made for the reconciliation and synthesis of all those elements? That's the *snag*. All the more so if it is a question of making such a man as would substantially unify moral life and mystical life, artistic life and corporeal life, into an evident and positive unity—not just a haphazard sampling of all the modes, but a realization of their unity as a being [*étant*]; and not just plurimodal, but simultaneously real in the synthesis of those various kinds of existence, in an existence that is at once superior, supreme, and singular. In considering such an astonishing and almost superhuman [*surhumain*] example, I will say that I certainly see an alternation between action and dream, between mystical life and virile action. But still, how *is* the saint the man of action, how *is* the man of letters the lover, how *is* the soul the body? That is what we would have to explain.

Returning to the great problem that accounted for this digression, we are therefore able, if we want, to posit the idea of a universal totality in the capacity of a transcendental ideal. We can even add, on the strength of a deduction, however abstract and notional it may be, that it would represent the maximum possible richness in reality. But let us be quite aware of the risk that we are accepting: we thus throw ourselves, in thought, well beyond the spiritually manageable regions of *surexistence*. In a single blow we do away with all the architectonic considerations that can lend a concrete and positive point of reference to the exploration of a metaphysical beyond of existence. By hypothesis, we unite, mix up, and efface so many differences—God and the world, moral transcendence and unitive transcendence, substantial union of the soul and the body and gnoseological union of the subject and the object—in a final involutive dissolution, by subverting and canceling any hierarchy (so as to imagine ourselves immediately at the summit) of the entities situated at the degrees of the Tree of Jesse or Jacob's Ladder: the order of *surexistences* being the only support for solid metaphysical investigations into these problems. Let us not move too quickly. Not only will we not get very far, but we will lose the only true fruit that can be philosophically reaped from these studies, and maybe also our contact with that which gives them their practical significance, which is to say, with the equally hierarchical and ordered experience of instauration.

§105. For in the end a final question arises, of which we will content ourselves with a quick sketch: that of the unification of unifications.

Indeed, it would be a shortcoming to content ourselves with a single conception of unity and totality (however satisfactory that conception may be), and to stop with the particular kind of existence or level of *surexistence* that it demands. As if that principle of unification was the only one possible.[136]

To this end, it is important to consider how the different efforts toward unity evoke different beings, according to the nature of the *surexistence* that each demands: bathic being, the foundation and origin common to all things, or terminal being, the culmination common to all things; the unity of a whole that reassembles the beings already perfectly determined in such or such a mode, and that includes all their accomplished truths of being; or the sum of all their accomplishments in the single plane of *surexistence*; or the common principle (however abstract) of their existence; and so on. What then is it to ideally posit the unity of all that under the name of being? To put the problem in its proper form is to postulate not the direct unification of the whole, but the unification of all the possible modes of unification. It is really to posit a *surexistence* of a kind still further removed from existence, and a problem of the third degree—without a doubt, the last degree our thought can manage.

---

136. This is the difficulty with which every effort to explain reality that follows a unique and uniform dialectic is met. Can we say that what is not encountered in this manner is non-existent? Hamelin was well aware of the difficulty. Whence his desperate (and vain) effort to prove: 1) That his dialectic is not intellectual (the intellect only arising, in its opposition to the practical and the affective, at the heart of psychological phenomena, at the end of the process of representation); and 2) That the dialectic of beauty or of goodness are not the principle of a recommencement *ab ovo* of his entire task on different bases (cf. *Essai*, 2nd ed., p. 445f. and 496f.). Whence the need for a purely notional aesthetics (447) and for the affirmation that "it could not have been necessary for Absolute Spirit to become absolute goodness" (496). For him, it is a question of proving (an impossible, almost absurd task) that what would only have existence in the name of an autonomous dialectic of art or morality would not exist; that after having followed the work of a mind that is divine, in the name of his Wisdom, we do not have to recommence the task in the name of Power, and then in the name of Love. Forgetting what is written upon the gates of Hell, according to Dante: *Fecemi la divina Potestate – La somma Sapienza, el primo Amore....*

§106. Should it be possible to perceive, in the preceding discussion, any outright rejection of some ancient or modern speculation concerning being or existence in their unity and totality, we will have made ourselves poorly understood: the case is quite to the contrary.

If in certain respects these speculations have an evidently critical aspect (they adjoin the problem of a general philosophy of philosophies[137]), they nevertheless have another face, through which we at least hope that they will come into contact with the most concrete reality.

For if any reality whatsoever occupies the points thus problematically or ideally defined—the various and specific keystones, the truly culminant summits, the actual heights of *surexistence*—that reality must be a concrete proposition on the part of the *surexistence* that responds to the implied conditions with a positive claim of its own.

In certain respects, Louis Lavelle's Being, Leon Chestov's God, Heidegger's man; or if we prefer, Spinoza's substance, Malebranche's God, Descartes' Substantial Union; or even Strada's Idea-Being, Gentile's Pure Act, Giordano Bruno's Human Maximum, etc.—are the mirror-images, reflected upon the plane of discourse, which represent definite positions where precise realities really reside in the *surexistential* domain. To such an extent that we can really investigate (through a critique that might find a useful arsenal in these reflections) whether these representations are adequate, whether they truly correspond to their objects, in short, whether they are true—the idea of truth being capable of intervening here, since these objects have a reality. The critique in question would first have to ask, by way of a purely metaphysical instance, which existential givens, in their intersection at the second degree, define in *surexistence* precise realities that are offered to thought as positive objects of speculation. And only after this would we be able to attempt the search for the point up to which such speculations remain credible and give us approximate images (under whatever name) that symbolically correspond to something of those entities in their conditioning of reality. The little book you now hold in

---

137. Cf. *Instauration Philosophique*, ch. V, p. 366f.

your hands has no ambition other than that of being an Introduction to a metaphysics thus understood. That is why, parting ways with the point of view that is tied to critique, and abandoning philosophies for reality, it simply remains for us to try, in several brief conclusions, to say how *surexistence* (as regards what it contains both of the positive and of the negative) adjoins existence, and what relations they maintain with one another.

⁎
⁎ ⁎

§107. What, in the first place, is the nature of the surexistent? What do we know of it? What world is that world?—Then: what bears witness to the surexistent on the plane of existence? What, here, is the fact?—Finally: what is the relation? What kind of structure is it that makes the existent and the surexistent bear witness to one another? Do they maintain one another mutually, or is one at the base of the other? And what need do they have for one another?

And these points settled (or glimpsed), what is it in the *surexistent* that implicates us; and how does it implicate us?

⁎
⁎ ⁎

§108. One thing is certain: there are many things, beings, and facts in *surexistence*, many Aeons in this Pleroma, not just the solitary One. This world is hierarchical and architectonic. This is even what we consider to be most certain regarding the subject. As we have seen: Tree of Jesse or Jacob's Ladder. There is an order and something like a genealogy of *surexistence*. As they variously come together, the modes of existence bend their branches so as to form places for occupants among the many vaulted arches. Is Malebranche's God or Nietzsche's Overman at the intersection of the body and the soul? We can have our doubts. Is it not to place God too low in the hierarchy of *surexistential* Aeons, placing him at that level? But is it not to deify the most real man, catching sight of him when we imagine him such as he must be if he is to realize the unity not only of corporeal and psychical existences, but of the two together and also of spiritual existence, and then even of existences of the ontic order and of the order of the event? "If God exists," Nietzsche asks magnificently, "why am I not God?" "I must become God," Novalis had already said. But one way or another—too divine to be called man, too human to be called God (and it is in giving names that the metaphysicians are cast into error)—that which we speak of in either case is the same being (the same entity), glimpsed vaguely in one manner or another, and yet designated precisely, with the exact content of its reality, by the metaphysical point that its existential coordinates define. Let us not therefore allow ourselves to go on to say, "it is the same being" [*le même être*], in the sense of, "it is being itself" [*l'être même*]; for to speak in this way would be to designate rashly the entire region of *surexistence* with a global name, abstracting from the order and architectonic that allow such diverse entities as, for example, God and the universe—but precisely this God and this universe, coordinating some particular plane of existence with some particular *surexistential* level—to be discerned and distinguished with precision. Nor should we accept too easily that by going straight to a sufficient height, we will ultimately discover complete unity, total coordination. For as we know (§105), it may only be a matter of a coordination of coordinations themselves (with all their possible varieties) and of that third degree, which may be abstract, may be purely theoretical, and which, in any case, would only be able to come into contact with the existential through the necessary mediation of *surexistences*, in accordance with the order of their Pleroma.

And let us no longer say that it is a matter of the ideal, and above all not of ideal existences. For, there is no ideal existence, the ideal is not a kind of existence. Or rather, it belongs simply to the imaginary, in the ordinary and most precise sense of the term. The ideal is the perfect imaginary. It would be more useful and profound for us to evoke the "transcendental ideal," in Kant's sense, namely, as a guiding principle. But we would still be wrong, for such a principle only articulates a problem posed (and for thought, in a critical sense). Yet what is really at issue is the problem resolved, in the reality of its solution. It is not the ideal, but the reality of this ideal that is in question.

It is true that, from our point of view, it may seem that the ideal has yet to be instaured (as is especially the case with the most real man); and it is in the experience of instauration that we most manifestly approach it. But that (which is a matter of our point of view) does not change its entirely real nature, which is not affected by our coming more or less close to it. At most, we can say that upon a complete approach, upon contact, it would cease being *surexistence* to become existence. But is this possible? In the meantime, we can above all say that it does not exist (as it has not yet been instaured), if to exist is to be on the plane of existence, it is to have committed to a mode of existence. At most it might be reflected in one of these modes—*per speculum in ænigmate*; and even then it is restricted to an existence that is modal and specular. Yet it is too rich in reality to be able to fit on that plane, or even on the various planes of existence that it assembles.[138]

§109. And how does it assemble them? This leads us back to the plane and to the point of view of the existential.

We now know the difference between a simple plurimodal assemblage—a *coacervatio*—and the synthesis (to use a dangerous word) that expresses and implies a *surexistence*. One further example of the latter will be useful and to the point; and moreover, of prime importance from the philosophical point of view, as it is nothing less than the problem of knowledge.

We become entangled in a false problem as soon as we outright oppose a certain idea of truth (not the only one, but one that is quite important and unavoidable): namely, the resemblance of thought and its object—our outright opposition being founded upon the exteriority of the object, which thought is therefore incapable of comparing with itself. For there is a certain aspect in which thought (or the claim) and the object are both exterior, or at least given to thought on a single plane. And this aspect is without a doubt the one in which the notion of truth was first formed or experienced. You are lying, because I see him alive, who you say is dead. Or else: one of you is speaking of a mastic tree, the other of an evergreen oak. *Tu sub schino, tu sub prino* (Daniel XIII). The irreconcilable mastic tree and evergreen oak of the old liars each evoke the higher reality of

---

138. Let us no longer say that it is a matter of an essence. It is certainly a matter of an essence, but that tells us nothing. There are also essences of existents, which reside in those existents (of which it is the existential quiddity). And here it is a matter of the essence of *surexistents*, residing in those existents (of which it is the quiddity of reality). The word essence therefore adds nothing, explains nothing, and only sends us astray in the direction of other points of view, which are not relevant to our problem. Once again, it is purely and simply a matter of reality—of levels of reality necessarily exceeding existence.

the true tree, that which would have sheltered the supposed sin of Susanna.

But however we grasp the problem, the idea of true knowledge always evokes something of this kind. Let it be a question of my own subjective thought and of its transcendent object: the *surexistential* reality, which would unite and coordinate what exists both in the mode of my thought and in the mode of the object (which is hypothetically different), is always evoked, all the same. Yet how can my thought, which (in wanting to be true) evokes that *surexistence*, actualize it, if not by inquiring into and modeling itself on that reality? In existence there is only a correspondence; not a resemblance between thought and its object, but a *response* from the one to the other, forming a couple. The fact of this response (it does not matter if it is right or wrong) is the only existential fact here. There is an echo. Some object is faced with some thought. The evergreen oak and the mastic tree call to, respond to, and confront one another. Such responses (in Goethe's or Baudelaire's sense) are inscribed in existence as a positive relation. But *how* do they respond to one another? Here we have the possible insertion of *surexistence*. With the intervention of the idea of truth, *surexistence* is formed not only from the idea of a being-together, but from the idea of a common reality having dominion over both of the two modes that respond to one another; involving both the fact of knowing in the subject, and the fact of being known in the object, as real qualities. "To be known such as one is!" is the wish (shout or sigh) of one of Gabriel Marcel's characters. "Such as one is" is quite useless, even dangerous. What I hope for when I make this wish wisely, is not for there to be, roughly speaking, some being (known or unknown) somewhere, who forms a true idea of me without me knowing or feeling that this is the case: it is to feel, as a real passion, as a submission that modifies me without changing me, the fact of being under a gaze, of being illuminated by this vision of myself—and of being truly presented in a new kind of existence, for this being would not be of the same kind as I myself am. The person alluded to here is indeed the one who would participate in both of these modes simultaneously, while also overcoming their constitutive diversity. This *surexistential* being does not exist but I myself can respond to him through an undergoing of the same kind as that by which he was defined. Undergoing the *surexistential*, in experiencing a modification that responds to it, and of which it is the reason (in the sense that the reason is the relation), is without a doubt the only way in which we are able to bear witness for it and be in a relation of action-passion with it.

Just as there are responses from mode to mode, which remain on the plane of existence as a direct relationship that assembles without increase, so there are also responses of existence to *surexistence*.

And there is no other manner of expressing and feeling them, than by observing that, in certain cases, the mode of response from existent to existent passes through the second degree, putting into play or involving the *surexistential* as reason or as law of response. It is a function of it.

Everyone knows that it is possible to undo a knot without touching its two ends—by passing through the fourth dimension. Likewise, the effective and concrete, practical realization of problems like those of knowledge or truth testify to some kind of passage through the dimension of *surexistence*. The fact of acting or of undergoing in accordance with the reality (even the problematic reality) of the *surexistential* is not its enigmatic projection as a mirror image upon the existential, but its experience. It is an experience of this kind that we have also seen in the instaurative action, through the effect of the anaphor. And it is the same when a strength arises in us, for which we cannot account without involving some *surexistential* reality as the key to our response to the occasion, to the situation. What made Michelangelo or Beethoven great, what made them geniuses, was not their own genius, but their attention to the qualities of genius residing not in themselves, but in the work. For works are also in *surexistence*, not only during the period of instauration, through the experience of the anaphor—which, as we have seen, puts the plurality of existential planes into play with the growth in the intensity of reality—but in their situation at the existential crossroads: where the spiritual conditionings of their intrinsic, formal realities meet all that is virtual in the demands of the age, in the noetic needs of the moment, in human attention, all of which outlines their counter-proofs and counter-reliefs in the mode of the virtual. The most real work is not only the one whose particular qualities give form to beauty or sublimity, but also the one that is the fulfillment of a call, of a desire that is indefinite and amorphous in itself; forms seeking their matter and materials seeking their forms.

But under this aspect, what is true of the great works of art is also true of the great moral works, or even simply of the human, vital, and practical works, yet to be instaured.

§110. And it is on this note that we would like to stop. For would philosophy be worth an hour's exertion if it failed to equip us for life?

Immanent justice: to exist in the manner of a body, is to be a body; in the manner of a soul, to be a soul. You will be a soul if, in the mathematical ratios of their architecture and the array of their sonorities, your interior harmonies outline virtual riches and make you greater, and also more indestructible and fulfilled, than you yourself are. But you will only also be a spiritual being if you can manage to live while bearing witness for the *surexistent* that would be the unique being, master of all three of these voices in concert, of these three modes of existence. This being does not exist, but you bear witness for its reality, which is higher and richer than that of any of those polyphonic voices, if your life is modified and modulated in accordance with this *surexistence*: the substantial union of the three.

Yet mind which reality you bear witness for in this way, whether it be rich or poor, leading to the most real or to nothingness. For if you bear witness for that reality, it is judging you.

To live in accordance with a God—as has been said—is to bear witness for that God. But mind also which God you bear witness for: he is judging you. You believe yourself to be answering for God; but which God, in answering for you, situates you within the scope of your action?

Only your charity (and we cannot say enough about the importance of this) can make a non-existent humanity stir. But take heed: will this humanity, which will thus, affectively, be *a humanity* to a greater degree, be the most real? It may at times be the case (take heed) that your severity (rejecting in yourself, rejecting in humanity that depravity of the heart, that baseness, or that material brutality of one's wishes!) *surexistentially* posits, in bearing witness for, a humanity that is higher and more real, and perhaps more spiritual and moral, while also being psychical and corporeal.

Is this a difficult calculus? Without a doubt. It is important for that very reason. It is moreover a calculus that can be replaced by experience, up to a point.

To resolve such problems in thought alone is to struggle to lend some existence to that which *surexists*, by offering it some existential mode as a mirror in which it would be in some way reflected; here, this mode will be thought. But this is not to say that this mode should have any superiority, perhaps other than a pragmatic one. And the very mode of the physical ontic and of the material and terrestrial world could rightly make like testimonies and support similar reflections. To establish both flesh and thought, spirituality and morality, in accordance with that more real man, and to establish dwelling places, social institutions, and cultural spectacles for him on this earth, is to bear witness for him as much as it is when we seek merely to catch sight of him in thought. And perhaps this engages more grandly and more forcefully in the paths of the instauration that is able to give the most certain experience of him.

But moreover, this progressive construction of the most real man, which constitutes one of our most obvious and most immediately present tasks, entails not only the invention of his reality, which is to be implicated in our own lives, but perhaps also the discovery of new modes of existing for concrete man— modes necessary for the harmony of the reality to which they contribute. This is one of the reasons for which the problem remains open and the *surexistence* we have evoked remains at a remove from existence: there are many experiences still to be had, many "to exists" still to be conquered, in order that the problem might finally be perfectly defined and begin to offer a virtual solution.

And that is why existence is, as we have said, quite rich and quite poor at the same time. It is a fortunate poverty, since it leaves room for invention, for the novelty of untried modes of existence; thus positing new possibilities, even for *surexistence*, which, in this respect, still depends on us and does not crush us beneath its hierarchical and sublime world. We have power over it; we can give birth to it, make new realities blossom in it, which would not appear there without us.

§111. Should we be surprised or frightened by what, in certain respects, is negative in this *surexistence*—which has finally been evoked as a necessary condition for some of the richest realizations of that multiple art of existing whose lineaments we have been seeking to grasp—let us make ourselves accustomed to it through the consideration of the old romantic theme of the kinship shared by love and death. One death is a plunge into the void; another is the dazzling incandescence of a life that comes to completion by burning up in the bright flame of a supreme sacrifice. One love is annihilation in a communion with a false reality, forged in its depths of nothingness; another is a veritable work, creative and fertile. We can be tricked. We can suffer tragic confusion. To know—through the very nature of the work to which we bear witness when actually working to instaure it, and through the direct experience of the instauration—how to isolate that which *really* is plenitude and richness, is to know that which is most capable, in existence itself, of approaching *surexistence.*

In any case, it is in our hands.

It is good that certain things do not exist, so that we have to create them; so that if they are to exist, they are in need of us. But we may be sure that beyond existence they have their reality. And however *surexistential* it may be, that reality is not without relations to us—relations of the same kind as those that a chord's harmony has with the distinct voices that perform it. It is through use that we play the polyphonic voices of existence, which are its various modes, and on the plane of which we find ourselves through our practice of the art of existing—it is through use that we can give back to that polyphony, as if from another world, the accents and chords that are our contribution to, as well as our participation in, the realities of *surexistence.* It is by Amphion's song that the City's walls are raised. It is by Orpheus' lyre that the Symplegades are stopped and transfixed, allowing the Argo to pass. Each inflection of our voice, which here is the very accent of existence, is a support for these higher realities. With just a few moments of existing, lodged between abysses of nothingness, we can tell of a song, which sounds beyond existence with the power of supernatural speech, and which may be able to cause even the Gods in their interworlds to feel a yearning for the "to exist"—as well as the longing to come down here by our sides, as our companions and our guides.

Of the Mode of Existence of the Work to-be-made

Étienne Souriau

OF THE MODE OF EXISTENCE
OF THE WORK TO-BE-MADE

I would like to put several ideas that are dear to me to the test today.[139] They are dear to me, and yet I would like to put them to the test by offering them up for your discussion. Why? Because one should not give in to the temptation of affirming such ideas too easily.

I will pose a problem. I will say that it implicates all of us, as men and as philosophers. How would I be able to make this claim if I did not obtain the assent of other philosophers, as diverse in their training and ideals as possible, to join me in affirming the urgency and universality of this problem?

And in order to attempt to resolve this problem, I will try to make an appeal to a certain kind of experience. But the more this experience appears to me to be decisive and invaluable, in-tervening in the framework of life and thought in order to sup-port and guide them, the more important it is for me to remain vigilant with myself, so as to avoid abandoning myself to a sort of superstitious reverie, in which I believe myself to have found solid footing and direction. What philosopher would want to

---

39. Extract of the Bulletin de la Société française de philosophie, 50 (1), session of February 25, 1956, p. 4-24.

affirm that a certain kind of experience exists if he were incapable of awakening the recollection and consciousness of a like experience in another? That is the precious fruit that I am seeking here today.

In order to ensure that my problem is well-posed, I will begin with a rather banal observation, which you will surely have no difficulty in granting me. This observation—and it is also a great truth—concerns the existential incompletion of every thing. Nothing, not even our own selves, is given to us other than in a sort of half-light, a penumbra in which only incompleteness can be made out, where nothing possesses either full presence or evident patuity, where there is neither total accomplishment, nor plenary existence. The table I touch, the walls that surround us, I who speak to you, and if you examine yourselves on the matter, each of you—none of this possesses an existence pronounced with sufficient force for us to be able to find its intensity satisfying. In the atmosphere of concrete experience, any being whatsoever is only ever grasped and experienced partway through an oscillation between the minimum and the maximum of its existence (to speak like Giordano Bruno); and these, truth be told, are only ever suggested to us by the feeling of that oscillation, of the growth or diminution of the lights or darknesses of that half-light, of that penumbra I spoke of a moment ago. Is existence ever a piece of property that we possess? Is it not rather an objective and a hope? So much so that in response to the question, "Does that being exist?," it is prudent to admit that we can hardly respond in accordance with the Yes-No couple, and that we must instead respond in accordance with that of the More and the Less.

To the extent that we ourselves are implicated in it, this existential incompletion is obvious. We all know that each of us is the sketch of a better, more beautiful, more grand, more intense, and more accomplished being, which, however, is itself Being to-be-realized, and is itself responsible for that realization. In such a way that accomplished existence, here, is not only a hope, but also responds to a power. It requires a making [un faire], an instaurative action. The accomplished being of which I spoke a moment ago is a work to-be-made [œuvre à faire]. And insofar as access to a more real existence comes at this cost, we cannot to the extent that we are ourselves implicated in it, escape the necessity of questioning ourselves about the mode of existence of this work to-be-made. It implicates us. Which is to say that such as we are, we are implicated by it, we endure, through a veritable undergoing, the "to act" that the active verb of the formulation, "the work implicates us," expresses. And we all know, of course, that it is the same if instead of thinking of our own individual selves, we think of Mankind *qua* still to be instaured.

But a moment ago I said that the case is the same for every thing. I said that this table and these walls are in a similar condition, such that we can only respond to the question, "Does this exist?," with More or Less, not Yes or No. And perhaps you will tell me that I am wrong or that I exaggerate, that those things have a positive, physical existence that does not admit of more or less, such that we must respond: physically, yes, those things exist.

It is true. I can respond to the question of existence with yes or no, but only because the yes attests to a sort of necessary minimum of an almost purely pragmatic nature, just barely in the control, at the macroscopic level, of some of the physicist's most elementary disciplines.

It is useless, for my purposes, to raise the more subtle questions that would arise if I were to make the physicist's point of view intervene in the conversation, but with respect to a scale other than that of the macroscopic. Such problems would be misleading. We must stick with the content of a concrete, common experience, lived by human beings. It is from this perspective that I say that despite its sufficient physical existence, this table has still just barely begun to take shape when I think of the spiritual accomplishments it is lacking. For example, intellectual accomplishments. Let us consider what it would be in the presence of a mind, capable of discerning all of the distinctive features and all of the human, historical, economic, social, and cultural meanings of a table at the Sorbonne! Meanings that are inherent in it, to be sure, and yet which are entirely virtual until there is a mind that thinks itself capable of embracing, of bearing the accomplished, intellectual existence of this table, of opening the way for that accomplishment, of making an effort toward the promotion, in this sense, of such an object's existence. This purely intellectual accomplishment is still only one aspect of the problem. There are other forms of spiritual accomplishment. Let us imagine the adventure that this table would live if its destiny was to be reprised [*reprise*] by the mind of an artist, and to pursue, in a painting, the objective existence (in the sense in which we all know Descartes understood the term) with which a painter would be able to reward it. Let us try our hand at this experience. Let us imagine the table treated with the intimate and almost interior style of which Vermeer held the secret; or such as it would appear as a prop in a Colloquium of Philosophers painted by a Titian or a Rembrandt. Or let us conjure it up in the dazzling destitution or the cryptic forthrightness that a Van Gogh displays somewhat savagely in his representations of some chair or some table in a small bedroom in Arles. These would certainly be instances of the promotion of existence. In such cases, the artist is spiritually responsible for beings that as yet have no soul—that have only physical existence, plain and simple. He discovers what this thing was still lacking in that direction [*sens*]. The accomplishment that he confers upon it is the authentic accomplishment of a being that only occupied the place reserved for it, so to speak, in the physical mode of existence, while still remaining poor [*pauvre à faire*] in other modes of existence. And it remains so to the extent that even if the woodworker has made this table, physically, it is still to-be-made to the extent that it implicates the artist or the philosopher. And if some of you were inclined to say that the accomplishment executed by the artist is something of a luxury, an unnecessary task that the object itself does not call for, I think that none of you would want to say that the accomplishment executed by the philosopher is a luxury and an unnecessary task. Thus, for example, we feel that of the various artistic accomplishments that I began to imagine a moment ago, one of them would probably be, if not more true, then at least more authentic than the others, which is carried out along a path that the object, in line with its existential destiny, really calls for, though without being able to provide it for itself. We also feel, as regards the philosophical accomplishment of the object, that we cannot discount the intellectual accomplishment of meanings, of which I first spoke. And will we ourselves be genuine philosophers if we do not feel ourselves to be implicated by the work that the spiritual promotion of objects of this kind represents? Is that not our task? Do we not feel ourselves to be responsible for this task, in somewhat the same manner as the artist feels himself to be responsible with respect to the kind of accomplishment that he is seeking on his side? When we spoke a moment ago of the individual or of mankind as works to-be-made, we simply noted that whomever this work implicates also find in themselves, believe themselves to find or to feel a power responding to a sort of obligation. Now, however, we are faced with beings whose existential content, reduced as it is to the minimum of physical existence, are only able to be accomplished completely through the power of another being. A profound difference, to be sure, which modifies the practical conditions of the problem, though without thereby modifying its essence. These kinds of beings must also be considered under the aspect of the work to-be-done, and of a work with respect to which we are not without responsibility.

But let us leave the question of responsibility aside for the moment. Let it remain here as an untied thread. We will come back to it in closing. What I just said suffices to pose the problem, or, more precisely, to note how the problem poses itself. If it is true, as we have just seen, that the as yet unmade work nonetheless imposes itself as an existential urgency—which is to say: both as deficiency and as presence of a being to be accomplished, and which manifests itself as such, as having a claim on us; if this is true, then the very manner in which the work to-be-made exists and the problem I am considering here are one and the same thing.

At this point, however, I cannot suppress a concern. He who really faces up to the fact that we have just set forth, he who feels how it is as if each being, grasped confusedly and poorly on one plane of existence, is accompanied by its own presences or absences on other planes, intensifying itself by seeking itself on them, and perhaps in this way even positing itself most intensely in its true existence—*he* will certainly be capable of being struck by the richness of a reality multiplied in this way across so many planes of existence. But when I speak of works to-be-made as of real beings, when I admit that it is as if a physical being—a moment ago I said this table, but I could also have said a mountain, a wave, a plant, a stone—is doubled by images that rise higher and higher above it in sublimity, I would be wanting in philosophical vigilance if I did not also ask myself: "This world, which now would appear to me to be so rich and ennobled as regards the number of echoing responses, and so pitiable as regards the number of responses that remain absent—am I not populating it with imaginary entities?" For in the end, we philosophers are all troubled by the memory of Ockham's famous razor and trained to ask ourselves up to what point we can multiply beings without necessity. I maintain, or I believed myself capable of maintaining, that there really was a necessity for this multiplication, and that it is not at all a logical necessity, but a necessity that we feel, that we undergo. But I will always be afraid of allowing myself to fall into the kind of superstition that I have been troubled by since the beginning of this talk if I do not succeed in finding an experiential contact with the mode of existence of the work to-be-made, and with the beings that exist (this is what I suppose, at least) according to that mode. In all good philosophical faith, as long as the work is still to-be-made in the concrete, I can only call this accomplishment virtual.

I must confess straight away—and with this I conclude my opening remarks—that it would certainly be a waste of our time to attempt to have an experience, whether direct or representative, of the contents of the deficiencies, of the lacunae to be filled in, of the remainder of existence that all those things that only half exist call to mind. It would be in admitting that all this falls within the purview of a sort of intellectual intuition that I would risk falling into reverie or philosophical superstition. I will even take strict precautions. I will avoid any appeal to the idea of finality—we will soon see why, for I will return to it. In seeking the relation between virtual existence and concrete existence (I ask that you allow me these necessary, provisional terms so that I advance nothing that is not quite positive and certain), it seems to me that I have only one existential hold, namely, that of the passage from one mode to another, and of that gradual transposition by which what at first was only in the virtual is metamorphosed in an instaurative approach, gradually establishing itself in the mode of concrete existence.

A metamorphosis.… You surely know the charming text by the Chinese philosopher Zhuangzi: one night, Zhuangzi dreamt that he was a butterfly, fluttering about without a care. Then he awoke and realized that he was simply poor, old Zhuangzi. "Yet we cannot know," he adds, "whether it is Zhuangzi who awoke after having dreamt he was a butterfly, or whether it is the butterfly who dreamt that he became the waking Zhuangzi. Nevertheless," adds the philosopher, "there is a demarcation between

Zhuangzi and the butterfly. That demarcation is a becoming, a passage, the act of a metamorphosis."

Nothing is more philosophical. And thinking about it as I must, I have in it the principle of a solution to my problem.

On their own, I can grasp neither the flat and simple existence of the physical—in any case, concretely given—thing without its halo of appeals for an accomplishment; nor the pure virtuality of that accomplishment without the confused givens that sketch it and call for it in the concrete. But in the experience of making, I grasp the gradual metamorphosis of the one into the other, I see how that virtual existence is transformed, little by little, into a concrete existence. Watching the work of the sculptor, I see how with each blow of the mallet and chisel, the statue, at first a work to-be-made, absolutely distinct from the block of marble, is gradually incarnated in that very marble. Little by little, the marble is metamorphosed into a statue. Little by little, the virtual work is transformed into a real work. Each of the sculptor's actions, each blow of the chisel on the stone constitutes the mobile demarcation of the gradual passage from one mode of existence to another.

Still, I do not truly have this experience when I study the sculptor. It is the sculptor himself who, in gradually accomplishing his instaurative approaches, both guides this metamorphosis and experiences it along its own paths.

I would not want to go so far as to risk saying that this instaurative experience is the only one in which we can find a foothold here. I would not assert—I do not even believe—that this active experience of making, such as the sculptor experiences, follows the only path of accomplishment. I would not want to remove, from the philosophical horizon, the kind of event to which others have believed it possible to make an appeal when they were disturbed by analogous problems: growth, evolution, dynamic schema, development leading to an emergence. Everything these words imply is quite worthy of attention. But whatever effort we are able to make in order to obtain a sort of intimate and concrete impression of what we might call the course of the internal flow of spontaneous instaurations, nothing can be as direct, as intimate, and as lived in the experience of the regulation of this course than what we discover in the personal experience of making. And what dangers arise the moment we claim to be consciously witnessing a somewhat panicked instauration within us, of which neither the powers nor the actions are truly ours. I repeat: I do not dismiss such experiences as impossible or illusory, nor do I dismiss the philosophies that have sought to base themselves upon such a consciousness as false or superstitious. I only say that they trouble me. While they are likely to appear more grandiose upon a first glance, since they seek to commune not only with particular becomings, but even with vast, cosmic becomings (at least in the order of life), we can be sure that they are actually in search of a conjectural reconstitution of such vast becomings, straying all the more from the direct and lived experience that they postulate. Whereas the experience of the instaurative making, which is intimately bound up with the genesis of a singular being, is a direct experience, incontestable by the instaurative agent, of actions, conditions, and approaches, according to which a being passes from that enigmatic and remote, but intense mode of existence I spoke of a moment ago, to existence on the plane of the concrete.

That is also why I remove the idea of finality from the givens of such a problem. I do not at all deny that it is a valid philosophical conception. I only say that it has no applicability here. It simply designates and summarizes the hypothesis according to which the same vectorial principle would be at work in the approaches of the instaurative agent, exercising his power of making, and in the spontaneous processes, which are formally analogous, up to a certain point, to those of the making, yet in which the freedom and efficacy of an agent are neither engaged, nor detectable.

I do not therefore speak ill of all the enticing speculations that can be taken up in the fields I mentioned a moment ago. But it seems absolutely certain, in the problem I am considering, that the practice of making, such as the instaurative agent practices and feels it, is the only intimate, immediate, and direct experience we have at our disposal. It is there—where, through our personal efficacy, we take responsibility for the fact that a being might be leading up to as plenary a concrete presence as possible—that we are dealing with a kind of experience, whose consequences for the vast problem I posed at the outset are, as you can see, evident.

And three characteristics are immediately evinced in this instaurative agent, to which we must now turn our attention—namely: freedom, efficacy, and errability.

First, freedom: at least a practical freedom, a power of choosing amidst indifference. The painter applies a touch of color to the end of his brush; he is free to put it here or there on his canvas; he is free to choose the blue or the red from his palette, and in one way or another, whatever the work to be instaured may be, it is in this complete freedom of choice that the action of this instaurative agent begins.

Another example, if you will excuse a comparison or a somewhat abrupt transition: the dialectic descending from Plato and the problem Aristotle posed asserting that it was a weak syllogism. Let us follow Plato when, with the approach of a demiurge, he instaures, so as to define, the Sophist. Or when he instaures the angler as a model, ceaselessly adding new determinations—the man who captures other beings, for instance, whether through cunning or through violence, and so on. Why does he choose these rather than something else? To respond to the question is to ask if a dialectic of instauration exists. But in any case there is no doubt that whatever the guiding principle of this instauration may be, the instaurator is free to choose. What is more, this is how Raymond Lulle responded to Aristotle. An experience we will analyze shortly guides the choice by allowing us to grasp the progress, toward its accomplishment, of the being that is in our hands in order to be completed. The painter has his reasons for choosing from his palette the color he is going to use. But it is in his power to choose.

In the second place, efficacy. Whether he acts manually or spiritually, the instaurator, the creator (if you allow me to employ these two words indifferently, in order to lighten my account), the creator, I say, *effects* the creation. In demonstrating to you, as I am attempting to do, that there is a being of the statue before the sculptor has made it, I am not at all denying, on the contrary, that the sculptor was free not to make it, and that it is indeed he who made it. Fichte said: every determination is production.

The statue will not be made by itself; nor will future humanity. The soul of a new society is not made by itself, it must be worked toward and those who work toward it really effect its genesis. The blossoming of a being in the world it may be, and yet it is a blossoming that is not possible if it does not feed, so to speak, on the effort, on the action of the agent. If our sculptor—weary, having lost faith in his work, incapable of resolving

227

the artistic problems that stand between him and the possibility of advancing—lets the chisel fall or stops striking it with the mallet, the work to-be-made remains in limbo, at the midway point, as if aborted. Eugène Delacroix said that if so many of Michelangelo's works remain incomplete, it is because he tackled insoluble problems. Or to use a different vocabulary, he did not feel that there was a sort of "lethal character" in his project. That precisely is the difference between the project and the instaurative journey. But I will return to that shortly. One thing is certain. If the creator—incapable of resolving the problem that stands before him at a specific stage of the creation, incapable of decision, invention, or action—stops acting, then the creation ceases its entrance into the world. It only progresses at the price of this effort on the part of the creator.

And in the third place: errability. This is the essential point. I insist upon it all the more so as, in all that I have read on the question I am speaking to you about, it seems to me that this was one of the most frequently overlooked points—that it has not, in any case, been paid sufficient attention.

After having brought his freedom and his efficacy, the agent also brings his errability, his fallibility, his submission to the test of the well- or poorly-performed. As I mentioned, he can place his brushstroke where he likes. But if he places it poorly, all is lost, it all falls apart. The use to which he puts his freedom can be good or bad. His efficacy can be that of promoting or of ruining. After having acted, he may hear the mysterious voice that says, "Harold, you were wrong!" And this mysterious voice is the tragic assessment that is known so well by all who have practiced the arts: the work that goes wrong, that miserably falls to pieces despite having seemed so good up to that point, all because of a mistake in the choice of words, in the stroke, in the thousand relations of taste that must be calculated on a moment's notice—in short, because that "poorly-performed" I spoke of a moment ago had, as its immediate consequence, an abortion, an existential recoil, the cessation of the promotion of being that ceaselessly secured the creator, touchingly hunched over the fragile genesis.

And I am not simply speaking of the minor adventure of the watercolorist whose stroke has dried too quickly, or of the sculptor who has cracked his marble by attacking it on a bad cleavage plane. I am thinking of things such as the following

Novalis said that there are ideal series of events that run parallel to real events. "Thus with the Reformation; instead of Protestantism came Lutheranism." I am also thinking of Pascal's wager, the spirit of which is not to tell us that we must choose, but to assure us that having chosen, we expose ourselves to the risk of having done so well or poorly.

I must insist upon the idea that as long as the work is under construction, it is in jeopardy. At each moment, with each of the artist's actions, or rather *as a result of* each of the artist's actions, it can live or die. The nimble choreography of the improviser, who, in the very same moment, is able to perceive and to resolve the problems posed to him in the work's hasty advance; the anxiety of the frescoist, who knows that a single mistake will be irreparable and that everything will have to be completed in the time that remains before the plaster will have dried; or the work of the composer or the author, seated at his desk, who is able to contemplate at leisure, to touch up, to redo—there is nothing spurring or goading these people on other than the expenditure of their own time, strength, and capacity; and yet, it remains the case that every one of them will have to respond, ceaselessly, to a more or less rapid progression of the ever-recurring questions of the sphinx: "work it out, or thou shalt be devoured." But it is the work that blossoms or vanishes, the work that progresses or is devoured. The poignant progression through the shadows, in which we grope our way forward like someone climbing a mountain at night, always unsure if his foot is about to encounter an abyss, ever guided by the slow ascent that will lead him all the way to the summit. Dramatic and perpetual exploration rather than abandonment to the spontaneous course of a destiny.…

If what I am saying appears to you to be right, you see that we find ourselves confronted by a sort of drama of three characters. First, the work to-be-made, still virtual and in limbo; then, the work in the mode of concrete presence, in which it is realized; finally, the man who is responsible for all of that, who attempts, with his actions, to realize the mysterious blooming of the being he has taken into his charge.

In this way, in this drama of three characters, I am led to speak of the work to-be-made as really being a character. I would almost dare say a person, save that it is something of a superstition of mine to feel the person-like character of the work to-be-made as strongly as I do. In any case, this duality of the work in limbo and the work already more or less sculpted, written, drawn in the eyes or the souls of men, this duality seems to me to be essential to the problematic of instauration in all of its forms and in every domain.

But how to designate, how to name, how to describe this work still to-be-made if not as one of the characters of a drama, inasmuch as it intervenes as one of the terms of a problem?

We are not saying that it is a "project" for reasons I ask your permission to explain in a moment; we are not saying that it is a futurity, since this future may not arrive if there is an abortion. I propose to you a term whose suitability can certainly be contested, and which, moreover, I submit to your critique: I speak of the "spiritual form" of the work. Elsewhere, I arrived at the expression, "the Angel of the work," simply in order to respond to the idea of something that appears to come from another world and to play a heraldic role. But you suspect, of course, that I only pronounce this word in the company of all those philosophical "as it were's" that go along with it. And for this comparison between the spiritual form and the angel, I would certainly be able to take shelter behind the authority of William Blake. In fact, and to use a more strict and technical language, I am really saying that the work to-be-made has a certain form. A form accompanied by a sort of halo of hope and wonder, the reflection of which is like an iridescence for us. All of which can clearly be interpreted through a comparison with love. And indeed, if the poet did not already love the poem a little bit before having written it, if those who think about a future world to be made to come into being did not, in their dreams of it, find some wonderful presentiment of the presence for which they call, if, in a word, the wait for the work was amorphous, there would doubtlessly be no creation. I am not indulging, here, in a sort of mysticism of the creative effort, I am simply observing that the creator hardly escapes from that sort of mysticism by which his effort is justified. There would be a sort of prostitution—especially in artistic creation—in the fact of making his own humanity into a means for the work if there was not something in the work that seemed to deserve the gift of a soul and at times of a life—in any case, of tremendous labors. That is what really allows us to speak about a reality of this work that does not yet exist, and perhaps never will. I am not postulating that which is in question when I implicate the being of the work in this double existence, as long as I maintain the latter within the action of the metamorphosis I am trying to grasp.

That is why, as I have said, I leave out everything entirely that could be connected with the idea of the project in the designation of this spiritual form. Just as, on the one hand, I dismissed the idea of finality with the futurity of the successfully completed work, so, on the other hand, I dismiss the project, which is to say, that which in ourselves sketches the work in a sort of thrust and throws it ahead of us, so to speak, in order to find it once more at the moment of its accomplishment. For in speaking thus, we eliminate, in a different way, every experience felt in the course of the making from among the givens of the question. We fail to recognize the very important experience of the work's progressive advancement toward its concrete existence over the course of the journey that leads there. Allow me, here, once more to take up an idea that has long been dear to me (I have presented it starting with the first work I published) by opposing the project and the journey in this way. In considering only the project, here, we eliminate the discovery, the exploration, and all the experiential contribution that occurs throughout the historial development of the work's advancement. The trajectory thus described is not simply the thrust we are given. It is also the resultant of all the encounters. An essential form of myself, which I accept as the structure and foundation of my person, does not exist without ceaselessly demanding, over the course of my vital journey, a thousand efforts of fidelity, a thousand painful acceptances of all that this form seeks to obtain through the world, and a thousand costly rejections of all that is not compatible with it. But particularly with regard to the development of the instaurative process, I cannot forget that over the very course of the journey of accomplishment, there occur many absolutely innovative acts, many concrete proposals, suddenly improvised in response to the momentary problematic of each stage. Without forgetting all the motivation that occurs with each decision and all that this decision itself adds. To instaure is to follow a path. We determine the being to come in exploring its path. In blooming, the being demands its own existence. In all of this, the agent must yield before the work's own will, must work out what it is it wills, and must renounce himself for the sake of this autonomous being, which he seeks to promote in accordance with its own right to existence. Nothing is more important in all forms of creation than this renunciation of the creative subject with respect to the work to-be-made. In the order of moral instauration, it is the obligation to leave the old man in order to find the new. In the social order it is a matter of instauring the ensemble of sacrifices that the development of the general spirit demands of all who participate in it. I could say analogous things concerning intellectual instauration. If I gladly take artistic instauration as a model in all of this, it is simply because it is perhaps the most pure of all, the most direct, that in which the experience I am seeking is most accessible and most clearly lived. But let us not forget that what we still have to discover is valid in all the domains of instauration.

Let us get closer to this experience. How does it allow us to speak, without superstition, without indulging in precarious hypotheses, of that spiritual form that was just in question, as of an experimental, positive reality which opposes the mind, on which the mind relies, and concerning which the mind alternates between active and passive interrelations?

Here, too, there are three essential points to be discerned.

One of the most notable ways in which the work to-be-made is present in this dialogue between the man and the work, is in the fact that it establishes and maintains a *questioning situation*.

For let us not forget that the work's effect upon the man never takes the appearance of a revelation. The work to-be-made never says to us: "Here is what I am, here is what I should be, a model you have only to copy." Rather, it is a mute dialogue in which the work seems enigmatically, almost ironically to say: "And what are you going to do now? With what actions are you going to promote or deteriorate me?"

What are you going to do? I imagine that to some degree this is God's name for man, for that man to whom God has given the freedom to do as he will, yet who is neither damned nor saved before the deed is done. Likewise, in a somewhat divine manner, the work orders us to choose, to respond. What are you going to do? Like the *deus absconditus*, it leaves it to us to work it out. Let us listen to the interior monologue of the painter, a monologue that is really a dialogue: "This corner of my painting remains a bit lifeless, you should add a vivid stroke, a burst of color. A bright blue? A touch of orange? … An area is no sufficiently filled-in here. Will I place a person there? Or a detail of the landscape? Or can I, on the contrary, remove these people over here, so as to better bring out the obscure space surrounding it?" Likewise, the author: "Here I would need a strange, rare, or unexpected epithet.… There, a noun that resonates with profound and intimate echoes.… After what my character just said, I must have this other character make a reply that will bring about an unexpected dramatic development… Or here I must have him make a witty remark.…" This witty remark is entirely to be invented. And yet, it is necessary. The work, that ironic sphinx, does not help us. It never spares us an act of invention. Beethoven is composing the *Fifth Symphony*. It is the last movement of the andante; the silence is setting in, little by little. Only the pulsations of the tympani fill it and make it live. And now it must rise up, cellos in unison, a great phrase with a calm and sublime melody. Yet this demand, which is certain and acutely made by the situation, is also a void to be filled. It is a void in which invention can be cruelly lacking, can exhaust itself in vain attempts without virtue. Perhaps a blessed moment will allow the phrase that the work demands to blossom, as if spontaneously. Perhaps the musician will long blacken his paper, his notebooks with sketches, will search amidst the jumble of outlines already made or of partially reusable works for the melody that must now ascend. There is an immense wait, which it seems impossible to satisfy, and which nevertheless will have to be satisfied, for at such moments failure is not pardoned. The work awaits us in this void, and if we fail it, it does not therefore mean that the work fails us. If we do not give the proper response, it immediately falls apart, departs, returns to the distant limbo from which it began to emerge. For it is in this cruelly enigmatic way that the work questions us, and in this way that it responds to us: "You were wrong."

At other times, the questioning situation presents itself in the following manner. The artist feels that what he has just made is usable, but that it is not quite there. It would need a new thrust. It would need to pass to a superior artistic level. Let us think of the three stages of Hölderlin's *Chiron*: first, the wait for day; then, the reprise of the poem, now transformed into a wait for death; finally, the immortal's thirst for the death he cannot have. In the first two stages, the poem is already beautiful. But it is not sublime. The poet, rereading his poem in its second stage, feels with an absolute certitude, with a direct and flagrant experience, that there is still a transfiguration to be performed, a last motif to be introduced into the work like a new leaven, which will raise it to the sky like a lofty summit. Yet I repeat that as clear and as obvious as the work's demand may be, it in no way excuses the inventor from inventing. Everything is still to be done, as Balzac's painter says to his disciple: "It is only the final brushstroke that counts." Those less grand than Beethoven or Hölderlin have sometimes felt that tragic moment when the work seems to say, "Here I am, fully realized to all appearances, though someone greater than you would know that I have not yet achieved my supreme radiance, that there is still something more to be done that you do not know how to do." That is why it can be said that genius so frequently arises at the last minute, in the ultimate moment when a final modification or even a complete reworking decides the work's access to its utmost grandeur. Let us not forget that Rembrandt began the *Supper at Emmaus* many times before arriving at the only Emmaus that bursts through art's ordinary ceiling and transports us to the heights of sublimity.

Such is the first form of the experience of the work to-be-made, which I have called the questioning situation. The spiritual form posits and defines with precision the nature of a response which it does not steal from the artist, but which it demands of him.

In the second place, I will indicate what I call the work's utilization of man.

The artist obviously draws his proposal, which he will have to make in response to the question posed to him by the work, from himself. He galvanizes all his powers of imagination or memory, he rummages through his life and soul in order to find the response that he seeks. Beethoven, as we know (I alluded to this a moment ago), seeking the musical motif that precedes the *Ode to Joy* in the *Ninth*, ended up rediscovering it in a work he had already completed, a "divertimento" of little significance, but which a simple change of rhythm raised to the heights required by the work. Lotte takes shape under Goethe's plume with the memories of his loves for Friederike Brion and Charlotte Buff, and so on. Yet it is the novel he is in the process of writing that rummages through his soul, that takes hold of it in order to nourish itself with the memories and experiences it

234

is able to use. Should we say that Dante used the experiences of his exile in the *Divine Comedy*, or that it was the *Divine Comedy* that needed Dante's exile? When Wagner becomes enamored of Mathilde, is it not *Tristan* that needs Wagner to be in love? For it is in this way that we are implicated and employed by the work, and that we throw everything we find in ourselves that is capable of responding to its demand and its call into its crucible. All the great works grasp the man in his entirety, and the man is no longer anything but the servant of the work, that monster in need of nourishment. Scientifically speaking, we can speak of a veritable parasitism of the work with respect to man. And the work's call is a bit like the call of the child who wakes his deeply sleeping mother. She is immediately aware that he needs her. Everyone knows the work's call because everyone has had to answer to it. It awakens us at night to make us feel the time passing by, the severely limited time that remains to us for all that remains for us to do. It is that which made Caesar cry, thinking that at his age, Alexander was dead. It is that which makes the sculptor go down to his workshop in the middle of the night to give the still moist lump of clay the three strokes of the chisel of which it was still in need. It is that, too, in moral instauration, which awakens those at night who feel responsible for the sufferings or miseries of others. A moment ago, at the outset, I said that it is essential to our problem that we feel the fact that the work to-be-made implicates us. And that is the way in which we feel it. I say that it implicates us: we are implicated by it. We feel ourselves to be implicated. And this is the very experience of the work's call. It is through this call that it utilizes us. And if at this point I am perhaps guilty of certain personal superstitions, I believe that even if I am refused the idea that the work is a person, I cannot, at least, be refused the idea that with respect to us, when it is completed, it is an autonomous being; autonomous in fact and by destination—and yet while it is being completed, and so that it may be completed, the work is sustained by way of the best part of us. The spiritual parasitism of which I spoke, the utilization of man by the work, is the other face of that abnegation through which we accept many sorrows and pains on account of that right to existence that the work claims with respect to us in its call.

Lastly, in the third place, I will attempt to discern a final aspect of the instaurative experience, the expression of which is less concrete and necessarily more speculative than that of the two aspects of which I have just taken stock. It is what I will call the concrete work's necessary existential *reference* to the work to-be-made. Or if you will permit me a pedantic term, the diastematic relation of the one to the other.

Here is what I mean to say. As long as the work is in progress.... Let us clarify. The lump of clay—already molded, already shaped by the chisel—is there on the sculptor's bench, and yet it is still no more than a sketch. In its physical existence, of course, this lump will always, from the beginning all the way up through completion, be as present, as complete, and as given as such physical existence can require anything to be. The sculptor, however, leads it progressively toward that final touch of the chisel, which will make possible the complete alienation of the work in its current form. And for the entirety of this development, the sculptor is ceaselessly calculating, in a manner that is clearly both comprehensive and approximate, the distance that still separates the sketch from the completed work. This distance is constantly diminishing: the work's progression is the progressive coming together of its two existential aspects, the to-be-made and the made. The moment the final touch of the chisel is made, the distance is abolished. It is as if the molded clay is now the faithful mirror of the work to-be-made, which in turn has become incarnate in the lump of clay. They are nothing other than one and the same being. Oh, never entirely, of course. The mirror that reflects the work to-be-made is distorted in accordance with the Pauline words, *ut in speculo per aenigmate,* for in every realization, whatever it may be, there is always a measure of failure. Whether in art or—and still more—in the great works of the instauration of oneself, or of some great moral or social work, we must settle for a sort of harmony, a sort of sufficient analogy, a sort of evident and stable reflection, in the work made, of what the work to-be-made was. A sort of proximity of the two presences of the being to be instaured, on the two planes of existence that nearly come into contact in this way, is enough for us to be able to say that the work is complete. But in the end, this sufficient proximity defines the completion. We would not be able to account for it without this feeling, this experience of a greater or lesser distance, which indicates that the sketch is still quite a long way off from the statue. And we cannot confuse this estimation of a distance, which spiritually measures the extent of the task that remains to be done, with any concrete evaluation of positive determinations. Let us not confuse the evidence of the completion with the work's finish, or with the stylistics of what are commonly, or in the terms of industry or commerce, referred to as "finishing touches." A crude confusion to which the artists of certain epochs, whose sketches or drafts are better than the finished works, have at times succumbed. And let us not believe, as we might in the case of the Platonic dialectic, that it is a matter of a successive addition of determinations, such that the number of these latter would measure the distance not with respect to the completion, but with respect to the point of departure. We all know that the physically and geometrically more complicated sketch sometimes has forms that are much less simple than those of the final work, which are often more pared-down and pure. So whatever solution of this kind we might seek to respond to the problem of completion, we would be thinking in a rather vulgar manner. I do need to tell you, however, that quite often, in every theory of instauration, this problem of completion is the stumbling block. I do not even recall having ever read an author, philosophical or otherwise, in whose work the problem of the instaurative dialectic was addressed, who responds to this problem of completion—I will not say in an adequate way, but—in any way whatsoever. Neither in Hegel, nor in Hamelin. What is more, this is not to say that even the most experienced and brilliant artist does not have his own worries and errors in this regard. Da Vinci was never one to abandon a work. And it might be thought that at times, for fear of going too far, Rodin abandoned a work a moment too soon. A difficult assessment, in which several factors struggle confusedly among themselves: such as the regret of giving the work up completely, of cutting the umbilical cord, of saying, "now I am nothing for it." Or the nostalgia for the work one dreamt of, the horror of that inevitable measure of failure I spoke of a moment ago. And sometimes also the fear of spoiling the work that is already almost satisfactory with a last-minute mistake. But in all these torments of the final moment which would rather not be final, or which trembles at the thought of going too far, it remains no less true that it is really a direct experience that intervenes in this final moment. It is an experience whose content, however it be interpreted, always implies the mutual reference, of the work to-be-made and the work made, in the assessment of their diminishing and ultimately almost abolished distance.

Not only do these three aspects of the instaurative experience thoroughly justify, I hope, the real presence of the work to-be-made, which I have been seeking here before you, and which yields three aspects like three rays of a single light. But I believe that the final aspect, which we have just considered, explains, in a manner that is not only positive, but I would dare say truly poignant, the richness of the real in those various planes of existence of which I spoke when posing my problem. For it is not a matter of a simple, harmonic correspondence of each being with itself, such that it is either fully present or else deficient across those various planes—a correspondence that I ask you to think of somewhat along the lines of the Spinozist attributes, in which the modes correspond to one another. We must realize, rather, that there are not only correspondences, echoes, but also actions and events through which these correspondences are made or unmade, are intensified as in the resonance of a harmony with many parts, or are undone and unmade. There, where a human soul has taken charge of the work to-be-made with all its might, there, upon a poignant point, two beings, which are only one, exiled from one another across the plurality of the modes of existence, regard one another nostalgically and take a step, the one toward the other, through that soul.

Now in such a case, the human soul lucidly and passionately helps this being, which is separated from itself, to reunite with itself. Let us not forget, however, that it, too, receives assistance in this task. When we create, we are not alone. In the dialogue in which the work questions us and calls to us, it guides and leads us in the sense that with and for it, we explore the paths that lead it to its final, concrete presence. Yes, in conversation with the work, we are not alone. But the poem is not alone either, provided it finds its poet. The great, immense poem that would fulfill the man of today, that would awaken the man to come, this poem is there, it only awaits its poet. Who among us will write it?

And that brings me to my conclusions. Here I return to the responsibility of which I spoke at the outset, and which falls to us with respect to all the incompletion of the world.

Indeed, our problem is not posed solely in the future; although it is assuredly in the form of a future instauration that i is most clearly set before our eyes, and that it most immediately entices us. But all that we have just said gives us a universal, philosophical approach to all of reality. And in the first place, it teaches us to discern, in all that is presented to us in the present or the past as fully made, a movement toward existence with the appearance of a work, which involves instaurative forces down below, and appeals and irridescences—in short, an assistance of which the apparently inert object is evidence—up above. The poignant aspect of the world, poignant or dramatic, of which I spoke a moment ago, and which appeared so clearly in the instaurative approach, subsists as a drama performed in all the real givens, a certain amount of which has already elapsed. And it is certainly not without philosophical importance to come to appreciate this. But there is more. That which we grasp in the state of being fully made, of sufficiently pronounced existence, nevertheless remains, from a certain point of view and up to a certain point, only partway along its course. We are not without responsibility for this incompletion if it is possible for us, especially by means of philosophical instauration, to confer upon it an as yet unrecognized accomplishment.

We must not defer too much to this temporalist tendency, to this tendency of going too far in considering all things under the aspect of an unfolding in time through a succession of spontaneous stages, of impulsions that extend themselves from the past toward the future. It is too easy to say, "That failed in the past, let us no longer speak of it…. That which came next is better." As I have already said, many things remain in a state of partial completion, in the state of a sketch. It is not certain that they are not salvageable, up to a certain point, for completions that still fall to us. I will explain what I mean. We are responsible before the child, before the adolescent we once were, for all that opened paths for us, which we failed to follow; for all that gave rise to strengths in us, which later went unused—ossified and withered by life, which is not always accomplishment. And if we think of a terrestrial world worthy of being inhabited by the truly accomplished man, this Accomplished Man, who has reached his sublime stage and become the master of the destinies of all the other beings of that world, takes responsibility for those destinies. I would love for this theme, which philosophically haunts me, to have made you feel a bit of its presence; namely, that from this point of view, there is no being—the most tenuous cloud, the smallest flower, the smallest bird, a rock, a mountain, a wave in the sea—that does not outline, as much as man outlines, a possible sublime state beyond itself, and thus that does not here have a say, by virtue of the rights that it holds over man, inasmuch as man makes himself responsible for the accomplishment of the world. Not only its philosophical accomplishment, as is obvious, but even the concrete accomplishment of the Great Work.

I could further comment upon such matters by posing rather technical philosophical problems. For instance, by evoking the Cogito in the form of a work, with all that this implies of making and of assistance received; by showing all the solidarities that this outlines between us, between the Self of the Cogito and all the cosmic givens that collaborate in its work in a communal experience where everything seeks its path to existence together—but that is another story. I would not want, at this point, to fall back into the sometimes rather dry daily bread of technical, philosophical discussions, in which the most vital aspect of our problems are too easily lost from sight.

I would like to have contributed a little, here, to accentuating what is really vital in the question I wanted to submit to your criticism. I said that I submitted these ideas to your criticism for my own personal benefit. But what is most important to me is that which is not at all personal in this, it is that which, on the contrary, if what I have sketched before you is correct, must be shared and felt by all of you. By which I mean to indicate the appeal that addresses itself so urgently to each of us as soon as he feels himself to be at the intersection of two modes of existence, and in living them—and this is his very life—feels that oscillation, that unstable equilibrium, that poignant trembling of all reality between the forces that support it from below, and a transparency in sublimity that from appears up above.

Univocal Publishing
123 North 3rd Street, #202
Minneapolis, MN 55401
univocalpublishing.com

ISBN 9781937561505

Jason Wagner, Drew S. Burk
(Editors)
All materials were printed and bound
in November 2015 at Univocal's atelier
in Minneapolis, USA.

This work was composed in Futura and Minion
The paper is Hammermill 98.
The letterpress cover was printed
on Crane's Lettra Fluorescent
Both are archival quality and acid-free.